Samuel James Stone

In and beyond the Himálayas

A Record of Sport and Travel in the Abode of Snow

Samuel James Stone

In and beyond the Himálayas
A Record of Sport and Travel in the Abode of Snow

ISBN/EAN: 9783337207298

Printed in Europe, USA, Canada, Australia, Japan

Cover: Foto ©Andreas Hilbeck / pixelio.de

More available books at **www.hansebooks.com**

IN AND BEYOND THE HIMÁLAYAS

Markhor

IN AND BEYOND THE HIMÁLAYAS

A RECORD OF SPORT AND TRAVEL
IN THE ABODE OF SNOW

BY

S. J. STONE

LATE DEPUTY INSPECTOR-GENERAL OF POLICE, WESTERN CIRCLE
NORTH-WEST PROVINCES OF INDIA

ILLUSTRATED BY CHARLES WHYMPER

EDWARD ARNOLD

Publisher to the India Office

LONDON
37 BEDFORD STREET

NEW YORK
70 FIFTH AVENUE

1896

CARPENTIER

PREFATORY NOTE

THE narratives of journeys contained in this book were published from time to time in *The Asian*, India's only sporting paper. They now appear in a new dress, having been revised, rearranged, and entirely rewritten, for the perusal of a wider public.

CONTENTS

PART I

ASTÓR, KASHMIR

INTRODUCTORY . . . 1

CHAPTER I

JOURNEY TO THE SHOOTING GROUND

Sopar to Bandpúra—Present condition of the village—A globe-trotter and his bag—The start—Lagging coolies—A Panjábi fakír on the tramp—My first brown bear—A tramp in the dark—Bagtór village—The Krishganga valley—A good find for stags—Elastic bridge—Sharafa's predicament—The Gagai nálá—Crossing the pass—A British colonel—A snowstorm—Marmai and its inhabitants—Procuring transport—Description of the place—Village of Diril—Village of Chhagám—Nanga Parbat—Colony of Kashmiri horse-thieves—Gúrikot—Wazír Rozi Khán's family—Evening tea—A British sportsman on his return—Astór—Wazír Rozi Khán—His wife subsidised by the Maharájah   4

CHAPTER II

THE FRONTIER DISTRICT OF ASTÓR

Boundaries of the district—The Astór river—The valley—General aspect of the country—The people of Astór—The Dárds—Their repugnance to the cow—Government of the Dárd nation—Forts of Astór and Búnji—Civil administration—The game animals of Astór—The márkhor—The ibex—The úrin—The brown bear—Localities frequented by game 17

CHAPTER III

MÁRKHOR SHOOTING

Start for márkhor ground—Tragic tale of "Bhúp Singh's Parhi"—My shooting establishment—My first stalk—Dangerous ground—Firing down a precipice—A good shot—Bag my first márkhor—Another hunt—Mysterious márkhor, not approachable—Leave Garai nálá—Weak-eyed Khúshál Khán—Bad road—A travelling bear—Kashmiri system of road-making—The Maharájah's sappers and miners—A heart-breaking road—Two sappers of the Kashmir Engineers in very bad case—Rámghát and its bridge—The guard in charge—Pass a bad night—The Búnji plain—Good úrin ground—Búnji—The commandant of the fort—He makes a lucky mistake—Cross the Indus—Reach Damót village—A pleasant spot—Wazír Búghdór Sháh 36

CHAPTER IV

MÁRKHOR SHOOTING—(continued)

Village of Damót—Compulsory labour—March up the valley—Good signs of márkhor—One killed by leopard—Theory regarding horns—A night out—A black bear's family—A fatiguing and useless ascent—Game not visible—Meet a brown bear, but lose my chance—Sight a márkhor at last—The stalk impossible—A tramp of thirteen hours—Find a fifty-two inch horn—Márkhor get the upper hand—An extemporised observatory—Begin a stalk of twenty-four hours—Failure at first—Great exposure—A bad night under a rock—Hard work again—Make bad shooting—A last and lucky shot—Bag a forty-seven incher—A "haláling" dispute—The theory of "haláling"—Dimensions of márkhor shot 50

CHAPTER V

MÁRKHOR SHOOTING—(continued)

Begin another hunt—Sharafa kills a snake—Eagles' chase after a snow-cock—Márkhor tactics—Watching game—Hard work and no reward—Mirza Khán in fault—Lose a splendid chance—Legend of the Major and the Saint of Ghór—Change our ground—Sight game—Our cautious (and ridiculous) tactics—Bag the márkhor at last—A candid confession—An undisputed "halál"—Mirza Khán's capacity for meat—Another shooting-box of Mirza Khán's—Spend a night in a watercourse—A bit of

CONTENTS

Kashmir in a rough setting—Inhabited by a microscopic but hugely vicious fly—Wily márkhor—Bad going—Mirza Khán makes a slip—Long shots—Very dangerous ground—Rain and snow in a tight camping-place—My rocky home—Cross the same dangerous ground again—Mirza Khán makes another slip—A bad two seconds on the brink of prospective eternity—Bad weather conquers—Márkhor shooting ends 64

CHAPTER VI

IBEX SHOOTING

Gluttony of my table-servant—Search for ibex—Grand view from a peak—A successful stalk—And curious shot—Mirza Khán is delighted—The Wazír is anxious for my safety—Suspect a conspiracy to frighten me—My servant's condition—Yearning for cooked food—Another unsuccessful hunt—A noisy camp—A conflagration in a tight place—Arrange for a hunt near the crest of the range—Try my hand at ibex-curry—Filthy Kashmiri habits—Limited quarters in a goat-shed—Bad weather beats us again—Leave the ground—Mark down three huge bucks—The stalk—Awkward position for a shot—Hill-crows are pleased —Very familiar and intelligent birds—Their manners and customs—A letter from the Búnji commandant—My supplies are stopped—Ibex shooting comes to an end—Square accounts with Mirza Khán and company 81

CHAPTER VII

BEAR SHOOTING

Return to Búnji—A nervous Kashmiri—The Indus and Kashmiri boatmen—My raw table-servant—Reach Astór—Settling with Rozi Khán and company—A bi-coloured stream—The Kashmir army at drill—The commandant—The major—Attained his majority before he was born—Reach Chhagám—Bad weather and great discomfort—The Mír Malik valley—Flower-carpets—Another difficult dining performance—Power of the evil eye—Shoot a musk-deer—Effect of the ·450 hollow bullet—The voice of young Bruin betrays his mother—Maternal love—A long stalk—Bag my first bear—A beautiful evening—A bear escapes—Stalk two others—How they disported themselves—Bag only one through a mistake—A splendid trophy—Proceed farther up the valley—A magnified fox—Cross the pass—Sharafa slips, but saves the rifle—In Gúrés again 101

CHAPTER VIII

BEAR SHOOTING—(*continued*)

The beautiful Phúlwáin valley—Good for stags in the season—A dangerous pathway—Reach Bagtour—Beautiful Krishganga valley—Anticipating a bogus thunderstorm—Waiting for an unpunctual bear—Sharafa's imaginary ailments—Shoot a musk-deer—Tremendous power of Henry's ·450 Express—Musk-deer numerous—How they are slaughtered—The Hánt valley—Nanga Parbat—Legends about it—How the "naked mountain" was named—The nomenclature of Himálayan peaks—Ibex not at home—A snow-cock's family—The power of maternal love—Delude a coolie—Waiting for a bear—A friendly hill-crow turns him out of cover—A painful stalk—Ends in failure—Wounded bear escapes—Two graceful hinds—Little flies cause great irritation—Hill-crows drive a musk-deer over me—A bear's bed-chamber—My shooting trip comes to an end—Return journey 117

PART II

CHANG-CHEN-MO, TIBET

CHAPTER IX

THE PROVINCE OF LADAKH, AND THE WAY THITHER

The happy hunting ground of the Englishman—How he takes his sport—General description of the country—Start from Lahore—Road as far as Sultanpúr—The transport difficulty—My travelling kit—Details of arrangements—Chamúrti, my Tibetan pony—Fifteen coolie-loads for a six months' trip—The Kúlú valley—Englishmen settled there—Flying-foxes—Destruction caused by them—Game in Kúlú almost entirely destroyed—A sporting tour round the Kúlú valley—The Ralah bungalow—Crossing the Rotang—Native servants—Chamúrti's pranks—My spirits rise with the elevation—Koksar bungalow—Reach Kailang 129

CHAPTER X

THE JOURNEY TO LADAKH

Kailang—Unavoidable delay—A difference in temperature—The Moravian Mission—Thakur Hari Singh—His travels—Lahouli

CONTENTS

Buddhists—The district of Lahoul—A sporting trip recommended—Resume the march—The last villages—A pass into Zanskar—The fall of a mountain on a village—Patsio annual fair and market—Filthy surroundings—Put up a bridge—Rather unsuccessfully—Zingzingbar—Halt at Choten-rong-jénn—A cold camping-place—Bad weather begins—Collapse of Indian servants—Alter my plans—Mules and servants dispensed with—Two Lámas turn up 142

CHAPTER XI

THE JOURNEY TO LADAKH—(*continued*)

We force the pass at last—Yákúb in a bad way—Height of Tibetan passes—A frozen lake—A grand snowy panorama—Water-parting of the Indus and Chináb—Nasman-Nisman camp—Saichú camp—Meet the first Tibetan traders to Patsio—Their sheep—Salt trade—Kiám camp—Enter Kashmir territory—Súmdo camp—More sheep—Láchálang Pass crossed—Effect of rarefied atmosphere—First game animal seen—Pangta camp—Ponies stray—Reach Rúpshú plains—A long march—Rokchen camp—Examine a sportsman's bag—Picked-up heads—Test of made-up trophies—Great cold at Rokchen—Coolies paid up—Yaks engaged—Plateau of Rúpshú—Meet a sportsman from Calcutta—Leave Rokchen—Tso-kar salt-lake—Sheldrakes—Their nests—Polokónka Pass—Tibetan cairns adorned with horns—The Púga valley—Raldong camp—Varying temperatures—Reach the river Indus—Delay in crossing—Yaha-jaha camp—Lámas' encampment—Shoot a black wolf—Description of him—First hunt after nyan—The valley of frozen lakes—Get on the wrong side of the pass—A Tibetan beggar—See some nyan—Reach the Mirpa-tso—Three impressions of Ladakh—Cross the Thaota-la—Reach Shúshal at last 154

CHAPTER XII

NYAN (OVIS AMMON) SHOOTING

The village of Shúshal—Its mud "bangla"—Arrange for the shooting—Old Tashi—Treatment of native shikáris—Hardiness of Tibetan ponies—Start for shooting ground—Saráp again—No post—One of the hardships of Tibetan travelling—Saráp deposed—My boy head shikári—The regular Kashmir shikár establishment—First sight of nyan—My first stalk—My boy shikári does splendidly—Bag my first *Ovis ammon*—Camp out—The Pangúrtso—On the border—Some more nyan—The old ram's cautious generalship—A successful stalk—Habits of the nyan—The valleys near the Pangúr-tso—Cloudy weather—Another nyan hunt—Six hours in a shallow trench—A trying ordeal—The nyan score this time—A desperate rush—Sight the nyan again—A long shot—Bag one—Return to camp—After nyan again—Nonplussed by idiotic kiangs—The hunting ground—An excursion suggested—Big heads are getting scarce—Causes of their disappearance—Old rams are adepts at concealment—Return to Shúshal . . 175

CHAPTER XIII

SPORT IN CHANG-CHEN-MO

Paljour, the old shikári—Saráp is "run in"—His iniquities—Leave Shúshal—The Pangong lake—Its absent beauties—Reverend Mr. Redslob—Dalgleish's murderer—Reverend Dr. Lansdell—Commissariat and transport for a month's trip—The "Great River"—Kiám camp—Bag my first Tibetan antelope—Description of the Chang-chen-mo country—Gograng camp—Madmar camp—Explore the Chang-lúng—Nyan at last—A fatiguing stalk—Another tramp—Miss chánkú (wolf)—Servants from Leh arrive—Yákúb's hard work comes to an end—A rare servant—A final exploration—Curious glaciers in Gograng—A weird and oppressive scene—Inaccurate maps—Return to Kiám—Correct name of Gograng—A change in the weather for the worse . . . 194

CHAPTER XIV

DONG (WILD YAK) SHOOTING

Start on the hunt—Shoot an antelope—The first dong track—Paljour takes up the scent—A black spot in the distance—Resolved into a bull-yak—Seventy yards range—I miss the target, four feet by six—The second shot tells—The bull slows down—Circumvent him at last—A butcherly business—The usual reaction—Piercing cold—The Tibetan gale—A snowstorm—Exhaustion—Tea and blankets—No remedy—The frozen dong—A splendid trophy—Bullets and their wounds—Hunting twenty thousand feet above sea level—The temperature falls—No water procurable—Yákúb's excitement over the dong's head and hide—Yákúb a keen sportsman—How he hunts the tailless Tibetan rat successfully—Weight of the dong's head—Length of the horns—The hunt continued—Tibetan grouse—More wild yak—A successful stalk—·500 bore bullets and their effect on the dong—Shepherds and sheep—How the Maharájah trades—The Champa robbers—Their depredations—Varying temperatures—Three wild yak bagged in a week—A record performance—Give up the hunt—Weights and measurements of heads and horns—Details of cost of expedition 211

CHAPTER XV

STAG AND BEAR SHOOTING IN KASHMIR

To Leh, capital of Ladakh—Route from Leh to Kashmir—Leave it at Shargól—March to Sórú—Story of General Zoráwar Singh and his death—From Sórú to Súknis—A human skeleton—Details of fatal accident to Dr. Genge and his party—The Súknis bear and his harem—Master of the village crops—Cannot find him —Stag-shooting in the upper Wardwan—Honking (driving) is unsuccessful—A stag calls—Go for him—Just in time—Difficulty in "haláling"—An hysterical coolie—A fine trophy—March for the valley—My first bear—Bad weather again—A forty-eight hours' snowstorm—Bear-shooting is ruined—A sociable snipe— Cross over into the valley—Five days' hard work—Result, a stag and a bear—Shooting tour comes to an end—Joined by Yákúb and Chamúrti—The latter's adventures—Yákúb lionised at home—Is fêted by nawabs—How he died 232

PART III

BEHIND THE HIMÁLAYAS—A PEEP INTO TIBET

CHAPTER XVI

THE BASPA VALLEY

A three months' tour—Description of the valley—The river—Villages — People — Climate — Theóg—Mattiana — Saráhan — Meet my friend—Rájah of Basáhir—He has tiffin—Is a keen sportsman —Well educated in English — Kilba — Headquarters of Forest officer—Large staff of woodcutters—How they are fed—Lay in my supplies—How I managed my transport—Enter the Baspa valley—Villages on the road—The course of the river—A transformation scene—Sángla village—The level valley—An ancient lake—The passes — Sheep — Sheep-stages — Difference between Tibetan and Himálayan sheep—The upper valley and river —Bad road—Miserable huts—Wild women—More information regarding passes, roads, etc.—Chitkúl 247

CHAPTER XVII

THE UPPER BASPA

Bad weather—A plurality of fathers—"Garókchs"—The village god —How he was propitiated—Proceed to the upper valley—My

PAGE

first barhal-stalk—A "bootless" tramp—A good shot—Anparh, the shikári, is not wasteful—The side valleys of the upper Baspa—Dangerous pathway—A stone-shoot—Narrow escape of my servant—Balti coolies behave well—A chance at a ram—A good shot—The wily ram shelves himself—Yákúb's ascent after lawful mutton—The ram is perverse—Halálcd at last—"Never again," says Yákúb—A grand panorama—Anparh's tactics—Temperature of the valley—Heavy snowstorm—Elevation of the camp—Of the Gúgérang Pass—Tibetans and their sheep—An ugly specimen of humanity—I fall ill—Uncertain weather continues—Flowers peep out with doubting hearts—Indisposition, blue devils, collapse—A quick recovery 257

CHAPTER XVIII

THE UPPER BASPA—(continued)

Another stalk—Ends in failure—But bag a ram next day—Excellent though unsanctified chops—The god Kardú is squared at last—Features of the upper valley—A tramp among the hill-tops—17,000 feet above sea level—Freezing cold and melting heat again—The Tibetan gale drives us back—Driven to bed in desperation—An airy bedroom—Nature freezes most audibly—Give up my intended tramp—Take a walk round the base of the peak—Return to camp—A snowstorm—Beautiful effect in moonlight—A dash for Tibet—Anparh—An enlivening episode—Garhwális try to trade on their own account—Tibetans object 270

CHAPTER XIX

FIRST STEPS IN TIBET

Dánam Panbóh recovers his sheep—A young Tibetan—His intelligence more apparent than his moustache—Tibetan officials—Anparh is unwilling to make a start—Makes up his mind at last—Arsamang camp—The way up—A scene of desolation—Rampant moraines mounting on each other—First view of Gúgérang Pass—Reach the crest—And enter Tibet—A Balti coolie falls ill—Too much "púltas" the cause—A new dish—Fraternal devotion—Péchang—The Baltis meet an old friend—Are greatly comforted—Ascend a side valley—No game seen—Unique scenery on the road—A disrupted mountain—Stunted trees appear—Ráná--Nánútatto—Green fields appear—Yellow furze 283

CHAPTER XX

AMONG THE TIBETANS

Camp discovered by two old women—First Tibetans arrive—Marriage customs—The real Panbóh of Záraug—He stands on his dignity—Tibetan manners—A Tibetan game described—Tibetan ponies—Her Majesty's silver countenance changes the aspect of affairs—Anparh's dilemma—The agreement ratified—The return visit—I hold an exhibition—Panbóh and pocket-knife—Tea and biscuits—Tibetan mode of expressing satisfaction—Napier Johnstone—Tandúp—His classical oblation—Primitive way of cleaning a dish—The Panbóh polishes his fangs—Tibetan humour—Preparing for a feast—Buy some curiosities—A welcome present from Mrs. Chering—Tibetan gratitude—The feast—The Panbóh and his followers depart—True version of the Garhwáli episode—Chinese exclusiveness—Lámas of Tángi interview me—A present of three articles—A regular passport system—How trade is carried on 292

CHAPTER XXI

A MARCH IN TIBET

Start from Tángi—A curious natural bridge—Tandúp, my guide—After rains again—A succession of blunders—A back view of the Himálayas—A Tibetan landscape—Force of the wind—The infant Ganges—The Sangyókh-la—Reach the regular trading route—Traces of barhal numerous—Run into a flock of rams—Make a large bag without any trouble—Púling Súmdo—Tandúp Zangbo—His manners and customs—His companion—Dismiss my Tibetans—Tandúp's wives—Presents for them—A good place for barhal-shooting—Rams about the camp—Meet the people from Nílang—I meet Paré—Information regarding game—First intimation of a wholesale murderer—Meet Bow Singh, the arch-impostor—Arrange a shooting trip with him—Bow Singh claims two nationalities—Meaning of the word "Jádh"—Bow Singh's temptation 306

CHAPTER XXII

THE LAST HUNT

A bad beginning—A very awkward ascent—Benighted—A good sleep and a square meal—An unsuccessful stalk—Massacre of the ewes—Twenty rams in view—The stalk—Forebodings of failure

—Bad weather—A sporting official—New way of stalking wild sheep—The official and the pig-tail—Traces of Tibetan game—Bow Singh plays me false—Return to Púling Súmdo—Dismiss Bow Singh with a flea in his ear—A Tibetan official appears at last—An *Ovis ammon's* head—Splendid trophy—Return journey begun—Nílang —A good game country—An airy bridge—The great pilgrim route to Gangótri—Jángla bungalow—The story of a murderous "Sahib"—Bhattári—Journey ends . . . 319

LIST OF ILLUSTRATIONS

MÁRKHOR	.	*Frontispiece*
SHARAFA HELD ME BY THE BELT BEHIND . .	*to face p.*	40
HUGE MÁRKHOR CAME TO LOOK AT ME DEFIANTLY .	,,	60
HE SIGNED TO ME TO LOOK OVER .	,,	82
SHARAFA HELD UP MY FEET	,,	96
THEY CAME SLOWLY TOWARDS THE ROCK ON WHICH WE LAY	,,	112
HUNTED BY A HILL-CROW . . .	,,	124
FERRY ACROSS THE INDUS AT NEUMA[1] .	,,	168
NOT LOOKING, BUT INTENTLY LISTENING .	,,	182
PANGONG LAKE[1]	,,	196
PANGONG LAKE, LOOKING WEST . . .	,,	202
THE INFURIATED BULL STOOD ABOVE THE ROCK	,,	224
BOUNDING THROUGH THE GLADE . .	,,	238
HE STOOD UP ON HIS HIND LEGS . .	,,	244
CROUCHED ON THE ROCK ABOVE, KNIFE IN HAND .	,,	264
I DISCOVERED THEY WERE ALL RAMS .	,,	308

[1] From original sketch by Major Henry Jones.

b

PART I

ASTÓR, KASHMIR

PART I

ASTÓR, KASHMIR

INTRODUCTORY

I PURPOSE in the following pages to attempt some description of sport I have enjoyed in and beyond the "Abode of Snow." Seven times have I journeyed for periods ranging from three to six months into and beyond the vast ranges of mountains, from the Indus, which bounds Kashmir on the west, to the Nipál frontiers of Kamáon on the east. The difficulties and troubles which fell to my lot, and they were not a few, bear no comparison with the pleasures of travelling through the grandest scenery, and following the noblest game, in the world. The mere sight of the journals I faithfully kept during my wanderings brings back to memory many of the most delightful days of my life.

My first expedition was undertaken twenty years ago, when I travelled along the present well-known route from Rawalpindi to Baramúla. In those days one marched along a rough mountain road, and progress was slow; and as tents and a full travelling equipment had to be taken from the very beginning of the journey in the plains, it can be imagined what time was lost before the impatient sportsman got within striking distance of his game. How changed now are the means of locomotion between these two points! The railway brings the tourist to Rawalpindi, within three days, from any point in India; a hill cart receives him at the station and whirls him away towards the blue hills without more delay than the pause to drink a cup of tea—for even the brewing of which he has not to wait. He reaches Murree in time for breakfast, and is off again on the long stretch of winding road which has been constructed for cart-traffic within recent years. Well-constructed staging-bungalows occur at every twelve or fifteen miles, and he can rest his weary body on a comfortable bed when darkness overtakes him. Only the old traveller, who has passed along the same road in years gone by, wearily tramping stage after stage for a fortnight, or wearing out skin and temper on a hired pony, can appreciate the change. At Baramúla the well-known boatman of the Jehlam, with his picturesque belongings,—wives, children, poultry-yard, and all that is his,—will be ready to receive the sportsman who has taken the precaution of telegraphing. Shikári, sporting-kit, and supplies, even the cash necessary for daily travelling expenses, will be on board the boat. The traveller has merely to step in, lie down, and be poled and pulled up the river. The people he employs have for more than a generation made it a study how to "do" (in more senses than one) the travelling Englishman. The latter has only to scatter his coin about with a generous hand, to find the road made smooth from the moment he steps on board to the moment he steps off six months afterwards, poorer in pocket than when he arrived, no doubt, but enriched with a store of health and pleasant memories whose value cannot be appraised in rupees.

INTRODUCTORY

The journey from Baramúla to Srinagar, the capital of Kashmir, is such a commonplace performance now, that detailed description may be omitted. Let us leave the beaten track as quickly as possible. It is not necessary to visit the capital if the traveller is pressed for time or intends touring in the western and north-western parts of the Kashmir territory. A visit to Srinagar means the loss of several days and the waste of money in the purchase of curios.

My first expedition was to the Wardwan valley and its famous ibex grounds;—that, as I have said, was twenty years ago; my last was undertaken within the last two years. But as it is not necessary to follow any chronological order, nor perhaps expedient that I should relate the events of *all* my various journeys, I will begin with the one which, to me at any rate, was the most interesting.

CHAPTER I

JOURNEY TO THE SHOOTING GROUND

Sopar to Bandpúra—Present condition of the village—A globe-trotter and his bag—The start—Lagging coolies—A Panjábi fakír on the tramp—My first brown bear—A tramp in the dark—Bagtór village—The Krishganga valley—A good find for stags—Elastic bridge—Sharafa's predicament—The Gagai nálá—Crossing the pass—A British colonel—A snowstorm—Marmai and its inhabitants—Procuring transport—Description of the place—Village of Diril—Village of Chhagám—Nanga Parbat—Colony of Kashmiri horse-thieves—Gúrikot—Wazír Rozi Khán's family—Evening tea—A British sportsman on his return—Astór—Wazír Rozi Khán—His wife subsidised by the Maharájah.

FROM Sopar, on the Wúlar, my boats took me across the lake to the village of Bandpúra, at the northern extremity of this beautiful sheet of water. It was the most convenient point from which to make a start for the district of Astór, my future shooting ground. In after years, when the Gilgit Agency was established, this small village became the base for all military operations in that direction, and it was transformed into a centre of activity which changed the face of the country for miles round. Sikhs, Gúrkhas, Panjábis, congregate here now in numbers; camels, mules, and military impedimenta are found in every direction; and what was once one of the best shooting countries in Kashmir is closed to the sportman.

There was the usual delay before I could make a start on the long and somewhat tedious journey to my shooting ground, nine marches distant. There was no made road then, only a rough mountain path, and travel was so slow that complete arrangements for the long march had to be made at Astór. I improved the occasion by visiting a "globe-trotter" encamped in an apple orchard close by. The gentleman and his "pal," who was out shooting at the time, were on their journey round the world, and had taken Kashmir in the usual course. They had been here for a month, and had bagged five stags and a black bear. People say, however, that they found two of the stags buried in last winter's snow. They dug out the carcases and appropriated the heads! This is one way of making a good bag.

A start was made at last, and Trágbal stage reached at half-past three, after a steady ascent of six hours. Though it was the end of April, snow still lay in great patches, and a level spot for the little tent was difficult to find. The ascent from this point was less steep than the one below, but the expanses of snow increased, and nothing could be seen but white sheets on all sides. The path wound along the hillsides, and I enjoyed my walk in the bracing atmosphere, though the wind was cold and cutting, and tramping in the snow almost froze my feet. The descent on the other side of the pass was steeper and shorter, but we had to travel for several miles along a narrow valley entirely covered with snow: the coolies lagged, and I was hungry; strong measures were necessary, and I birched the men on the legs with thin and stinging twigs from the trees. The effect was stimulating, and also lasting. Below the pass I met a Panjábi fakir going to Kashmir. He said he was once a Hindu; he had left home twelve years ago, and had wandered ever since. He said he had studied all religions, and talked with some knowledge of the Bible and the Korán. His emaciated body was covered with a tattered coat and a pair of torn pájámas; in his hand he held a ragged cap which he never put on his head—yet he sat in the snow in seeming comfort, and talked to me quite at his ease. He was, he said, a *charasi*,—a smoker of the hemp drug,—and the only thing he regretted was the want of this stimulant during his lengthened wanderings. Though the Indian of the plains is a stay-at-home, it is surprising, when he does wander, how he manages to reach the most out-of-the-way places on earth, without means, wretchedly clad, in the most trying climates, and without any commissariat whatever.

Some distance farther down, Sharafa, my head shikári, discovered a brown or snow bear feeding on the opposite hillside; but, alas! the second shikári, who carried the rifle, had gone on ahead. The birching I had given the coolies, two hours previously, had put so much life into them that they had gone straight ahead without a halt, and the rifle-carrier was with them. Sharafa ran on for the rifle, while I sat down, glass in hand, and watched the animal for half an hour. On his return we made a successful stalk, and got within forty yards. I hit the bear on the point of the left shoulder, but rather low; the bullet smashed her fore-leg, split up, and then made a hole in her side. She fell back off the rock she had just mounted, stood for a moment very sick, then collapsed, and rolled down the hillside on to the snow at the bottom of the valley —dead. This was my first shot with a new ·450 Henry Express which I had received just before starting on this expedition. Five drams of powder were behind the bullet, which was the usual hollow Eley Express, weighing 270 grains. The whole business did not take fifteen minutes, from the moment the rifle was brought. It was getting late, and camp was some distance off, so we had to do everything at best pace. The bear was a small one and very thin, but the fur was in splendid condition.

It was fast growing dark, and, what was worse, the coolies had not halted at Kanzalwan, but had gone on three miles farther to the village of Bagtór—the birching seemed to have inspired them with perpetual motion. We hurried on for Bagtór, but the darkness soon obliged us to go slowly, for the path in one place went over a plain so wet and boggy that I floundered over it in growing ill-humour. A dense forest of pines on the left increased the gloom, and little rivulets of snow-water had to be jumped every ten minutes: the rushing Krishganga was on the right, a good distance below, and the path often led along the edge of the steep slope that overhung the river. A slip, and I should have rolled down to the river—perhaps into it. A twinkling light in the distance was a welcome sight, but it turned out to be only a pine-torch in the hands of a little boy thoughtfully sent out by the good old lambardár (head-man of the village) to guide me.

We reached Bagtór at 9 P.M. The tent was behind with some lagging coolies, so I spread my bedding on a thick layer of hay, and something to eat and a glass of whisky soon put me in good spirits. I had been on the march from five in the morning, and it was now nine o'clock, so I was not particular as to how I got my rest.

Early next morning I was on the tramp again along the left bank of the Krishganga, a lovely stream amid splendid scenery. The whole valley looked as if it contained game, from the rocky ridges above the right bank to the undulating slopes that fell gently to the path I travelled. Sharafa informed me that the forests about Bagtór were certain finds for stags during September and October. They begin to "call" as they start from their summer quarters in the valleys on the right bank of the river about the 15th September, and take about three weeks to reach the wooded slopes on the Kashmir side. The best plan is to reach their summer haunts about the middle of that month, and to stay all through the calling period. It is waste of time to wait for them in certain localities which they frequent during these migrations. They will be found there for a few days, then suddenly disappear, and the precious days of the calling season will be lost hunting after them in an abandoned forest. The difficulty, however, is to follow them from valley to valley without trespassing on ground already occupied by another sportsman. The universal custom in Kashmir is for the stag-hunter to secure a likely valley and stick to it, taking his chance of getting a few shots during the short calling time. The method I suggest would be considered downright poaching, and would engender much bad blood, and create endless disputes; but it is certainly the likeliest way of securing good heads.

Marching up the Gagai stream next day, I came to the tent of a gentleman, who, though camped here for a month, had shot only a single bear. Went on and came to a bridge—to wit, a fine sapling of slender girth, and oh, so elastic! The coolies passed over, load and all, some splendidly and some badly. Sharafa was A1 at this business: he crossed it over and over again, carrying the loads of those who had not nerve enough for the undertaking. My turn came last: Sharafa came to help (very unnecessarily), and took my hand. When half-way over, the sapling began to spring up and down: tight-rope dancing was nothing to it. Sharafa fell into the stream and was carried away a couple of yards, but soon recovered his legs, while I clung on with hands and legs under the sapling, like a monkey. Sharafa came up again, and with his aid I got across at the expense of some skin and an essential part of my attire. Sharafa was in a sad plight, as the water was icy cold. It was early morning, and there was no sun, so we had to make a fire for him, and toast him at it. After a time we turned up a small stream called the Chhota (small) Gagai, and crossed another pole bridge, much narrower than the first, but with very little spring in it.

The valley now contracted gradually. There were rocks and rocky ridges on either side, very ibex-looking, but it was too late in the season to expect them so near the path now. We reached Búrzil at 3 P.M., and had to camp on the snow. This is the much-used Gagai Pass. The dak-coolies of five sahibs were with me going up to Astór and beyond. The wind was piercingly cold in the evening, and some snow fell. Our march next day was a trying one, and the ascent to the crest of the pass occupied five hours. The most heart-breaking part of it was the alternation of hope and disappointment during the whole time. After painfully ascending a long distance, a sharply defined crest appeared above me. I made certain that the end of the journey was within sight ; but I gained the sky-line only to find a farther stretch of snow and painful ascent lying before me, with another well-defined crest cutting the blue sky at a farther elevation. The pass, of course, this time, I thought ; but no, that was only crest number two ! Four times was I disappointed : the fifth slope was the last, and the fifth sky-line was the actual *col* beyond which the descent into the next valley began. The descent for some distance is very sharp. I tobogganed down this slope, and nearly obliterated the colonel of a British regiment in my descent. He was lying in the snow muffled up, and I mistook him for one of the coolies. It was not till he sent for me that I discovered his identity. I lay down alongside of him and had a talk. After a rest he continued his way up, and I went down. The descent was gradual, but the snow was very deep everywhere.

When we reached the Riàt encamping ground at five, the snow increased and the wind was more cutting than ever; but we pitched camp somehow on the snow in a young birch forest—a very uncomfortable shelter indeed. It must have snowed for several hours during the night; its weight so bore down my little tent that the coolies had to come out twice to shake it off. The morning light showed a splendid winter scene: the leafless branches of the birch trees wore a snowy dressing, each branch standing out distinctly from its fellows; an hour's sun, and this fairy scene vanished. I awoke early and called for my servant; I had to shout loudly and often, receiving a muffled reply each time, as if the man were smothered under a dozen blankets or two feet of snow. I began to get alarmed, but the rascal had not been snowed up; he was too comfortable in his blankets to rise in a hurry.

Packing was a terrible business. The tent was frozen stiff as a board; but we had to get out of this snow-bound land, and proceed farther down into more genial regions. At least twelve inches of snow must have fallen during the night; and travelling was difficult and dreadfully slow. The slope of the valley still trended gently downwards, and we at last reached Loyón-harrar, a pretty plain. A large stream runs through it, which I at first mistook for the Astór river, but it is only a tributary. The main stream is farther north, but the volume of the river I had reached was much greater than that of the former. The main road from Gurais to Astór, which makes a great bend a good distance to the right of the short cut I had taken, crosses the stream here by the bridge, so that I was again on the principal line of communication between the two districts. Marmai is the highest inhabited spot in the valley, and the porters I had brought with me from the last village on the other side of the Gagai Pass had to be relieved here.

When I arrived it was in possession of women and children only—not a man was visible, and such an assortment of old hags it has never been my misfortune to see together. One old lady attracted the attention of my party at once; she grew a beard of which no man need have been ashamed—neither was she; the beard was dominated by a hooked nose, and the furrows in her face held, I should say, a century of dirt. The old woman was so much out of the common that the curiosity of even my fagged coolies was excited, and everyone went round the corner to have a good stare at her—each returning with an amazed look which dissolved in a broad grin and loud guffaw as his dull comprehension grasped the sublimity of the dame's ugliness. Three or four young women were comely, and, but for the hereditary dirt, would have been pleasant to look at. They wore a curious woollen hood, a broad metal button at the point, and a loose woollen sack down to their heels. This is their full costume. The dress is worn till it rots away from the wearer's person—a process of denudation that was in progress in the garments of the fair ones before me.

No man being visible, and time being a consideration, active measures were resorted to. A burly Kashmiri dakwála (letter-carrier), belonging to a gentleman shooting in Astór, who was accompanying my party, was most useful, as former experience had familiarised him with the proper *modus operandi* in such circumstances. He at first gently appealed to the women to say where the men were: they answered energetically, and in full chorus, that all the adults were away; the Makadam (head-man) had gone to one village, the Kotwál (village watchman) to another. The dakwála looked incredulous, but, to avoid hurting the feelings of the ladies, did not express himself—he simply dived into the huts and made search. He was unsuccessful, so in more determined language addressed himself to the Bai Makadam (Mrs. Makadam), the best-looking of the lot. This harangue took time to deliver, but was evidently convincing, for the lady went to the entrance of the huts and shouted, " Kirim Khan, come out,"—and in a second out came Kirim Khan, a stalwart youth with rather a sheepish look, and clothed in woollen rags. Amazement and satisfaction mingled in the smile that illumined the features of the postman—he had just that moment searched the three huts and found no one. Hope now rose in the breasts of the tired porters, but no more men emerged from the cavernous depths below us.

Kirim Khan was a big-boned young fellow, with reddish hair and honest brown eyes—in appearance a thoroughbred Dārd. He enjoyed the situation as much as any of us, and took up his task of a beast of burden with great good-humour; he had been an actor in this sort of play many times before, I suspect. As no more men could be drawn from the huts, Mrs. Makadam was persuaded to despatch Kirim to bring her husband from the next village, while we rested on the housetops, about four feet above the level of the ground. The coolies were talking to the women, when suddenly a whisper went round that men were still concealed below. A general rush was made into the huts, and another man brought out. He resigned himself to his fate, and fell to mending his leather stockings at once. Shortly afterwards there was more whispering among the women, another rush down, and another man was revealed to the light of day, blinking like an owl. It was now rumoured that the Makadam himself was concealed below. This was too much for me. I lighted the lantern, and myself went down to explore the nether regions; but there were no more discoveries—the human mine was exhausted.

DESCRIPTION OF THE PLACE

These poor people live in a most extraordinary fashion, as nearly like brutes as possible. The village consists of three houses (families, I suppose), and the following is the ground plan: one roof covers the whole village—the entrance only is open to the sky. The walls are about four feet high; the eaves sloping down almost to the level of the ground.

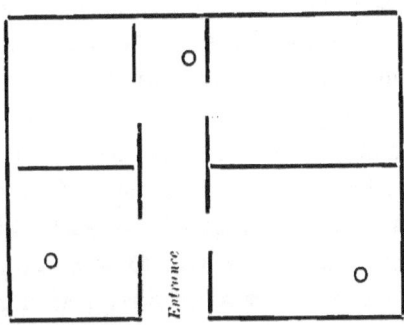

The three points marked o are holes in the roof which let out the smoke. The dotted lines mark a stick partition running the length of the room, dividing it into two: in the back portion the family live and keep their chattels; the front shelters the cattle, cows, sheep, goats, and ponies. The entrance is a shining cesspool, into which the combined dwelling and stable drains. The cattle-room is ankle-deep in filth, through which one must wade to get to the human dwelling-places. It is hardly possible to imagine the state in which these people exist during the eight months of winter, when they must lie buried several yards below the surface of the snow.

My search for the Makadam was very short indeed, and he was not within after all. The Kotwál (village watchman) appeared after a time from a village across the river, and the dakwála pounced on him at once, tied his arms behind his back, and with his alpenstock belaboured him on his posteriors till he was tired. After this preliminary he spoke to him. The matter-of-fact way in which the Kotwál took this punishment was extraordinary; he was evidently used to it! With his arms tied, he was sent down to the river bank opposite the next village to shout for coolies. Shortly after appeared the Makadam himself, with two men. Still there were not sufficient porters for the loads; I was therefore obliged to make the Makadam and Kotwál carry a load each, as the sun was setting, and I was determined to make at least five miles more before halting for the night. These two men had not gone a mile when two others came running up from the next village and relieved them of their burdens! This was how we travelled in this part of the world ten years ago. The people of Marmai are said to be Shías in religion—Ráfizis or heretics; and the orthodox Kashmiris evidently treat them in the manner I have described, as a matter of religious duty. They are said not to be Dárds, but emigrants from Baltistán who have settled in this valley.

We reached Diril village late in the evening. Our next march was to Chhagám. Some distance from Diril the road crosses the river and goes along the left bank. After crossing the bridge and going some distance down the left bank, we turned a shoulder and came on to Gabar Maidan (fire-worshippers' plain?), a curious undulating plain running down towards Chhagám; the road passes over it. An open and level valley, the Mír Malik, comes down to the river from the left. It is pretty, and a good find, I am told, for bears and úrin (wild sheep). From Chhagám the river takes a sharp turn to the right, going completely round the spur of the range on its right bank. The range ends abruptly in this bend. Just opposite, on the left bank, is the mouth of the Rúpil nálá running down from Nanga Parbat, of which there is a grand view from the bridge which spans the muddy stream at this point. Ibex are said to be found up this valley, and márkhor later in the season. There is a penal settlement of Kashmiris a little distance up this valley: it consists of people who gave so much trouble in the valley stealing ponies, that the Maharájah banished them to this spot, under the shadow of the naked mountain, several years ago. Gúrikot was reached at seven, a very hot march from Chhagám. Rozi Khán, Wazír of Astór, had his house and family here, as Astór is not a nice place to live in.

I sent for the Khán at once to arrange my shooting trip, but he had gone to Astór. In his stead came his little son with a tray of sweets and a samovar of hot tea, —quite the Central Asian custom,—which brought home to me, very pleasantly, the fact that I was now far from Hindústan and its exclusive customs. Rozi Khán has an older son who is Thánadár (police officer) of Astór, so that the civil government of this district is entirely in the hands of this family. I reached Astór at nine next day, meeting on the road a British officer returning from his shooting: he had bagged six márkhor; very good heads they seemed to me, but he said he was not satisfied, and was afraid his colonel (the gentleman I met on the pass) would not be very well pleased with him. Soon after my arrival, Rozi Khán paid me a visit, and we had a long talk. He promised me a good man and a good place for a certain consideration, which I agreed to, with the stipulation that I must be satisfied with my sport. The fort is on the edge of a deep ravine, at the bottom of which flows a stream. The road from Gúrikot descends to the water, and there is a very stiff pull up again to the fort. A small tank lies in front of the fort gate, and a few poplars shade its banks; on the other two sides are the houses and huts of the garrison. My tent was pitched on the right bank of the tank, a narrow place not ten feet wide. The sanitary arrangements of the cantonment were much neglected; consequently my camping place was not an agreeable one.

This fort, I may observe, was taken by the Sikhs from the Därds in the usual treacherous Asiatic style. Rájah Guláb Singh being unable to make any impression on it, the Därd Rájah was at last beguiled by solemn promises to give himself up. As soon as he passed through his fort gate he was made a prisoner, and the fort entered. The Rájah was given a jagir (a grant of villages), and was still living in Astór. I received a second visit from Rozi Khán in the evening. He is a stout middle-sized man, past middle age, and of dark complexion, with the manners and deportment of a native gentleman. He is well-educated and intelligent, and has travelled about this frontier a good deal, and has a very exceptional knowledge of the peoples and countries beyond the Maharájah's territories. For any political work in that direction he would be most useful, and, I think, could be trusted. It would be interesting to know what has been the career of this capable man since the changes which have taken place in Kashmir within the last few years. His salary as Wazír, or Deputy Commissioner, of this district when I met him was sixty rupees a month, and four villages in jagir. He has two wives: one of them, the favourite, bore the reputation of a very wise and able woman, who helped the Wazír a great deal with her counsels in the affairs of the country. Her influence was recognised by the Maharájah, who paid her a salary of forty rupees a month. This novel system of administration should find favour with the Government of India in its present straits. It would be a premium on marriage, ensure dual control, and be a soothing concession to the raging lionesses in the old country who are fighting for women's rights.

CHAPTER II

THE FRONTIER DISTRICT OF ASTOR

Boundaries of the district—The Astór river—The valley—General aspect of the country—The people of Astór—The Dárds—Their repugnance to the cow—Government of the Dárd nation—Forts of Astór and Búnji—Civil administration—The game animals of Astór—The márkhor—The ibex—The úrin—The brown bear—Localities frequented by game.

THE district of Astór comprises the main and side valleys of the river of that name which takes its rise on the water-parting line dividing it from Gúrés in the Krishganga valley. The course of the river is from southeast to north-west, and its length is about ninety miles. From the Dáskirim Pass, above its western source, to its junction with the Indus below Rámghát, it has a fall of 9274 feet, or an average of more than one hundred feet per mile. The descent of the waters for the first two-thirds of the river is not so abrupt as the fall in the last portion of its course, from Astór to the Indus. The passing traveller will be often reminded of this difference on his downward journey. The frantic dash of the waters within their pent-up course, their deafening roar during the whole distance to Rámghát, suggest the blind career of a herd of mighty beasts rushing to their destruction.

The general aspect of the country is dreary in the

extreme to the traveller from Kashmir. After crossing the path from the Gúrés direction, a wilderness of snow has to be traversed for several miles, even in the month of April: no vegetation of any kind is visible. Willows and stunted birch trees are the first to welcome you after your weary trudge through snowland, and lower down a patch of pines here and there struggles for existence. As you reach a lower level, the green turf gives a pleasant spring to your steps; and, after passing the first village, the greenery of wide-spreading walnut is a treat to your sun-scorched eyes. From the village of Chhagám fruit trees are frequent, and large patches of cultivation surround each village. After leaving Astór the scene changes again. The steep sides of the mountains are clothed with pines, and the prospect on every side is much confined; and the traveller has only one desire—to proceed as rapidly as possible to the happy hunting grounds now within view.

The people of Astór are called Dărds. According to Drew, they are separated into five divisions: Ronú, Shin, Yashkan, Krémin, Dúm. The Dúm, the lowest of all, is no doubt the same as the Dom or Mirasi (musician) of India. Drew is of opinion that in all these cases we have remnants of the early pre-Aryan race that inhabited India. "This is a new and unexpected fact, the existence of this race among the high mountains and in the snowy country." The Krémins are the potters, millers, etc., of the country, and correspond in function with the Kahárs, Jhíwars, etc., of India. The similarity between "Krémin" and the Panjáb word "Kamin," which is used to designate the same class of people, is certainly curious. The Yashkan are the most numerous, and are owners of the soil. They and the Shin may be considered the bulk of the Dărd nation, who invaded the country and took it from the earlier inhabitants. The Ronús are found in Gilgit only, and are accounted the aristocracy of this people. They are not numerous. The Dárd race are spread over a great extent of country, including Astór, but are not found beyond its limits towards the south, except a few scattered families in Gúrés. "In physique they are broad-shouldered, moderately stout-built, well-proportioned men; active and enduring, and good mountaineers. In faces hardly handsome, but with a good cast of countenance, hair mostly black, sometimes brown, complexion moderately fair, eyes brown or hazel, voice and manner somewhat harsh."

In disposition they are bold and independent, by no means soft-hearted, but not disobliging. They are decidedly clever, clear-headed, and quick, and exhibit in no small degree a pride of race which is refreshing after intercourse with the cringeing, soft-mannered, and ever-deceitful Kashmiri.

"Their dress is a woollen pájáma (trousers), choga (long coat), waistband, and cap. The latter is a bag half a yard long, rolled up outwardly until it fits the head. The roll protects from sun and cold nearly as well as a turban. This head-dress is characteristic of the nation; it is never discarded. They wear strips of leather round their feet and legs, as far as the knee, secured by thongs. The skins of wild animals are generally used for this purpose."

There is one custom among the Shin caste of Dárds that deserves particular notice.

"They hold the cow in abhorrence; they look upon her in much the same way that an ordinary Mahomedan regards a pig. They will not drink cow's milk, nor do they eat or make butter from it, nor will they even burn cow-dung, the fuel that is so commonly used in the East. Some cattle they are obliged to keep, for ploughing, but they have as little as possible to do with them. When the cow calves, they will put the calf to the udder by pushing it with a forked stick, and will not touch it with their hands."

The Därd nation is also peculiar in its government,—that is, of course, in those places only where they have not come under the yoke of the foreigner. The Astór Därds under Dógra rule are governed according to Dógra ideas, but across the border, in some districts, the government is a despotism, "untempered, absolute." These latter are generally found on the right bank of the Indus. The republic is governed by a general assembly called Sigás. The executive consists of a few men, five or six, chosen by the people in their assembly: these are called Joshteros; they can formulate a policy, but have no power to carry it out without the sanction of the Sigás. They can, however, settle minor disputes. The usual advantages of monarchies and republics, on a large scale elsewhere, also exhibit themselves in these small governments among the Därds. The village of Thaliché, consisting of seven houses only, which can be seen across the Indus from the road to Búnji, enjoys the distinction of being the smallest republic in the world.

Since the establishment of the Gilgit Agency and the conquest of the districts of Húnza and Nagar, great changes have been effected in this portion of Kashmir territory. When I passed through the country, the forts at Astór and Búnji were the only places of any importance in the district. Búnji was beyond its limits at that time, but, being situated on the left bank of the Indus, communication with Astór was much more frequent than between it and Gilgit, to which latter district Búnji was subordinate. The Astór garrison consisted of six hundred men, and a "general" commanded the troops. A few guns were mounted on the fort walls. There were about two hundred men in the Búnji fort, under a commandant, subordinate to the general commanding the Gilgit district. Near each fort were collections of huts which formed the cantonments. All the officers and men lived in them; only a small number at a time garrisoned the forts. The civil administration was then distinguished for its simplicity; the governor was called the Wazír; in him was centred all civil authority, and under him was the Thánádar, the chief officer of police. These two officials managed the affairs of their charge through the medium of jagírdárs and lambardárs, the great and small landholders of the country. The military and civil administration was entirely alien, though Rozi Khán, the Wazír at that time (a very capable man), had strong sympathies with the population, as his family had been settled in Gúrés and Astór for the last two generations.

Let us now turn to the game of Astór and the places where they are found. The list is not a long one, but it comprises the two animals for which this corner of the Kashmir territories has always been famous—the markhor (*Capra megaceros*) and the ibex (*Capra sibirica*). Besides these there are the úrin (*Ovis vignei*) or wild sheep, the brown or snow bear (*Ursus isabellina*), and the musk deer (*Moschus moschiferus*);—a short list, no doubt, but every individual worthy the rifle of the best sportsman in existence.

The markhor is called *Bŭm* in the Dárd language: *bŭm maziro* is the male; *bŭm ai* (pronounced "eye") is the female. Sterndale (page 441) after Kinloch divides them into four varieties: we are concerned at present with the fourth, or Baltistán and Astór márkhor, distinguished from the rest by "large flat horns branching out very widely and then going up nearly straight, with only a half turn." It is impossible to give a description of this animal that will strike the experienced man as accurate. Sterndale says: "The general colour is a dirty light blue-grey with a darker beard, in summer with a reddish tinge." Ward, though he gives no detailed description, says (page 14): "In their winter coat of grey they are difficult to discover." Jerdon describes the animal's colour (*The Mammals of India*, page 29) as "in summer light greyish-brown, in winter dirty yellowish-white with bluish-brown tinge." My experience of the Astór animal, recorded on the spot, inclines me to think that the male, in the month of April at any rate, wears a dirty-white coat on his back, which hangs some distance down his sides, making him a very conspicuous object indeed among rocks, the "light blue-grey or greyish-brown" hardly visible on the body. These were the old males; the young bucks, herding with the females, were decidedly of a muddy-red, that made them, when they were motionless, undistinguishable from their surroundings at even a short distance. Two weeks later, in another locality, across the Indus (Damót valley), the old bucks had only a broad streak of dirty-white along their backs, and the light blue-grey was very conspicuous. In the figure at page 442 of Sterndale's *Mammalia of India and Ceylon*, the whitish streak along the back of No. 1 variety illustrates exactly what I mean. It is evident that the colour changes according to season, locality, and age. The dirty-white coat doubtless belongs to winter, and disappears more or less quickly according to the early or late arrival of spring. Perhaps the young bucks have not this distinguishing colour to the same extent as their elders. The size of the márkhor varies according to locality. Ward, in his *Sportsman's Guide* (page 14), says: " This (the Astór márkhor) is larger than its representative in Kashmir proper.

Many stand as much as eleven hands high, whereas the largest I have seen in other localities barely reached ten and a half hands." Jerdon and Sterndale agree in fixing the height at eleven and a half hands. Ward thus continues: "The curves of the horns are bold and flat, the divergency at the tips great, and the massiveness, which is shown to such advantage in the single twist, leads this variety to be considered by most people the handsomest of the four." Single horns of sixty-one and sixty-three inches have been found in Astór, but complete trophies range from fifty-two inches and less; the length, girth, and divergency of different sets of horns vary considerably. It may be laid down as a general rule that the longest are always the most slender, while the shortest are the most massive, and have the greatest divergency. This will be found to be the case with most horned animals. I have noticed it constantly among antelope, gazelles, and ibex. It would seem that nature had fixed a certain *quantity* of bony and horny matter for the head ornaments of each male, which, according to individual circumstances, is developed into long and slender, or short and massive, horns. Length and massiveness will rarely be found together. The best specimen measured by Ward gave the following dimensions (page 15): "Length along curve, 52 inches; girth at base, 12½; divergency at tips, 43 inches. Trophies of this kind," he continues, "are rare, . . . rare indeed is a head with horns much over 50 inches in length." He speaks truly. The best trophies fall to the goatherd's rickety matchlock, or the surer onslaught of the mountain leopard, which are the ever-present enemies of the márkhor and ibex. The keen-eyed goatherd, not many degrees less wild than his quarry, always takes his matchlock when his flocks mount to the grassy uplands for their summer pasturage. In a few days he has marked down all the game within reach. He bides his time, and when a certain opportunity occurs, he bags the biggest márkhor or ibex on the hill. But he has not been mentally measuring the splendid horns, or stroking the flowing beard of the patriarch of the flock; his one idea is meat, accordingly he singles out the largest animal. He may become possessed of the most splendid trophy, but his first act is to smash the horns with his hatchet, split open the skull, and throw the brains on the blazing logs of his camp fire; that is his *bonne bouche* for dinner. The remains of the head and horns find their resting-place at the bottom of the glen—to be picked up years after, perhaps, by the casual Saxon, who sighs over the lost splendour of "the largest horns he ever saw."

The márkhor is an ungainly animal: his long back and disproportionately short legs rather detract from his appearance as a game-looking beast; his shaggy coat and long hair, which conceal the upper portions of his limbs, make his ungainliness more conspicuous. Even in his gait he is not graceful, but none can deny his wonderful activity among the rocks and precipices of his favourite haunts. A venerable buck, standing solitary on a rock, contemplating the world below him, will make the blood of the most *blasé* tingle in his veins; or a herd of long-bearded seniors, gravely crossing a patch of snow, perhaps just out of range, is a sight that will recur to mind for many a year after. And the amount of fatigue and labour it will cost you to bring a forty-incher to bay will certainly inspire you with a wholesome respect for the márkhor's sense of smell and vision, and for his alertness.

Kinloch says (Sterndale, page 443): "The márkhor inhabits the most difficult and inaccessible ground, where nearly perpendicular faces of rock alternate with steep grassy slopes and patches of forest. It is very shy and secluded in its habits, remaining concealed in the densest thickets during the daytime, and only coming out to feed in the mornings and evenings; . . . early in the season the males and females may be found together in the open grassy patches and clear slopes among the forest, but during the summer the females generally betake themselves to the highest rocky ridge above the forests, while the males conceal themselves still more constantly in the jungles, and very rarely showing themselves."

My experience is that the márkhor is not a cold or snow-loving animal like the ibex, though nature has been generous in supplying him with winter clothing. He passes his life at a much lower level, at all seasons of the year, than the other animal, and the heat of the early summer months seems to cause him no inconvenience, though he still wears his winter suit. As summer advances, he is driven higher by the village flocks that graze gradually up as the snow-line retreats; and also by the swarms of flies, gnats, midges and what not, that make life a burden both to man and beast at a lower level. The fresh and tender grass, too, can be found only near the snow-line, and these influences combine to keep him constantly moving upwards, till he reaches the open slopes near the top of the range, where he may then be seen in close proximity to the ibex. The rutting season overtakes him here by the end of September or beginning of October; and he has his short season of madness at this high elevation, where cover is scarce and precipices infrequent. Native shikáris have informed me that the rutting season is the time for márkhor shooting, and they themselves hunt him most frequently at this particular period. His shy and retiring habit, I am inclined to think, is due in some measure to those ever-present pests, the flies. The cool shades of the forest and thicket preserve him from their attacks during the heat of the day when these insects are liveliest. In the morning and evening, when the cold impairs their activity, the márkhor is not loth to take advantage of the opportunity. The old bucks are decidedly lazy, and if a flock be watched, a decided stiffness and slowness of movement will soon discover the seniors. The younger bucks are full of life and play, quick in their movements, and have a set-to after every dozen mouthfuls of grass; the elders are always feeding or resting. The native shikáris say the old bucks keep these youngsters with them for the sake of their keener sense of sight and smell; they are quicker to detect danger, and so warn their seniors.

The ibex (*Capra sibirica*) is called *Kíl* in Astór (*Kél* in Kashmir), *kíl mázáro* and *kíl ai* for male and female. He is much more plentiful and more easily found, stalked, and shot than the márkhor. Sterndale's description of him is as follows:—

"General colour light brownish, with a dark stripe down the back in summer, dirty yellowish-white in winter; the beard, which is from six to eight inches long, is black; the horns, which are like the European ibex, are long and scimitar-shaped, curving over the neck, flattened at the sides, and strongly ridged in front; from forty to fifty inches in length. Under the hair, which is about two inches long, is a soft down, which is highly prized for the manufacturer of the fine soft cloth called *túsc*. Size, height at shoulder, about 44 inches (11 hands)."

The ibex is not the ungainly animal I have styled the márkhor. He is lord of the mountain-tops, and looks every inch the monarch of all he surveys. But I must protest against the caricature of this animal at page 445 in Sterndale's book. The head shows none of the massiveness of the living animal; and where, oh, where is the beard "from six to eight inches long"? As for the legs of the figure in this book, they are truly a libel on the sturdy limbs of this the gamest of mountain game. Those spindle shanks would snap like pipe stems if they were used as I have seen the ibex use his legs, jumping from rock to rock in his mad career. And I must take leave also to protest against that silly-looking animal at page 443 labelled "*Capra megaceros.*" No. 1 variety, looking at No. 2 upon the opposite page, wears an air of contempt that has been shared, I am sure, by every reader of the book who has seen the animal as nature made him. It is fair to say, though, that No. 2 was drawn from a stuffed specimen in some museum.

The ibex is the pleasantest animal to hunt within the limits of Kashmir. Pursuit of the ibex has afforded me more real pleasure than that of all the rest put together. Márkhor takes it out of you in a very short time; after you have secured a reasonable trophy, you are apt to cry. "Hold, enough!" But the ibex is a gentleman in his manners and customs as compared with his spiral-horned cousin lower down mountain; he gives you all the chances that a fair-minded animal should give an honest foe. He is nevertheless "all there" when treading his ancestral hills, and, after you have circumvented him, you feel that he has been a worthy opponent. Kinloch's description of the habits of the ibex is by far the truest I have seen (p. 446, Sterndale): "The ibex inhabits the most precipitous ground in the highest of the ranges where it is found, keeping above the forest (where there is any), unless driven down by severe weather. In the daytime it generally betakes itself to the most inaccessible crags, where it may sleep and rest in undisturbed security, merely coming down to the grassy feeding grounds in the mornings and evenings. Occasionally, in very remote and secluded places, the ibex will stay all day on their feeding grounds, but this is not common. In summer, as the snows melt, the old males retire to the highest and most unfrequented mountains, and it is then generally useless to hunt for them, as they have such a vast range, and can find food in places perfectly inaccessible to man. The females and young ones may be met with all the year round, and often at no very great elevation."

The most wide-awake animal in creation is certainly the female ibex, and she seems to exercise her vigilance solely for the benefit of the ungrateful male, who is by no means so watchful; in fact, if he is old and lazy, he keeps no look-out at all after having comfortably laid himself up for the day. That duty falls to his mate, and admirably she performs it. Uncomfortably perched on a jutting rock far above the rest of the flock, securely sleeping on some soft patch of level or gently sloping ground below, she lies keeping her tireless watch. The patient native or Kashmiri is used to her sentry duty, and, after taking in the situation, he too falls asleep like the bearded males he is trying to circumvent; but the impatient Saxon fumes and swears in the intervals of studying the little animal through his glasses. The case is perfectly hopeless; there is no approach nearer than a thousand yards, without instant detection—for several hours to come at any rate; and the language that contaminates the mountain air is truly awful. How often have I resolved, in these moments of desperation, to shoot that one female in particular, and allow the long-horned careless ones, sleeping just beyond range, to go in peace, purely for the satisfaction of the thing. That feeling is not peculiar to myself; I am sure others similarly placed have felt the same. The female ibex is the *bête noir* of the sportsman; she has spoiled many a careful stalk, and at other times has forced him to trudge many and many a weary mile to escape her all-seeing eye;

when, if she had been absent, a walk of a few hundred yards would have placed him for his shot.

The report of the rifle has its counterpart in so many sounds of common occurrence in these elevated regions, that ibex are little alarmed by it. "Falling rock" or "thunder" is the first idea that occurs to them, and their first thought is to get out of the way of those familiar dangers. When a good stalk is made, and the sportsman has his wits about him, several shots can almost always be obtained, and instances of three of four animals having been bagged at one stalk are not rare. The ground, too, generally is so favourable that the stalker can get within very short range—always provided that the sharp-sighted female has been successfully dodged. I have shot bucks at five, ten, and fifteen yards distance, and a sportsman has informed me that on one occasion he could have *touched* the animal with the muzzle of his rifle!

The úrin or oorin (*Ovis vignei*) is the only representative of the wild sheep in Astór. I have never shot him, and I cannot therefore speak of him from personal acquaintance. Sterndale (p. 435) gives a very short notice of him: "General colour brownish-grey, beneath paler, belly white; a short beard of stiffish brown hair; the horns of the male sub-triangular, rather compressed laterally, and rounded posteriorly, deeply sulcated, curving outward and backward from the skull, points divergent. The female is beardless, with small horns. The male horns run from 25 to 35 inches, but larger have been recorded.

"This sheep was for some time, and is still by some, confounded with the oorial (*Ovis cycloceros*), but there are distinct differences. . . . It inhabits the elevated ranges of Ladakh, and is found in Baltistán, where it is called the oorin."

"Úrin" is, I think, the Astór, not the Baltistán name.

This animal is not fond of snow, and I should say would seldom be found at elevations of 12,000 to 14,000 feet as stated by Sterndale. From all accounts, it is a most difficult animal to stalk, as it generally frequents level plateaux, where it cannot be approached within easy rifle range. Large horns are now scarce in Astór.

The Himalayan Brown Bear. Sterndale's description of this animal is as follows: "A yellowish-brown colour, varying somewhat according to sex and time of year." Jerdon says: "In winter and spring the fur is long and shaggy, in some inclining to silver-grey, in others to reddish-brown; the hair grows thinner and darker in summer as the season advances, and in autumn the under fur has mostly disappeared, and a white collar on the chest is then very apparent. The cubs show this collar distinctly. The females are said to be lighter in colour than the males."

The brown bear is always found close to the snow, at very high elevations. He is most impatient of heat, as he well may be in view of the tremendous quantity of hair that clothes him! Grass, roots, and berries are his food.

I must confess to feelings of regret as I contemplate the figure of this old acquaintance on page 110 of Sterndale's book. He has been persecuted for a generation in Kashmir by the English sportsman, and has yielded his splendid furry coat year after year amid groans and grumblings that cannot be soon forgotten. An old male mortally wounded and fast dying at your feet, uttering his protest in his own bearish language, seems to say: "Why have you murdered a harmless creature like me? I keep far away from the human species, and have done them no harm—even the roots and berries that are my food cannot ever be of any use to you and yours." And after he has been deprived of his coat, his stark and naked body lying on the bare hillside resembles so much the human corpse that few can look at it without feelings of compunction. Moreover, the sport itself is so tame, that, after obtaining a couple of good skins, the majority of sportsmen leave him alone and turn their attention to worthier game. Nevertheless, a certain class persecute poor Bruin perpetually; and, besides, every tourist, whether sportsman or not, must be able to say that he has "shot a bear." The 'native shikári, too, can always secure a good price for his skin, and he is constantly on the lookout for the poor animal.

Although my sympathies are entirely with the bear, I cannot deny his occasional mischief. In a sheepfold he is apt to be very destructive, and if he makes regular visits to a field, a decent crop need not be expected; but these are rare occurrences. Bruin is by nature timid, and by habit a dweller remote from human habitations; he cannot tolerate man or his belongings. When the shepherd with his flock enters a valley, the brown bear promptly makes tracks for the opposite crest in search of solitude.

The localities in the Astór district where márkhor and ibex abound are so numerous, so well-known to the local shikáris, and to several from Kashmir, that the sportsman will never have any difficulty in finding them; the earlier he goes in the season, the better his chances of securing a good place; if he arrives somewhat late, he will have to travel a good distance towards Búnji and beyond, before he can find a vacant valley. Again, if he goes very late, that is, towards the end of the season, he will find many good nálás available, but the game will be hard to find and most difficult to circumvent.

As regards márkhor, the shooting grounds are divided into two distinct portions in Astór proper by the river of that name. First is the range of mountains that begins from the Nanga Parbat peak and runs down directly north to the junction of the river with the Indus, below Rámghát. This range on the west drains into the Indus, on the east into the Astór river. The whole length may be about thirty miles; the side valleys ten and fifteen miles. Those running down to the Astór river are not good for márkhor; but those on the opposite side towards the Indus are sure to yield trophies, the best that are to be found in this country. The Búldar, however, is the most widely known. It runs into the Indus a little below the point where this river takes a turn at right angles to the west. It contains a greater extent of shooting ground than any other valley in Astór, but is most difficult of access. First, there is no road to the valley; it must be entered by a path from the Astór side, after a difficult climb, or by the Huttú Pír, which is a longer way; and secondly, the valley is scarcely within Kashmir boundaries, and the officials are always reluctant to assist sportsmen to get there, for fear of complications with the tribes just across the Indus; nevertheless, it is sure to be occupied very early in the season. The large village of Ghór is just opposite the opening of the Búldar; the slopes of both valleys can be minutely examined, even by the naked eye, from either side, and the inhabitants of that village are a notoriously turbulent lot. Even if the diplomatic sportsman can "arrange" matters with the Wazír at Astór, it is certain that the latter will pester him with messages to the effect that some disturbance has occurred across the river, and that the gentleman had better return. I believe this state of affairs continues to the present day, though the fort and garrison at Chilás has been established for some years on the left bank of the Indus a few miles lower down, and a good road connects it with the main line between Búnji and Gilgit. The márkhor in the

Búldar are disturbed least of all, as it is no man's land and is seldom visited; for this reason, large heads are sure to be found there at the beginning of the season.

Second is the mountain range that culminates above the Parishing stream, and, running first in a north-westerly and then in a southerly direction, past Búnji, ends in the loop formed by the Indus opposite the village of Haramosh. This range drains on the south-west into the Astór, and on the north-east into the Indus from Rondú in Baltistán downwards. The whole length is about fifty miles. The valleys on either slope are numerous, but they are not of any length and are generally confined. Those on the Astór side are the most known, and have been shot over so much year after year that a good head has become a rarity. The animals have no refuge on this side, as they have in the Búldar on the opposite range. They are constantly harried, not only by sportsmen from Kashmir, but by every local shikári who has a gun, by shepherds wandering with their flocks, and by sepoys from the garrisons at Astór and Búnji and the troops passing up and down this route. Most of the shooting is done by the natives during the winter time, and by the European sportsmen during the summer months. The former never spare the females, and so the márkhor are slaughtered all the year round in these Astór valleys without any intermission. It is no matter for surprise, therefore, that good heads have almost entirely disappeared. The following valleys were the best localities on the side of the Astór river:—(1) Garai and Amátabar; (2) Dichal; (3) Shaltar; (4) Dachnár, Dachkat, or Missigan; (5) Búnji valley: and on the Indus side, or north-eastern slope of the range—(1) Jachi; (2) Daroth; (3) Baltari; (4) Ballachi.

I have not visited these grounds during recent years.

3

Probably they have been entirely cleared out since the occupation of Gilgit by a British garrison; the information, therefore, that held good a few years ago would now be misleading.

These are the famous márkhor grounds of the Astór district of years gone by. Game used then to be found during the end of the season round the broad base of Nanga Parbat, and in plenty in the Damót and Jagót valleys across the Indus, opposite Búnji. Behind Nanga Parbat, in the direction of Chilás, between the Indus and the Kashmir border, good márkhor used to be found. But the Kashmir officials were unwilling to allow European sportsmen to occupy those valleys, for the reasons already given, and the British Resident in Kashmir generally limited the wanderings of his countrymen in this direction by ruling that the Kashmir border should be the boundary of their excursions. From the Lolosar lake on the road to Chilás, from the Upper Panjáb to the bend in the Indus below Rámghát, is a distance of seventy or eighty miles. The frontier line runs along the water-parting of the range; the Indus is about fifteen or twenty miles from it. The valleys that drain this extent of country were never visited by Europeans in former years. I have no doubt that, under the new régime, they are now open to sportsmen, and good heads should be obtained there.

Of course there are large tracts of country in the neighbourhood of the Astór district where márkhor abound; but they are hardly yet available. In a few years, no doubt, they will become accessible, and then the mountain hunter will have a vast extent of new ground to range.

It should be taken for granted that ibex will always be found where márkhor abound, but at a much higher elevation. They are numerous on all the higher ranges,

HAUNTS OF THE URIN

and can be hunted in many localities on the route from Kashmir to Astór, Búnji, and beyond.

Úrin are found from the Búnji plain along the range on the left bank of the Astór, across the lower slopes of the Nanga Parbat, above Chhagám, and as far as the Mír Malik valley. I do not think they wander beyond this river. They are restless animals, and are on the move constantly backwards and forwards between the limits named. They spend their winter in the Búnji plain and the low hills in its neighbourhood. As summer approaches, they wander up the spurs from the Hattú Pass, proceed along that range, round the base of Nanga Parbat, as far as the Mír Malik. They reverse this order on the approach of the cold months. These journeys are regularly performed by well-known pathways; in consequence, the patient local sportsmen lie out for them at favourable points along the route, and bag a great many without any exertion or trouble whatever. The Kotwál of Búnji (son of Wazír Rozi Khán) was a well-known hand at this kind of pot-shooting.

Brown bears are most numerous in the upper valley of Astór to the south, along the routes leading from Gúrés to that district. They are rare in the markhor grounds.

CHAPTER III

MARKHOR SHOOTING

Start for márkhor ground—Tragic tale of "Bhúp Singh's Parhi"—My shooting establishment—My first stalk—Dangerous ground—Firing down a precipice—A good shot—Bag my first márkhor—Another hunt—Mysterious márkhor, not approachable—Leave Garai nálá—Weak-eyed Khúshál Khán—Bad road—A travelling bear—Kashmiri system of road-making—The Maharájah's sappers and miners—A heart-breaking road—Two Sappers of the Kashmír Engineers in very bad case—Rámghát and its bridge—The guard in charge—Pass a bad night—The Búnji plain—Good úrin ground—Búnji—The commandant of the fort—He makes a lucky mistake—Cross the Indus—Reach Damót village—A pleasant spot—Wazír Búghdór Sháh.

I LEFT Astór at a quarter-past five in the morning on the 3rd May, and after a long march came to the Garai nálá, and camped some distance up. This was the place said to contain large márkhor. It looked promising, but I did not believe that large horns were to be found here. Sharafa told me the story of "Bhúp Singh's Parhi," or rock. This is a large flat rock on the road from Búnji to Gilgit, on the Gilgit river. It overhangs the bank, and a large number of men can obtain shelter under it. Bhúp Singh was a colonel in Gúlab Singh's service, and had a thousand men under his command, whom he was taking to Gilgit. He camped under the flat rocks for the night; next morning he found himself blocked up in this rat-trap by three Dárd brothers—rebels. These three brave men kept the colonel and his regiment shut in for several days. At last, after a parley, Bhúp Singh and his men were allowed to come out, on condition that they left their arms behind. All did so except two *Púrbiás* (southerners—men from Hindustán), who refused to give up their arms. The defenceless men, being well away from the rocks, were surrounded by the three brothers and their retainers, who butchered them on the spot. The two Púrbiás jumped into the river with their swords and swam down to Búnji, the only survivors of Bhúp Singh's regiment. This is the native account; the authentic story may be read in Drew's work, *Our Northern Barrier*.

I had brought with me only one servant from the plains —a Khidmatgár, or table servant, a weak-kneed and slim young Mahomedan, whose first experience this was in snow travelling. He did not like it at all; the night he spent in the snowstorm at Riát, he said, was the most wretched he had ever passed in his life! He stood in great awe of the shikári Sharafa, whom he called Bara Mián ("Great Sir"), and treated with the greatest respect. He addressed the coolies as "my brothers" whenever he asked them to mend their pace or do anything for him, and in consequence was frankly laughed at. Altogether he had a bad time of it, being completely out of his element. I had given him an old cloth coat and a pair of warm trousers; they were a very bad fit, but gave him a certain air of distinction. With a blue pugri round his head and a pair of blue goggles, he had the appearance of a decayed Persian gentleman. Sharafa, the shikári, should have received attention first, as the most important man of my following. I engaged him a month before my expedition began, on the recommendation of the author of that most useful book *The Sportsman's Guide to Kashmir*, whom I have to thank for his good selection, as well as for the very valuable information he gave me. Sharafa was a handsome man, tall, well-made, and very gentle, but manly withal in his bearing and manners. He had honest soft brown eyes that inspired confidence. He was good-tempered, very tactful, and managed the coolies and people of the country in a manner that I have never seen excelled by any Kashmiri shikari.

Next was Gharíb Káká, or "old cock Gharíb." He was small and slightly built, past middle age, weak-looking, and troubled with a bad cough. The most remarkable features about him were his bushy eyebrows and the keen steady eyes that belong only to the born shikári. He had two weaknesses—he was very garrulous and too fond of the hukka (native pipe); the latter was a bond of union between him and my table servant, as no one else in camp smoked. Gharíba was a Dárd, and had accompanied other sportsmen after márkhor; his local knowledge was most useful. The Wazír also gave me a sipáhi (soldier) to look after supplies, an arrangement that saved me much trouble. Manawar Khán was a Kashmiri, who had a thorough knowledge of the country and villages on my route. I hired nine coolies from Kashmir to carry the baggage, at a monthly wage of five rupees each; only two of them deserve particular mention. Jamála (or "Jamál dín," as he was called when he stood on his dignity) was "tiffin coolie," to accompany me when after game, carrying the food, spare grass shoes, etc. Jáfar Báta was the bhísti (water-carrier) and general assistant to the table servant; he was a strong, square-built man, with a determined countenance, and a bullying manner that brought him to the front. The others were mere baggage animals. My camp equipage consisted of a small tent six feet square for myself, and a smaller one for the servant and his cooking operations. When starting from

Bandpúra, I found the carriage difficulty so pressing, even at that early stage of my journey, that I left my camp-bed, table, and chair there in charge of the contractor who provided travellers with supplies. I had to leave there also all my tinned provisions and other superfluities, arranging with the contractor to send out small quantities by the postman who was engaged to bring out my letters every fortnight or so. In this way I lightened my baggage considerably, and secured a constant supply of provisions. All necessaries were contained in three waterproof "ruchsacks," or Swiss shooting-bags (most convenient things for this kind of work). The provisions and cooking apparatus were carried in kiltas (wicker baskets covered with leather), and kept in the servants' tent. These kiltas were the weak point in my arrangements—they were too large and heavy; the coolies were always shirking them, and those carrying them always came in last. My tent was generally pitched on the most level spot to be found, and the cooking tent on one side of it. The shikáris and coolies put up wherever they could find shelter, but very often they slept out in the open round a blazing log fire.

I started early the next morning, and went up the slope just above camp; then turned down towards the Astór river and got on the ridge dividing the Garai from the Amátabar nálá. After searching the opposite side of the latter ravine for a long time, I saw some ibex only. The two shikáris went farther down on the Garai side, and after an hour Sharafa came back and said he had marked down some márkhor. I went with him, but no márkhor were to be seen! Sharafa looked puzzled, as he had not been away more than fifteen minutes; but after watching for an hour I gave it up, found a soft place, had a sleep, and then breakfast. I had just finished when the márkhor were seen again; they were much lower down on the ridge we were on, and we had to watch them for a couple of hours, as they were restless and could not decide upon a place for their mid-day rest: they did come to an anchor at last, but in terribly difficult ground. In fact, it seemed to me, unacquainted with the locality, utterly impossible to get within shot; but Gharíb Káká was equal to the occasion: he took us back a little, and then descended below the level of the off side of the ridge, out of sight of the game. The going was awful—loose crumbling rocks all the way, in most places ground into gravel and sand, and the slope down which we had to slide was very abrupt: I could hardly get any footing, and the gravel and stones rolled down at every step, making noise enough to frighten away game a mile off. It took us a long time to get down; and the blazing sun right overhead added to my distress. The heat was something frightful, and there was not a tree anywhere until we were nearly over the márkhor. We came then to some stunted pines, and halted at once.

After a short rest we moved on again; the ground was the same crumbling stuff, and as we were now nearing our game, additional caution was necessary to prevent noise, and the going became very slow and aggravating, as, tread gingerly as I could, the stones *would* roll. We did at last reach the precipices below which we had marked down the game, and, after dangerous and painful (and very cautious) craning over the brink, I saw one young márkhor lying in the shade of a tree more than two hundred yards off. The others, the larger ones, could not be seen—they were evidently right under us, below the precipice, and out of sight. Gharíba at last found a way down a short distance to a lower ledge, and we followed. From this point we could see one more, and here we had to wait patiently on the brink of a sheer

precipice till the markhor moved into a better position. The heat was so terrific that I soon gave in, and went up again to the shade of the trees, though there was very little of it. After long waiting the markhor moved, and I went down again ; but to fire down almost perpendicularly was impossible without following up the bullet in person, and I was not so enthusiastic : nor could a rest be found for the rifle. Three of the markhor at last moved lower down and farther away from the precipice, and I became anxious, as they were getting out of range. The fourth and largest, the one on which I had set my heart, had not yet been seen : he was still lying down right below me. After screwing about and craning over, I did at last see him, but my struggles attracted his notice : he looked up, rose at once and ran down to the others, who also became alarmed and began quickly moving off. In desperation I went as close to the brink of the precipice as I dared, made Sharafa hold me by the belt behind, and covered the biggest. He stood for a moment facing to my left, and I fired. The bullet hit, and I could see the animal's legs fly from under him, as he rolled head over heels down the hillside and fell into the ravine out of sight. I was rather astonished at my good luck. The distance was certainly two hundred and fifty yards, and I used the first sight. The ·450 Express did its duty—all honour to Henry. This was the No. 2 rifle of the pair—the one with which I killed the bear. It was my second shot at game, and I had bagged both times. Ghariba went down and brought up the head, and we returned the way we came. It was a frightful pull up hill ; but since we had not now to mind the stones rolling down, it was not so bad as the descent. The sun, though it was evening, still punished me, and I wanted a drink sadly ; some shouting brought Jamala down, but of course he left the tea bottle above, and had to go up again for it, as I refused to stir till I had had a drink. Gharíba got some snow for himself and Sharafa. He plastered it on a rock facing the sun, and the water was soon dripping from it into a hollow, from which they drank—a very slow process for thirsty people; I had finished all my tea by the time they had had a couple of mouthfuls. Having enjoyed my tea, I marched very contentedly back to camp, though the grass shoes had punished my feet severely. Grass shoes in this dry stony country are certainly not the best things to wear; a day's work wore out two or three pairs; they soon get loose and twist over on to the instep in a very aggravating manner, when one is walking along a hillside.

I stayed in camp next day, as my feet were sore, and Sharafa had to prepare the head and skin of the márkhor. The horns were 30·5 inches long, and the girth round the base was 11·5 inches; divergence at tip, 26 inches. The length was below the average, but the other measurements were good, and the horns were a handsome pair. When the coolies brought in the carcase, we found that the bullet had hit the márkhor behind the small ribs, touching the spine, which was not much injured; the shock, however, must have quite paralysed it. We found this flock of márkhor very low down, much lower than I imagined they ever went. The two largest had white coats, the other two were very small, and of a dark colour: I got the largest of the lot. The shikáris went up Amátabar to look for márkhor. By the way, when I got out rifle No. 1, I found I had been using the barrel of No. 2 on the stock of No. 1—proof of the perfection which the gunmaker has attained.

I heard to-day that the Dichal valley was not likely to be vacant for some time, or indeed at all. Every one of the usual márkhor valleys was occupied; so I had simply to go on and on until I came to good ground which I could occupy. The shikáris returned in the evening, saying they had seen two large márkhor—one very old and emaciated, and with horns of three curves. Accordingly I got up early and went straight up hill above camp. After a long pull we got to the top of the ridge dividing the Garai from the Amátabar, and after some searching with glasses the shikáris spotted a large márkhor on a ridge of rocks on the opposite side, but he was not the three-curved one. I never saw this animal the whole day, and for a very good reason—he existed only in the imaginations of my men. Gharíba said there was no way of getting at the márkhor opposite, unless we went up the valley a day's journey, and then came back on the other side. If we went straight down and up, the quarry would see us before we had gone a hundred yards; so there was nothing to do but study his manners and customs during the day, in the hope that he would get into a more favourable position by evening. I examined him carefully through the big telescope; he was not much larger than the one I had shot, but his horns perhaps were a few inches longer. I could see plainly that they diverged outwards in a very remarkable way. He seemed very uneasy and alarmed; he did not graze for more than five minutes at a time in any one spot, though it was his feeding time, but kept to the rocks, looking about. It appeared to me that he was either ill or wounded, or had very lately been fired at. The shikáris said a shot was heard here the day we came up —most likely a shepherd's. We saw a flock of ibex higher up the valley, but no big horns.

In these valleys the wind blows upwards from sunrise to sunset, and the reverse way during the night. Sharafa had studied this part of his work thoroughly, and was always correct in his conclusions regarding the wind's direction. Ibex are always found higher up the valleys than márkhor: the latter seem able to endure heat better than ibex, but they stick much more closely to rocky precipices and dangerous ground than the ibex, who generally graze and wander about on level grassy hillsides for longer periods than márkhor. It was an unsatisfactory business watching that márkhor, as it turned out : having studied the wary brute all day while he kept to his rocks, he crossed the ridge and disappeared from sight just as the sun was setting; no doubt he went across to have his evening's feed, and must have come back to his citadel for the night after we left for camp.

On the following day I went up early to the ridge where I shot the márkhor, but could see nothing for a long time. At last there was a great rattling of stones under the precipice I was sitting over, and soon after some females and one small márkhor were sighted far below. The buck was last—a very small fellow, hardly full grown. Wanting meat, I had two shots at him, and gladly put on record that I missed. I returned to camp at noon, turning a deaf ear to the shikári who tempted me with stories of magnificent ibex higher up this valley ; I wanted márkhor first, and so prepared for a move to other ground.

Returning by the road we came, we reached Dashkin at two o'clock. Coolies were not procurable, so I remained for the day. No tent was put up, so I had to dodge the sun round a bush. While I was having tea under my bush, an old man from the village came up; he told me that he was formerly one of the lambardárs of Dashkin, and was turned out because he was out-bribed by the present holder of the appointment. It seems the Wazír makes him the head-man who bribes highest. My visitor had weak eyes, and wanted medicine for them, so I told him to wash them often in fresh goat's milk. He remarked he was strong enough otherwise, though eighty years old. He remembered Hayward very well, and mentioned his name. He passed through Dashkin on his way to Yasín.

We left Dashkin at half-past three in the morning; it was very dark, as the moon was behind the hill; we had to use the lantern for an hour or so. After starting, we came on the fresh droppings of a bear on the pathway. He was travelling in the same direction that we were going, and could not have been far ahead of us, but the lantern and the noise we made no doubt soon alarmed him. We reached Tor-billing village (three huts only) soon after six. From these huts there is a short cut to the Búldar nálá, a famous ground for márkhor; it was, of course, occupied. There are a great number of roads about here; I noticed this in many other places on my journey up. The explanation given was that when the Wazír of the district was hard-up for money, he wrote to Kashmir that he had discovered a new line of country, by which a much better and shorter road could be made, if the funds were supplied. The funds generally were supplied, a new path was made by the people of the country, and the Wazír replenished his private treasure-chest with the cash. At Doín village there was another road much higher up than the path I was on, called the "Mule Road"; there was another below, and I could plainly see a third across the river, on the opposite edge of the valley. Half-way between Doín and the highest ridge, about the middle of one of the zigzags along a precipice, we met two Sappers of the Kashmir Engineers coming from Búnji. One was leaning against the rocky side of the path, looking so sick that I thought him at the point of death; his companion was sitting close by almost as helpless. The former had given out at this point, and could go no farther, so the two had made up their minds to pass the night here. Such a place to spend the night! The wind was blowing cold, there was a slight drizzle, and the men were clothed in the scantiest rags; stones and rocks were constantly falling from above, and crossed the path with a whiz like that of a bullet; but these poor creatures were too apathetic to care. They had some rice, but could not cook it, having neither wood nor water. Sharafa rose to the occasion: pulling some sticks from the floor of the path (which was laid along beams fixed in the rock), he made them a fire, filled their pot with water, and arranged for the cooking of their rice. As it was getting late, we had to leave, advising the two Sappers to move lower down to a safer place after their meal. Both were Báltis (natives of Baltistán or Little Tibet).

I was informed that the whole corps of "Safar maina" was recruited from that country — that is to say, were forcibly taken from their homes, sent under an escort to some distant part whence they could not desert, and formed into regiments of Sappers for work on the roads, etc. They never saw their country again! Several times during this journey I met parties of these poor creatures carrying their tools, a long-handled matchlock, cooking-pots and several days' provisions, in the shape of a bag of flour, and toiling along the road to and from Astór. Their dejected air and humble mien were distressing. They were all *Shías*, and consequently heretics, and treated by the *Súnnís* (orthodox Musalmáns) as the scum of the earth. We reached Rámghát at 7.45 P.M., rather fagged; the descent was rough, but nothing in comparison with the path on the other side. Rámghát is a bridge on the Astór river, with some sepoys' huts about it—a most horrible place. The hillsides come straight down to the water's edge on both sides, and there was no level space for anything. There was one hut near the bridge, and a large cave higher up. The sepoys have to fish in the river for passing logs to use as fuel. I had to put up here for the night, as there was a bad place just beyond the bridge, and the coolies refused to cross in the dark. My quarters were unsavoury, to say the least; but I was tired out, so was not altogether sorry to stay. I did not get much sleep; a hurricane was blowing down the river, and the sand and grit hailed upon me the whole night, like charges of small shot; it was very hot, too, and altogether I had a disagreeable time of it.

We started at three o'clock, and, following a very bad road, came out upon a plain, sloping down from the range on the right to the level of the Indus. The ground is very stony, and cut up by narrow channels made by the rush of rain-water down to the river. This is the famous Búnji plain, where úrin (wild sheep) are so numerous during the winter. It is a very ugly bit of country, without a tree or blade of grass to relieve its monotony. After toiling two hours along this seemingly endless desert, we came suddenly to the brink of a deep, broad ravine, with a small stream running at the bottom. This is the Búnji nálá, and on the other side is Búnji itself, smothered in green trees. There were green fields, too, and lots of running water: what a contrast to the country we had just passed through! We reached Búnji at half-past six and, after a rest, visited the post office, and made the acquaintance of Commandant Bágh Singh, in charge of the fort at Búnji. He was very kind and obliging, owing to a happy mistake on his part. After making a few inquiries, he suddenly came to the conclusion that I was an old friend of his who used to be very kind to him in the plains a few years ago. He said I was not altered in the least after so many years' toil in the heat, and recognised me, nay, every feature in my face, at once! I had never met him in my life before, but did not feel called upon to correct the lucky mistake. The result was that my arrangements were completed in an hour, and I was allowed to cross the Indus and make for my hunting ground without any opposition. There was a standing order that no sporting gentleman, nor any other, was to cross the river, as the country on the other side was considered dangerous. All I was asked to do was to write a few lines, saying that if anything happened to me on the other side, no one was to be blamed, and that I went entirely on my own responsibility. There was, however, I think, another reason: a sportsman had already crossed. That being the case, it was rather difficult for the officials at the fort to make objections to my crossing. I was informed that my precursor had had some difficulty, but he arranged it by some management on the part of his shikári. I had no particular desire to have my sport across the Indus—I was simply driven in that direction by force of circumstances. All the good Cis-Indus shooting grounds were occupied, and I did not care to go farther up the river in the direction of the Bara Lóma, as I had already come far enough, and my leave was for three months only. Hearing that there was a vacant valley on the right bank of the river, I made for it at once, and the excellent Commandant Bágh Singh, by his mistake, facilitated my movements in no small degree.

We crossed the Indus at mid-day, and went on at once to the village of Damót—the valley that was to be my hunting ground. The sportsman before me had been shooting for the last fortnight, but, as he had bagged nothing, I thought there was a chance of picking up a couple of good heads. We moved up to the next valley, Jagót, where I heard he was equally unsuccessful. My tent was pitched under a beautiful wide-spreading walnut tree, round which had been built a broad and clean platform. The Damót stream flowed below, a few paces off, and there were a few houses of the village some distance above. It was a pleasant spot. I made the acquaintance here of Wazír Búghdór Sháh, the head-man of this and the neighbouring villages, and the Kashmiri official in charge of affairs on this side of the river. The Wazír was a tall, well-made, gentlemanly-looking man, of very dignified deportment. He was an agreeable old fellow, fond of saying his prayers, and very conscious of his dignity.

CHAPTER IV

MARKHOR SHOOTING—(*continued*)

Village of Damót—Compulsory labour—March up the valley—Good signs of márkhor—One killed by leopard—Theory regarding horns—A night out—A black bear's family—A fatiguing and useless ascent—Game not visible—Meet a brown bear, but lose my chance—Sight a márkhor at last—The stalk impossible—A tramp of thirteen hours—Find a fifty-two inch horn—Márkhor get the upper hand—An extemporised observatory—Begin a stalk of twenty-four hours—Failure at first—Great exposure—A bad night under a rock—Hard work again—Make bad shooting—A last and lucky shot—Bag a forty-seven incher—A "haláling" dispute—The theory of "haláling"—Dimensions of márkhor shot.

I FOUND the surroundings so pleasant at this village that I halted here to rest and to make the necessary arrangements for my shoot in the valley above.

Búghdór Sháh has all the villages as far as Chakarkót under his charge. They are all on or near the high road to Gilgit, and the begári work (compulsory labour) fell heavily on the people: there was a constant stream of officers and men to and from Gilgit, and their baggage had to be carried by the villagers, who did two marches in either direction before they could be relieved. In the Astór direction they went as far as Dashkin, and by result they were constantly absent from their fields for three and four days at a time.

As this went on during all seasons of the year, the people were very hard pressed. Many homes were broken

MARCH UP DAMOT VALLEY

up; the men ran away across the border, which is, here, only a few miles off, and settled in villages beyond the influence of this tyranny. The Wazír complained bitterly of the difficulty of his position. On the one hand, he had to satisfy the constant demands for carriage; on the other, he had to see to the cultivation of the fields by means of the men he had to send away as porters. The system of compulsory labour is very oppressive in every part of Kashmir, and it is greatly aggravated by the numbers of English travellers who wander about this country for eight months of the year. Rozi Khán of Astór was also very bitter on this subject. Every head-man I met and spoke to brought it forward at once as the grievance of the people, and I myself have been witness more than once of the hardships they endured through it: for instance, the coolie difficulty at Marmai.

The Damót valley is easy going along the streams for some distance. I passed the family mansion of the Wazír in a shady grove of fruit-trees, surrounded by a stone wall, water sparkling and murmuring in every direction—a pleasant spot. Mulberry trees and cultivation were scattered along the waterside all the way, flocks of goats were feeding about, wild rose trees were in full bloom, and a gentle breeze blowing in my face brought the fresh scent of the flowers. The morning was cloudy and cool, and I enjoyed the walk immensely. The valley is narrow; steep, rocky hills on either side, without a trace of vegetation on them; the green bits along the water's edge are real gems in a very rough setting. Our camping place was about four miles from the village, and on reaching it I sent back three coolies, reducing the party to six—Sharafa, Gharíba, Mirza Khán (local shikári), breakfast coolie Jamála, and two others. I left the tent and heavy baggage behind, also the khidmatgár. All my

supplies came from the village, so it was well to reduce
the number of men with me. My own food was cooked
at the village and sent up daily. The shikáris went on
after we camped in order to view the ground higher up,
and I remained behind. Towards evening, while lying on
the ground, my eyes wandering over the steep hillside
before me, I saw a female márkhor on a rock a few
hundred yards above, sharply defined against the sky. I
went down with Gharíba to a ravine on the left of the
main stream, to watch in case there might be a buck close
by, but we saw only three females coming down the ridge,
under which a flock of goats were grazing. The márkhor
evidently wanted to come down for a drink, but were
afraid to venture so low. After watching them for a while,
we came back to camp and found there Sharafa, who said
he had seen only two males, a great distance off, high up
on the ridge above camp.

We started early, and went straight up a nálá, turning
up the hillside over our camping place, a steady ascent
for more than two hours. Many old signs of very large
márkhor were visible, but no trace of the two bucks seen
on the previous evening, so we crossed the ridge and
descended to the next nálá. Having had breakfast at a
spring, we scrambled down the face of a precipice, holding
on to ledges, and went up the valley, which is a very
narrow one; but the wind began to blow very strongly
upwards, that is, from us, and as there was also slight rain,
we lay up for a time until the wind abated. Sharafa found
the head, horns, and backbone of a márkhor that had been
killed about twelve days previously, evidently an old buck,
judging from the long beard; but the horns were only
thirty-four and a half inches long, and were quite joined
together at the base. This, and their shortness, Mirza
Khán said, was due to the owner being one of a pair of

twins—an item in natural history that should be noted.
My informant meant that when a female markhor brings
forth only one kid, the horns, if a male, grow to great size;
but when two are brought forth, the horns are small. He
said a leopard had killed it, and, as we saw fresh traces of
a leopard on the ridge above, the absence of markhor was
probably explained. The ground was first-rate for them,
and Mirza Khán said this nálá was always a sure find. I
sent down Gharíba and a coolie to bring up bedding and
food, as I intended staying out the night, so as to be on
the next ridge and valley early in the morning. Mirza
Khán said the markhor must be there, as they had been
driven out of this by the leopard. Rain began again in
the evening, accompanied by a very cold wind, but my
shelter was dry and comfortable. It was a hollow under
a huge rock, nicely cleaned out, and dry grass spread at the
bottom. Mirza Khán said this was one of his "shooting-
boxes." At certain times of the year he concealed himself
here, and when the markhor came down to drink at the
spring, he shot them.

I passed a fairly comfortable night, and the morning
was bright and clear. We went up the left side of the
valley above the spring and on to a ridge, whence we looked
for markhor, but saw none. Sharafa discovered two very
small black bear cubs playing at the mouth of a cave;
there was no sign of the mother. I watched the cubs
climbing and wrestling for nearly two hours from the top
of a rock, twenty yards off; the white half-moons on
their chests were distinctly visible, and the point of the
under jaw was of a reddish colour. Sharafa said some
have the point of the lower jaw white, and that those with
the reddish colour were always the fiercest. We came to
the conclusion that the mother was in the cave, as it was
unlikely she would go far from such young cubs. So I

got the rifle ready and had stones thrown into the cave. No result. We did not proceed to extremities, as I was not anxious to shoot her, for the youngsters would certainly have died of starvation. Higher up the ridge we came to a forest of birch and fir, with rocky places here and there —just the spots for márkhor, but we could not find a sign of them. We went up higher, close to the snow-line, saw nothing, and descended into the valley. A short distance down we passed many places where márkhor droppings lay in heaps, but all of old date.

Next day we were out again at five o'clock. Soon after seven we sat down on the first spur, and searched the hillsides carefully, but saw nothing. My predecessor must have frightened all the game farther up, for, though he bagged nothing, he had had a good many shots. We now changed our direction and toiled straight up till we reached a ridge of flat slate rocks, four and a half hours from starting. This was the greatest grind I yet had, going straight up without a halt. When I got to the pine forest I was thoroughly done. This seemed to me to be quite over-doing the business; two days at least should have been spent over the extent of ground we did this morning. I saw traces of márkhor now and then, but all old. I was certain we had come too high; this ground must be their headquarters later on, in July perhaps, when it gets very hot lower down. It was too cold for them so high up just now: there was a good deal of snow lying about still. All the places we visited were splendid for márkhor, and they must be numerous here at the proper season. Mirza Khán was in the habit of hunting them later in the year, when he had harvested his corn and came up to the grassy slopes to graze his goats during the rutting season (October). He had found them here then, and so concluded they would be found in the same place in May. After breakfast, and half an hour's rest, we went along the hillside; and after going some distance, and getting low down, we heard a cry, which Sharafa said was that of a very young bear cub. Soon after, we sighted the mother and youngster very low down. We at once went for them, but it was very difficult ground, and we had to go slowly and cautiously. It now began to rain and sleet; the bears, too, began to move towards us for a short distance, and then crossed to a slope on our right. We waited for them to come up opposite us, when they would have been only fifty yards off, but, unluckily, they went straight along the hillside, and did not ascend in our direction. Sharafa entreated me to fire when they were a hundred yards off, but, feeling certain they would come closer, I lost my chance. The wind was most uncertain. The bears must have scented us, for we never saw them again, though we followed their tracks at a good pace, on fair ground, for some distance. This was very disappointing, for the female was a very large one, and had a splendid dirty-white coat; the hair on her sides almost touched the ground. The cub was half-grown. I was very savage with myself for not taking my only chance of a shot. I was rather fagged now, and my left knee was painful, as I had given it a bad knock in the hurry of following the bears—it was the knee I smashed in an exactly similar manner ten years before; my feet also were very sore from so many hours of continuous walking, so we made for camp along a very rough and steep goattrack. When we got round the shoulder of the hill, we were in sight of, but still far above, the camp on the main stream. Sharafa had seated himself to have a rest and to examine the rocks, when suddenly he spied a large male márkhor among the cliffs on the right, about a thousand yards off, above us a little and in a most impossible-looking place. He came suddenly round a corner on to a sheet of sloping rock, and kept turning and looking about, showing all his grand points, as if in derision. He had a splendid pair of horns, with two curves, wide-spreading, and with a grand sweep. They were at least fifty inches in length; he looked a veritable monster, with his great flowing beard, and shaggy coat hanging down his sides, light in colour on the fore part, darker on the hind quarters, quite different from the dirty-white colour of the one I shot in the Garai. We saw only this one, but Mirza Khán insisted that there were several others, and that this was one of the flock we had been seeking all day. While we had been toiling and sweating at the back of the range looking for them, they were quietly feeding about these cliffs, not half a mile from the camp, and actually in sight of it! When we made the first halt in this morning's ascent and searched this hillside in this very direction, they could not have been farther from us than they were now; they must then have been feeding in some grassy ravine out of sight. It was now four o'clock, and too late to do anything, for to get at the márkhor it would be necessary to go back and up the gorge where the bears had bolted, then round the top of the ridge to the edge of the precipice below the place where we saw the márkhor. This could not be done before night set in. The grand old buck came down a little way, fed for about five minutes, went up again and disappeared round a projecting point, and we did not see him again. I had the tents and the khidmatgár brought up here, and made this the base of my operations, for the shooting grounds were too far from the village to be convenient. I was now in the centre of the valley, about six miles from the village, and the same distance from the line of watershed on the main range. I was on the tramp this day for thirteen hours (too much for pleasure), and my feet were very sore. I must add that about an hour after leaving camp, Sharafa picked up an old márkhor horn, which measured fifty-two inches! A shepherd told us he had seen a flock of ten márkhor two days before on the left of the main stream a little below camp.

I remained in my tent for a rest next day, sending Gharíba and Mirza Khán to search for the flock seen by the shepherd. They returned in the evening, having seen nothing, though they came across plenty of fresh tracks, etc., but about the same time Sharafa sighted a flock of seven márkhor on the opposite hillside, some distance up, just above our camp. There was great excitement in consequence—fires were put out, coolies crawled about on hands and knees to get under cover, and spoke in whispers. An observatory was extemporised at the tent door, and the binocular and telescope were permanently focussed on the animals above us. These observations began at 4 P.M. and went on till 7 P.M. The single márkhor seen the previous evening must have been one of this lot—they were nearly in the same place. They grazed down gradually in a slanting direction, and came very low, evidently wishing to come down to the stream for a drink, but afraid of the camp. They were last seen on a hill slope, half a mile from camp, up stream; but as we were below them all the time, we could not stir, and watched them patiently for a chance which never came.

The márkhor were in the same place next morning, and we started in a very hopeful frame of mind, but had great difficulty in getting along, as they were in sight, and we were below them. The wind was blowing from our direction, and, as we had to push along without viewing the game, the stalk failed; it could not have been otherwise under such conditions. The márkhor had the better of us, both

as to wind and sight, simply because they were above us—
and they scored. After going along cautiously for a time,
we heard their note of alarm, and knew we had been
discovered. Shortly after, we saw them making straight
for the precipitous rocks on the sky-line. When they
were out of sight, we followed and went along below the
cliffs, scrambled up some ugly places, and soon after came
on our footmarks of the 14th, and up we went again
along that same toilsome ascent. We followed our old
footsteps till we came to the fir forest, then Mirza Khán
took us along the hillside; but when we came to the
rocky ledge overlooking the spot where the márkhor had
been last seen, they had vanished. I had breakfast and
started again at ten, Mirza Khán, who knew every inch
of the ground, and also all the dodges of the wily
márkhor, leading; he concluded that they had topped the
ridge, crossed the fir forest, and made off for a fresh
resting-place higher up, and behind the ridge bounding the
pine forest on the other side. His forecast was perfectly
correct. After going a short distance, we came on fresh
tracks, showing that they had run fast through the forest.
They must have crossed here while we were toiling up to
the steep, and have got our wind again. We followed the
tracks to the opposite side of the valley, bounded by a
rocky ridge, terminating in a very precipitous hill, up
and round which the márkhor had gone. I remained
below, while Mirza Khán and Sharafa followed up to see
if they could see them on the other side. This was a
dangerous piece of work, and evidently Sharafa did not
like it. Mirza Khán, knowing the ground, went first, and
the last I saw of them was climbing a pine-tree in a
narrow cleft between two rocks, which apparently was the
only way of doubling round the hill: from the top of the
tree they jumped out of sight. An hour afterwards they

reversed the performance and came *down* the same way. They had not seen the runaways, but reported a solitary márkhor sitting on a rocky ledge on the other side of a ravine. Mirza Khán now led us over some very awkward ground, an open spot in the forest, where we stopped and examined the rocks where the solitary male had been seen, and by good luck sighted our friends, the seven, at once!

For two hours we watched them from this breezy ridge. The snow lay in large patches, and the wind was cutting, and I suffered severely from sitting so long in a cramped and exposed position; but the márkhor at last grazed away down the slope, crossed the ridge, and disappeared: this was about 5 P.M. I got off the ridge and into my overcoat at once, and had something to eat with a sip of tea, then walked briskly up and down hill to get warm, but it took time before my teeth stopped chattering. Jamála had been sent down for food and bedding in the morning, as soon as we had made certain that the márkhor would give us a long chase, and I was now determined to follow them till I got a chance. Mirza Khán was on his mettle too, and vowed he would track them till he brought me within range. The coolies were heard below in the forest just as the márkhor had crossed over, so we went down a short distance and whistled them up. We then went along a goat-track till we reached the ridge a good way above the point where the márkhor had disappeared, crossed it, and went down the other side for half a mile, until we found a suitable place, and camped for the night under some rocks, late in the evening. It had been raining during the day, and it now began to sleet and snow. It was the more disagreeable, as the rock I was under only half protected me, and I could not keep my bedding dry.

Dinner was a difficult performance under the circumstances. I was established on a shelf two feet wide, beyond which the hillside fell away abruptly, while at my back the rock rose perpendicular. Dinner consisted of two lumps of tinned beef and two chapátis (cakes) cooked the day before. It was dark, and the lantern had to be lighted, then the umbrella had to be opened, and it had to be held—trifles which become serious tasks in a high wind. My attention was equally divided between the lantern, which threatened every moment to take a header down hill, the umbrella, which tried to elope with every gust that came round the corner, and my own mouth. I managed them all, for I was hungry, but I have enjoyed more comfortable dinners. However, after the eating apparatus had been put away, the umbrella folded, and a glass of whisky and water stowed away over the dinner, I was contented. The sense of comfort that creeps over the sportsman at this hour, just before he sinks into the sleep that is fast approaching, is well worth the twelve hours' previous toil.

I had not been asleep long when I was brought back to a sense of my awkward position by snowflakes falling on my face. My faithful umbrella, that usually formed part of my pillow, saved my head, but snow was slowly piling on the waterproof sheet over my blankets, and, while I was speculating on the probable depth that would cover me by morning, I fell asleep again; but my slumbers were disturbed. Fear lest my good umbrella should vanish in an extra strong gust, prevented sound sleep. Its loss would have been serious. I held it with one hand all night, awaking several times—sometimes to see a twinkling star overhead, sometimes to feel the steadily falling snow. I had a series of dreams—demons were rushing away with my helpless self and umbrella, or huge markhor came peeping over the ledge of rock to look at me defiantly, and my rifle not at hand! I was well

"HUGE MARKHOR CAME TO LOOK AT ME DEFIANTLY."

nightmare-ridden, and was awake, and longing to be up, a couple of hours before dawn illumined the sky.

As soon as we could see to pick our steps, we made a start after the márkhor. Reaching the top of the ridge, we followed it till we found their tracks, and carried these down steadily for four hours. Going down this ridge was terrible work—I am sure we did not cover over a mile in that time. The whole distance was one mass of crumpled rocks with great gaps between—the rocks were knife-edged, the slope below was frightful, and ended in sheer precipices. Mirza Khán led us over this dangerous ground at a good pace, always some distance ahead, carefully peeping over the precipices on either side, and searching the hillsides below with the binoculars. Sharafa looked serious, not relishing the work at all, for Mirza Khán was a perfect cragsman, and beat him at it out and out; so my head shikári had to play second fiddle throughout.

I gave in after 9 A.M. and sat down, blessing the márkhor with all my heart, and keeping an eye all the time on Mirza Khán a good distance below, quartering the ground like the best of trained dogs. At last came his faint whistle—it galvanized us like the shock from a battery, and the excitement began. I reached Mirza Khán in less than no time, and learned that he had sighted the flock far down below the precipices. He led on for half a mile, and then we had the márkhor below us: they were feeding at the foot of the cliff on a patch of young grass.

It was impossible to get a shot from this point, so we went farther along the ridge to take them in flank, though the range was greater. We came at length to a projecting rock with a stunted fir-tree by it, which served for cover, though cover was not necessary, as we were above the animals this time, and they were so intent on the tender herbage that there was no danger of detection. I got into position and picked out the largest pair of horns I could see; waited some time till I got a broadside shot, fired and—missed. Fired the second barrel and missed again! Then I took the second rifle, and at the third shot broke a fore leg. Another large márkhor now came into view, and I fired the fourth shot at him—missed again! Sharafa handed me the first rifle reloaded, and I fired again at the wounded one, who was now making off—and missed once more. The agony of that moment! The brute was limping off; he would be round a projection out of sight in ten paces. Just at the turn he stopped for a second to look back; it was my last shot and my last chance. Desperation steadied me; I put up the second sight, and placed the bullet behind the right shoulder; the márkhor rolled down the slope and was brought up dead. The range could not have been less than three hundred yards.

Firing downwards at an angle of thirty degrees is very ticklish work, and many misses must occur unless one is well practised in this kind of shooting. At the last shot, the animal, though farther off, was nearly on a level, so it was an easier shot. Mirza Khán and Gharíba, with knives drawn, started off at a frightful pace to perform the *halál* (cutting the throat), but they had to go down round one slope, cross the ravine, and up the opposite hillside, and it was at least fifteen minutes before they reached the victim—too late, for the old buck was dead long before they arrived. The halál was a failure; but would not have been if Sharafa had not been so scrupulous. He shouted that the animal was dead, and no halál was possible, but to be careful about cutting well below the throat, etc. —he was mindful of the "setting up" and its requirements. Gharíba in a rage shouted back that he would halál. Sharafa then said the meat would be *makrúh* (unlawful), and that was the end of it. I now found out from

Sharafa that, in this country, the game is always considered "halál," provided the hunter, after shooting the animal, follows him up at once, and does not sit down till he has cut its throat, though the cutting may be performed hours after the animal has been hit, or is dead. This convenient interpretation of the law saves a good deal of meat which would otherwise be wasted in a difficult country like this. Musalmáns always have some convenient dodge like this for circumventing the law. Sharafa superintended the cutting-off of the head, through the telescope. The dimensions taken at camp, whither we now returned, were—length of horns round curve, 47 inches; girth at base, $11\frac{1}{4}$ inches; divergence at tips, $26\frac{3}{4}$ inches. I measured the hoof of one of the fore legs—length, $3\frac{1}{2}$ inches; breadth at heel, $2\frac{1}{4}$ inches. Of my six shots only two took effect; the third broke the left fore leg at the knee, the sixth was through the right shoulder—a splendid shot at three hundred yards, if not more. This márkhor's coat was quite different from that of the one first shot; the colour of the latter resembled the dirty white fleece of a sheep. The pelage of this one was the same as that described by Ward in his book, page 17—a reddish or brownish hue, mixed with white in front and a darker shade towards the hind quarters. The hair was not long, except that of the beard, which waved down splendidly. He looked thin, and had a tucked-up appearance, due perhaps to old age, for his teeth were worn nearly to the gums, and the horns were battered and chipped. When Mirza Khán and Gharíba appeared with head and skin, they used strong language to Sharafa for causing so much meat to go waste. I think he made a mistake by interfering with the halál.

CHAPTER V

MARKHOR SHOOTING—(*continued*)

Begin another hunt—Sharafa kills a snake—Eagles' chase after a snow-cock—Márkhor tactics—Watching game—Hard work and no reward—Mirza Khán in fault—Lose a splendid chance—Legend of the Major and the Saint of Ghór—Change our ground—Sight game—Our cautious (and ridiculous) tactics—Bag the márkhor at last—A candid confession—An undisputed "halál"—Mirza Khán's capacity for meat—Another shooting-box of Mirza Khán's—Spend a night in a watercourse—A bit of Kashmir in a rough setting—Inhabited by a microscopic but hugely vicious fly—Wily márkhor—Bad going—Mirza Khán makes a slip—Long shots—Very dangerous ground—Rain and snow in a tight camping place—My rocky home—Cross the same dangerous ground again—Mirza Khán makes another slip—A bad two seconds on the brink of prospective eternity—Bad weather conquers—Márkhor shooting ends.

THAT night it snowed and rained heavily, so I took a day off, and enjoyed the rest. A large márkhor was seen from the camp in the evening, and next morning we went after it, making a start at five o'clock. After following the stream along a narrow valley on the right, we came on tracks of márkhor which had just come down the hillside we intended to ascend, and had gone up stream; we sighted them soon after on the ridge. They must have seen us, for they were alarmed: had we been fifteen minutes earlier, we should have met them face to face. Turning up the hillside, we came across numbers of márkhor tracks, quite fresh—no doubt made by the flock we had just seen. Going on, we disturbed three females among some rocks: there was great hurry and excitement getting the rifles out of their cases, but no buck appeared. We went up higher and higher, and at last crossed the dividing ridge where the márkhor was seen last evening; there was no sign. Along the hillside up the valley the ground was very bad and very slow-going,—precipices and rocks,—but just the place for the game we were after. Some more females were in sight and two bucks with very small horns; shortly after two more, but not worth stalking. One of these was lying on a rock just under us, but out of range; he was looking down the valley with a most steady gaze, never dreaming that his greatest enemy was above him. Sharafa made a slight noise, and the buck vanished like a phantom, and we never saw him again. This youngster had a dirty white coat similar to the buck I shot in the Garai. These animals, like all hill game, watch downwards and listen upwards, the organs being admirably placed for the purpose. During the whole of this dangerous journey we saw nothing more, and descended to the bottom of the valley over ground worse than any I had crossed during the day—and that is saying a good deal. We did not go over much ground, but it was slow and dangerous work for the latter half of the day.

Next morning we were out again at six, bound for the ridge where we saw the large márkhor yesterday—those that had crossed our path a short time before we came up. An ascent of three hours to the top gave us a sight of their tracks, but nothing more. Sharafa killed a large snake (viperous) among some rocks, catching it by the back of the neck. He said he was not afraid, as he knew a *mantar* (charm) that would protect him even if bitten. Many natives pay for their belief in a mantar with their lives, but faith in the potency of charms survives.

Two large dark hawks, or eagles, passed a few yards over my head in full pursuit of a large snow-cock; they went at a terrific pace, but the snow-cock had a good start, and I think got under shelter on the next ridge before his pursuers could catch him: it was a grand sight, though it lasted only for a few seconds. The weather was very muggy and hazy since the rain and snow. We could not see any distance distinctly. Sharafa, who had gone farther up, came back to report seven large márkhor in a small valley to the left, but they soon fled out of sight round a rock, and Mirza Khán said there was absolutely no way by which we could follow them. About two o'clock we sighted the same lot of márkhor on the hillside right across the valley, and shortly after another flock of three smaller animals some distance lower down. It was most provoking. Yesterday we were on that side of the valley on the very ground these animals now occupied, and sighted the márkhor on this side. To-day, after toiling up to this ridge, we saw the bucks on the very ground we went over yesterday. There was no way of getting near them, so we lay down comfortably under the shade of pines, and studied them till it was time to go down.

This watching of the game and noting their habits is, I think, only less pleasant than the actual stalk and the successful shot at the end of it. The seven males were immense brutes, every one with splendid horns and long shaggy beard and coat that seemed, through the telescope, to sweep the ground as they grazed about. These old gentlemen, like humans who have passed the meridian of life, found their only pleasure at the table, and were very intent on their dinner, never for a moment ceasing to feed till it was time to retire: they then grazed their way slowly up, towards some rocks, where doubtless they passed the night. Two of the other lot were more lively;

after a few mouthfuls of grass they would turn to and have a friendly trial of strength, butting each other, locking and unlocking their horns, retiring, then standing on their hind legs and clashing their horns with a report that could be distinctly heard. These games went on till one gave in and turned, when the victor would give the vanquished a parting butt in the rump and turn to grazing again. This performance was enacted several times.

We had intended sleeping in our old resting-place under the rock higher up, but Mirza Khán changed his tactics after sighting the markhor in the other valley, and brought us down to the main stream. We slept under the trees where we had camped the first day when we were coming up from the village.

The weather was very cloudy and rainy when we started at five o'clock, and the wind could not be trusted. After waiting for an hour the sun came out, and we went along the ridge to get above the spot where the markhor had been seen. Mirza Khán worked hard, never leaving a rock unsearched, though he risked his neck more than once to do it. We saw no sign of the beasts, however, and at last gave up the search, disappointed and disgusted. We were returning exactly the way we had gone up three days before, when the usual *contretemps* occurred. It was about five o'clock, and we were all going carelessly, and looking anxiously to the spot at the bottom of the valley where the coolies should be with the bedding, etc., when Mirza Khán, who was leading, topped a swell on the hillside, and came bang on to the seven large markhor we had been hunting for all day! They were not more than seventy yards off. The animals rushed down the slope, and by the time a rifle could be got out of the case, where they had been put as it was wet, they were on the opposite hillside, six hundred yards distant at least: they actually ran over the camp by the stream where the coolies were lying down! After glaring at each other for some time, we descended to camp, and the márkhor ascended to theirs. Language could not do justice to the occasion, and I recognised it, but I was so wild that I lost my appetite! A few minutes before, my imagination had been revelling in the pleasant prospect of dinner—tinned beef and chapáti though it was. When I reached camp, the very thought of food made me sick, and I went to bed at once, without a mouthful of any kind. Mirza Khán was no doubt most to blame; but he looked so miserable that I had not the heart to say a word to him. He threw himself on his face, and remained motionless as long as I could see him. I believe he, too, went to bed without any dinner.

The weather next day was horrible, and very unusual for these parts at this season. It rained till one o'clock, when we went up the main stream to have a look at the ground, and saw five young márkhor and several females: farther on there were three large rams, but we did nothing.

We went after those three large márkhor next morning, and reached the spot at nine o'clock. There was no trace of them excepting a few hoof-marks, but there were small márkhor in sight in three different places. They were so placed round us that we could not move an inch without being sighted by one or other of the flocks. It did not matter much so far as the small bucks were concerned, but if these were alarmed and bolted, the large ones would surely take the hint and bolt too. Patience and sleep were the only alternatives, and eventually we returned without seeing the game we were after, though we lay most of the day on the very ridge where they had been twelve hours before.

Mirza Khán told me that a few years ago the "Major Sahib" who was engaged in the survey of this valley, wished to map the country on the Ghór village side, but the Ghór people objected. The Major Sahib insisted. The Ghórians, however, were strong in possession of a powerful fakír, who could command the elements, and that very night, while the party were encamped here by the stream, he sent a tremendous flood, which rushed down the valley with an awful roaring. Most of the Major's followers were swept away, and he himself only escaped by rushing up the hillside with a lantern in his hand. What a sight it must have been—the Major in his pájámas, bolting up-hill with a lantern in the dead of night! The Wazír and his men lost all their traps while saving the Sahib's. The latter, however, got his way after all, for I have the map he made.

Just as the story was finished, there was a brilliant flash of lightning overhead, followed by three deafening thunderclaps. Their suddenness, close overhead, after Mirza Khán's story, was very startling, and had a telling effect on the men. The thought in everybody's mind must have been—"The Ghór fakír again angry at another Sahib's intrusion!" And he was no common magician, content with flash and sound only; the thunder was followed by a heavy hailstorm. It ceased when we were within a mile of camp, and could not have lasted more than twenty minutes. This was the first time since my arrival in the valley that I had seen lightning or heard thunder; it is not the season for them—more credit to the holy man!

The postman turned up on the evening of the 24th May. How I had longed for his appearance! He had taken more than twenty days to go to Srinagar and return, when he should have done it in fifteen. He was a snuff-taking old scoundrel, and too old for quick travelling: I made a mistake in taking him on. I wrote letters till noon, and, having despatched the postman on his return journey, took bedding and food and went down the main stream to the field, a mile or so above Damót village, and camped under a solitary tree. This was quite fresh ground, and Mirza Khán was confident of showing sport.

He said large márkhor were always seen on the last spurs of the range, between the main stream and the Indus, but higher up the hill we sighted a flock on the farthest ridge overhanging the river, and went after them at once, ascending and descending very cautiously about half a dozen intervening ridges and deep ravines. When the animals were first sighted they were coming down, apparently towards us, so that, after the third or fourth ravine had been crossed, we moved along with greater caution, expecting to meet them face to face as we topped each ridge. After creeping slowly to the top, and making careful survey of the ground below us, we rushed down the next slope at best pace, and repeated our tactics on the next hillside, and so on till we came to the last ravine, just above which we had sighted the flock. All our trouble was wasted, however, for when we arrived within a short distance of the spot where the márkhor had been last seen, we saw by their tracks that they had gone along grazing up the ravine, out of our view all the time, and had crossed over to the slope running down to the Indus.

Feeling rather done, I sat down while Mirza Khán followed up the track, step by step, to the top. I watched him creeping along ledges of rock, and holding on like grim death, and thanked my stars I was not with him! But fifteen minutes later I was working my way along the very same ledges, regardless of anything but the fact that the márkhor were just below the ridge in front of me and within range. Mirza Khán signalled the news after a careful peep over the hilltop. It was about ten o'clock, and the sun was very hot, and the márkhor were resting within a semicircular rocky enclosure, and were apparently looking down intently right into the Búnji fort, across the river, not a mile off. I was splendidly placed for a shot, but only one male márkhor was visible, lying in a corner on a ledge of rocks that protected him from the sun. He was so snugly placed that I could not make him out for some time, though he was not over a hundred and thirty yards off. The largest male, which we had noted when we first sighted the flock, was not to be seen. After a careful and unsuccessful search for him, I determined to loose off at the one before me, so rested the rifle on a rock and took careful aim—result only a broken fore leg. Nothing better could be expected when the animal was lying down. He looked up stupefied, and my next missed him clean; the third broke a hind leg. These shots disturbed the big one, and he rushed down the rocks towards the river at a frightful pace. After going down about two hundred yards, he stood for a moment on a projecting rock, and I had a snap-shot at him and missed. I had put up the second sight, and the bullet went over him. The wounded one was still standing on the ledge where he had been sleeping: he seemed paralysed, and kept shaking his wounded legs, as if endeavouring to get rid of something that was holding him down. My fifth shot was a miss too, but it moved the márkhor; he came hobbling down the rocks and stood in the sunshine on a smooth sloping slab of rock, looking quite bewildered, and not ninety yards away. He gave me a good broadside, and I put the sixth bullet through his shoulder. He rolled down the sloping rock for fifty yards, his horns rattling and banging in a way that made me tremble for them, but happily they escaped with only two or three bad gaps along the edges of the curve, and the tips somewhat damaged. So many misses disgusted me, and I looked on my two Henrys with anything but affection; but they were not in fault. In this instance I made the mistake of keeping the muzzles of the rifles in the shade of a bush to keep the foresight from catching the sun, but in the endeavour to effect this my position became awkward, and I could not place the foresight true on the animal's shoulder—hence the misses. I perceived my mistake at the fifth shot, and fired my last with the sight in the sun, and the bullet struck within three inches of the point aimed at. The horns were $35\frac{1}{2}$ inches long, 12 inches round base, 26 inches between tips. These horns quite met at the base behind, then curved out gracefully; they are massive, but the tips were ruined by the fall down the rocks. Mirza Khán, after examining the teeth, said the buck was six years old—half the age of the 47-incher; but the horns of the younger animal are much thicker. Mirza Khán and Jamála went down and did the halál, Sharafa making no objection this time, though the animal was of course dead before its throat was cut. The meat was stowed away in a hole and carefully covered with rocks, Mirza Khán saying he would send his brother up for it next day, we bringing away only the head and skin, as I thought, but Mirza Khán, it turned out, had the heart, liver, and saddle carefully packed up in the skin. He had great capacity for meat, and could eat any quantity without accompaniments, even without salt. On the way down we came to the bottom of a narrow valley, with a small spring of water oozing from beneath a rock. This was another shooting-box of Mirza Khán's. Water is scarce in these barren stony hills, and the márkhor came to this spring to drink. Just above the rock Mirza Khán showed me a small cave, nicely floored with grass, where he sat and potted the márkhor; the spring was just below, so the game approached within ten yards of his gun muzzle. It is not surprising that the márkhor disappear so fast when such murderous practices are followed.

The next was a blank day; we moved again, and camped in a small patch under a splendid pine, just opposite the rock where I had spent such an uncomfortable night before I got the 47-inch márkhor. This was the pleasantest camp I had in the valley, and my happiness would have been complete but for the attacks of a ferocious little fly. It was hardly big enough to see, but wherever it stung it left a minute blood-spot that itched dreadfully.

Next morning saw us making our way straight up from camp for the ridge above—a stiff ascent of two hours—where we had to remain an hour till the sun fell on the other slope. This delay is always disagreeable, as it is generally cold and windy, and there is seldom any protection. One dare not move down the other side as the wind is blowing downwards, and every head of game, down to the bottom of the valley, would scent you before you had gone a hundred yards. When the sun has warmed the hillside, the current is changed, and the winds blow upwards. You are then safe, and may walk up to a bear, and pull him by the ear before blowing his brains out. If the day is cloudy, however, you may as well give up stalking—the wind is everywhere. The shikári constantly halts, pulls some fluff from his woollen coat, and floats it away on the wind, watching the tiny speck anxiously. Then call patience to your aid, and wait, sit, sleep, do anything but move about. A cloudy day in the hunting grounds of Kashmir must give the recording angel above a busy time of it. At nine o'clock we descended the next slope, and saw two márkhor feeding on the hillside, near some birches, about six hundred yards off. Had we crossed earlier, we should never have seen these animals, as they would have got our wind at once. We made for them very cautiously, as they were in low jungle, and we were not aware of their exact whereabouts. Cautious as Mirza Khán and Sharafa were, they, or rather the first, made a mess of the stalk; it could hardly have been otherwise in such bad ground. As we crossed the top of a swell, covered with bushes, there was a crash below as of a large animal rushing through jungle. We rushed down five paces in the direction of the noise, and came upon the fresh tracks of a large márkhor. Following them, Mirza Khán again sighted the animals in an open space on the opposite side of a narrow valley, and down we went again. The slope was steep, the rocks were loose slates that answered with a metallic tinkle every time I put my foot down. Where there was no rock the ground was slippery from recently melted snow, and I had more than one agonising slip; but Mirza Khán crowned the record of accidents when, we having arrived within twenty yards of the animals, who were still out of sight, he slipped and rolled down the slope. The rifle which he was carrying nearly came to grief; it was plastered with mud, and showed some bad scratches on the barrels. Of course the márkhor were off, and I gave up following them after this. They were again sighted, but were much lower down, and going at a good pace. They did not seem to be very large ones after all—sour grapes!

We put up for the night in a goat-shed, and at five o'clock next morning went up the nálá above the hut, and had a cold time of it in the sun and wind for an hour. A young márkhor which came on the ridge in front of us, and about three hundred yards above, was all the game we saw that day, and I did not get a shot at him. Next day we went up Salat stream, and camped on its bank, about two miles from the tent. Mirza Khán said this was his pet nálá, and that he would show me some real old bucks very shortly.

We were on the move very early in the morning, and, crossing the stream to the right bank, went up a very steep and narrow gorge. It took us three hours to get to the top of the ridge. When we were more than half-way up, I saw a márkhor on the sky-line; he had seen us long before, and disappeared behind the ridge, after rolling down some stones, from which the coolies had a narrow escape. Leaving the men behind, in a depression, we crossed over and came to patches of snow on a hillside, with broken rocks scattered about a very bad bit of ground. Then an awkward scramble through a dense patch of young birches. We breakfasted at a snow stream, and then toiled on to the next ridge. Here we saw the márkhor again; he was lying in the shade of a birch-tree on the ridge we had just crossed, but lower down; he gave the alarm, and disappeared on the other side whence we had come. Disgusting! We had been looking for him all this time, and he had been lying comfortably at the foot of a tree not a dozen yards from the place where we had last seen him while toiling up the gorge. I put up for the day under a rock overlooking a bit of dense pine forest, while the two shikáris went lower down to look for game. I had a nap, and then took out a *Civil and Military Gazette*, more than a month old, and read it word for word nearly to the end. I was just getting through a report on cholera, by a Dr. Richards, and was wondering what "alvine choleraic discharges" meant, when a pebble fell on the paper. Looking up, I could just see Sharafa peeping over the rock above me. I crept round with all caution, to hear that there were three márkhor just in front of the rock where I had been sitting, not two hundred yards off, but invisible from that point on account of the trees. I went lower down with the men and watched these márkhor for more than an hour, for they were in a bad place, and we could not get closer as the ground was covered with dry birch leaves which crackled loudly under foot. After a time the márkhor moved, and we had to do so too. We went as far as we could, but the beasts were still more than three hundred yards off, and were feeding up, while we had come down, under the impression that they would feed down, as their custom is. The sun was blazing straight in my face, while the márkhor were in the shadow of the opposite spur, so I decided to fire before they grazed out of sight. I had eight shots, all at over three hundred yards, and missed every time! I simply could not see the foresight through the blinding glare of the level sun, and the shots went high. I saw only two of the márkhor—one a venerable old fellow with flowing beard and shaggy sides, whom I ought to have nailed at the first shot.

We had a troublesome march next day when we moved. The ground was so difficult and dangerous that we did not make more than a mile in two hours. We had to cross a ravine with perpendicular rocky sides, fifty feet deep at least; we had to scramble down rocks on one side and climb up a straight wall on the other. A fall, perhaps, would not have hurt anyone much, as the bottom was full of snow; but the risk lay in the certainty that if one did fall on the snow, he was likely to roll down the very steep ravine for about twenty yards to the edge of a sheer precipice of—heaven knows how deep. It came on to snow and rain after mid-day with a very cold and cutting wind. There were fresh márkhor tracks all over the place, but the weather shut us up, and we moved down to the bottom of the next valley and camped under a rock. The rain and snow continued till dark, but I was snugly placed under a huge rock that kept the rain and snow off my bedding; after a time the water did begin to trickle and drip. We remedied this by an elaborate arrangement of waterproof sheet, which carried off the rain and dropped it just beyond my bedding. This device having been completed with much care and pains, the rain and snow naturally ceased.

The morning brought rain and snow again, so I sent coolies down for more food and the small khâki tent, as I intended remaining where I was for several days.

For want of anything better to do, I examined my journal, and discovered I was two days behind time, making the 3rd June the 1st; a mistake that might have consequences when on privilege leave. When the snow or rain ceased, it became foggy, which was just as bad. The coolies brought up the tent in the evening, but we could find no ground level enough to pitch it, though an eight feet square would suffice. I was obliged, therefore, to spread it on the rock, and to secure it with a couple of ropes tied to a pine close by. This afforded more dry space, but no extra room, as the slope was very abrupt. I made a roaring fire of birch logs under the pine, a few feet from my rock, and toasted myself. I had to stand (there was no sitting room), and, as the wind never blew from one point for more than two minutes together, I was constantly moving to escape the smoke from the wet birch logs, which was most pungent and trying to the eyes. My revolutions round the fire soon became tiresome, and I was driven to the rock again. In this manner I passed the day. My companions were much worse off: Sharafa stowed himself away between two large rocks, roofed in with sheets of birch bark; Gharíba and Mirza Khán were crouched in a hole under a small rock, a few paces off, just big enough to hold them, curled up like a dog when he is very cold. The space into which these people can screw themselves and remain, asleep and awake, for hours, without change of position, is truly wonderful! The coolies managed the best way they could, mostly covered with their blankets round a huge log fire, as there were no more rocks to protect them.

The weather next day was as bad, but after breakfast I could hold out no longer, so made the shikáris come along the ridge towards the main stream; we saw nothing, as usual. The rain and snow, I fancy, had driven even the márkhor under cover, for the place we searched was the one where the nine large bucks had been seen from the opposite side of the main valley a few days before: we saw their tracks all over the place, and huge ones they were. I sat on the top of a conical hill under my umbrella for a couple of hours, while the shikáris hunted above and below, and then, convinced that the rock and roaring fire were more comfortable, returned to camp. It drizzled, snowed, hailed, sleeted, and rained alternately, but not for long at a time. This variety was no doubt interesting from a meteorological point of view, but not from mine. It cleared up at night, but clouds still hung about.

A comparatively clear morning was welcomed, and we started at five for the ridge where I had missed the márkhor eight times. We all agreed it was best to make the ground good in that direction, as during this bad weather the márkhor might have gone round there again. We had a very bad time, both going and coming, and saw nothing for our pains, though we did find the footmarks of some brutes that had actually walked over our tracks only a couple of days old! Going, we went along the hillside to avoid the ravine we had crossed before, and thus got into the snow and among huge rocks. We walked through this with frozen feet and aching fingers; then came to a steep hillside, one sheet of snow, down which we had to slide sitting. For punishment let me recommend this mode of progression when the snow just conceals numerous points of rock. Coming back, we shirked the ascent through the snow, and concluded to take our chance over the dangerous ravine. We had a bad five seconds crossing it. Sharafa, having better nerve on snow than Mirza Khán, went first; then the latter crossed, but, being too proud to use the foot-holes made by Sharafa, tried it a little higher up, while I followed Sharafa's track. About half-way across, Mirza Khán being a few feet above me, his feet slipped, and, as he felt himself losing his balance and coming down on me, he uttered a despairing groan, thinking he was slipping into eternity over the precipice a few yards below, and taking me with him. But Sharafa was watching us from the edge of the snow, and, coming back a few paces on his old track, held Mirza Khán up till I had passed. Had Mirza Khán slipped a couple of feet more, he must have had me down, and we should both have swished over the precipice in a second. There was absolutely nothing to stop us, if once started. Mirza Khán looked very yellow after, and it was very evident that his nerves had been shaken. It rained off and on during the whole day. The wretched weather played the mischief with my shooting in this direction. I had no more time to spare for the márkhor, as I intended to devote some days to the ibex, and secure a couple of good heads before I left. The large fires we made and the smoke from them must have had something to do with the disappearance of the márkhor from these hillsides, for though we came across innumerable tracks, a few days old only, every time we went out, we never saw a single animal.

After a last and despairing search for the nine large males next day, during which we never saw a horn, I gave up the markhor for good, and tried for ibex higher up the range for the first time. We soon sighted a large flock of females, but no bucks, so crossed down to a pleasant grassy hillside and fixed camp in a green hollow commanding grand snow views on all sides. I was out of sorts, probably from my enforced idleness under the rock on the other side. So the little khaki tent was put up, and I occupied it for the first time. It was very snug and comfortable, just the thing for this kind of work. How enjoyable it was to lie level, and be able to stretch out one's legs after so many nights cramped under the rock.

CHAPTER VI

IBEX SHOOTING

Gluttony of my table-servant—Search for ibex—Grand view from a peak—A successful stalk—And curious shot—Mirza Khán is delighted—The Wazír is anxious for my safety—Suspect a conspiracy to frighten me—My servant's condition—Yearning for cooked food—Another unsuccessful hunt—A noisy camp—A conflagration in a tight place—Arrange for a hunt near the crest of the range—Try my hand at ibex-curry—Filthy Kashmiri habits—Limited quarters in a goat-shed—Bad weather beats us again—Leave the ground—Mark down three huge bucks—The stalk—Awkward position for a shot—My trophy can be patched up—Hillcrows are pleased—Very familiar and intelligent birds—Their manners and customs—A letter from the Búnji commandant—My supplies are stopped—Ibex shooting comes to an end—Square accounts with Mirza Khán and company.

THERE was a storm of snow and wind during the night (6th June), but the four-feet high tent withstood it gallantly. The shikáris and coolies had a bad time of it, as they had no shelter, and were obliged to crouch round a huge fire, for it was very cold. I heard that the khidmatgár, down at the tent on the main stream, was very ill; large blisters had broken out on his stomach, he had pains in his loins, and his body was swollen. The men said he had been gorging himself with mulberries and a whole leg of márkhor, sleeping day and night, and not moving an inch from camp all the time! He had had absolutely no work, and this was the consequence. I sent Gharíba down with five rupees to carry him to the village, where he could be treated by the local doctor, as I heard there was one there. I started from camp early and went a long distance over the grassy, undulating slopes, just below the top of the ridge, looking for ibex, and saw a couple of small ones, but let them go. At about ten o'clock, when the sun was getting hot, Mirza Khán sighted a flock of large males in a stony ravine, a great distance ahead of us. They had evidently just finished breakfast, and were now making for the rocks above to enjoy their mid-day sleep. We watched them until they walked out of sight, and then followed them up, sighting them again from the ridge they had last crossed. They were on the opposite side of the ravine, about three hundred yards off, some lying down, some grazing, and a few going up the slope. They had evidently not yet found a comfortable place for their rest. Examining them through the telescope, I saw there were two large fellows with horns between forty and fifty inches; the rest were a little over thirty. The biggest was also the laziest, and he was lying lowest on the hillside. When all had crossed over the ridge, the old fellow got up and followed them. Though they were all out of sight, there was no following them straight across the ravine, as three females had appeared some distance above the point where the males had crossed, and were keeping a very sharp look-out in all directions but above. They had chosen their position so well that we should have been discovered instantly if we had put even our heads above the rocks behind which we were concealed. They could not have been more than eight hundred yards away. It was provoking: it obliged us to go back, get a ridge between ourselves and the sharp-eyed females, and then climb straight up to the dividing ridge, turn the flank of the females, go round and below the ridge out of their sight, and then come down again to the place where the

"HE SIGNED TO ME TO LOOK OVER."

bucks had last been seen—a formidable task. I fortified myself with breakfast before attempting it, as did the shikáris, and we began the toilsome ascent about eleven, the sun blazing on our backs as we went up. It took me an hour to reach the top, and I was thoroughly done when I got there. After a rest we crossed over to the northern slope, and found ourselves on a vast sheet of snow, which the sun had softened to such a degree that we sank above the knees at every step. This was very slow and tiresome work, and we had to do over half a mile of it before we dared to put our noses across the ridge. Coming up I had been almost melted by the sun; on this side I was nearly frozen by the snow, and my feet were quite benumbed! We had another rest after crossing the snow, and, getting under cover on the other side of the range, descended with all the caution inspired by ignorance of the exact locality of the bucks, and dread of the watchful females. No ibex were visible, though we were nearly on a level with the spot where they had last been seen. We were certain that they could not be more than one hundred and fifty yards from us, but whether to our right or left, or below, was the question. The suspense, the extreme caution, and the very careful and slow pace we were forced to adopt affected my nerves, and I knew I should make a bad shot when we sighted the game, if I had not had time to recover myself. Sharafa and I halted, and Mirza Khán went on alone to locate the ibex, which he did in about ten minutes. Coming up to the rock behind which he stood, he signed to me to look over, and there were the seven bucks, lying in all attitudes, perfectly at home, on a small patch of sloping grass about a hundred yards off across a small ravine—my first chance at ibex! How careful I was to rest the rifle and take deliberate aim, and how clean I missed the largest-horned buck in the flock, and the next, and the next! Life was not worth living for the half-hour after this disaster. I had aimed at the largest-horned one while he was lying down—a very great mistake indeed. I was still bilious and out of sorts, and the ascent in the blazing sun had not improved my nerves. The shikáris looked disgusted, and I am sure I went down several degrees in Mirza Khán's estimation. After a rest, we came down to the stream at the bottom of the valley, and then along the next hillside down to camp on the stream.

At six o'clock next morning we started to go straight up the stream, then turned up to the left on the spur dividing the two streams of the valley, and passed the hillside where I made such bad shooting the day before. We saw only one small ibex high up near the head of the valley, and let him alone, to go up the hillside on the left of the larger stream for a long distance, then round the head of the stream on snow for more than a mile, to a stony ridge where we had seen some ibex yesterday evening as we were returning, but found only their tracks. We ascended to the very top, a rocky hill-point on the dividing ridge of this valley, and had a glorious view all round. Mirza Khán only was with me, as Sharafa had become ill, and was lying down on the rocks below. Nanga Parbat was to the south, its massy proportions looking right royal among the low peaks and ranges around. On the north and north-west, facing Nanga Parbat, but fifty miles apart, were the snowy peaks of Rikhi Poshi, Dobanni, and Haramósh, inferior only to the mighty mass on the south from this point. These three peaks seemed to be on one range, and almost in a straight line. Behind them, far away, could be dimly seen another snowy range, like a massive white wall. Below, on this side, were the districts of Húnza and Nagar, on the other

—space. At our feet was a wide open valley, a level plain apparently for a long way down, the head of the Jagót valley, very stony, barren, and desolate. I was now standing on the extreme frontier of the British Indian Empire. Chilás and Darél were below the next ridge on my left. The Chilásis bring their cattle to graze on the slopes below in summer, a little later on. It was rather lucky that they were not here during my shooting excursion.

Descending from the rocky hilltop, we had breakfast, and followed the ibex tracks down again. It must have been the very flock I missed yesterday. We ascended the low central ridge, and carefully searched the opposite hillside, but saw nothing. On the top of a spur we came upon the fresh tracks of a bear, which must have come down the same way that we had gone up. We followed his tracks for a while, then gave him up, as he was evidently travelling fast. After crossing some dense scrub and bad rocky places, Mirza Khán sighted a buck coming in our direction, and then another a little distance from the first, so we went higher up the hillside to get above the game, and then began the stalk. Crossing a slatey ledge, the rock under my feet gave way, and the slates went down with a terrible rattle that, I imagined, must be heard a mile off. I held on and found footing again.

The ibex were not alarmed, for, as I have said, noises of this kind do not frighten hill game. We lost sight of them for some time, but did see one at last, and managed to get within one hundred and fifty yards of him. He was on the slope above which we had just come, and was evidently going to the rocky places we had just crossed for his night's lodging. He was in no hurry; he halted every ten paces and grazed about, sometimes looking right and left, evidently for his companion, who was not visible.

I took careful aim as he stood showing his left flank, and made a capital shot, which to some extent atoned for my blundering yesterday. Mirza Khán shouted for joy when he saw the animal roll down. The ibex stood looking down the valley. When the bullet hit him, he rushed up hill with tremendous bounds for about forty yards, then fell and rolled down again. The bullet struck him in the centre of the chest, so he must have turned in my direction just as I pressed the trigger. The buck was of enormous size, but young, for his horns were only $32\frac{3}{4}$ inches. He was soon skinned, and we set out for camp as fast as we could go, for it was rapidly getting dark.

The next was an off-day. Sharafa had been suffering from severe headache, etc., for the last two days, something like myself. Manawar Khán, the sipahi (my commissariat officer), brought a message from Wazír Bághdór Sháh, to the effect that I should return to the village, as there was a disturbance across the border among the Yághistánis (rebels), and they might come across and loot my camp. This inconsequent reasoning did not impress me much. The khidmatgár was still very ill, but was able to move about, and could eat a little. This man's illness I suspected to be another plot. I had no doubt that all my party above and below were getting very tired of the rough life, and they had conspired to frighten me down to the village with these stories. I found that my servant had eaten a whole leg of the last márkhor which had been given him for my use—the glutton! I never tasted a bit. Every-one said he was an enormous eater, though he had but a small body. He said he had pains all round his body, he was dying, and he was always crying; but his harrowing tales had no effect on my obdurate heart, for I was determined to have my ibex hunt. I began to suspect even Sharafa; his pains and aches, too, seemed to be assumed.

The coolies brought in the remaining portion of the ibex, which had been safely stowed away by Mirza Khán for the night, and I now began to feel the want of a cook. My *chef* had become quite useless as a cooking animal ever since I had taken to lodging out under the rocks in these upper regions, and all this time I had been living on chapátis, tinned beef, and jam. My interior craved something cooked and warm. My sleep was disturbed by visions of splendid dinners, that were only an exasperating memory when I awoke. I tried my 'prentice hand at ibex chops, cooked in the cover of the only pot I had with me, but my success fell very short of my hopes. I forgot to record in the proper place my first experience of "black dál" (pulse). It was an agreeable surprise; very palatable when boiled long enough, that is, for five or six hours, and eaten scalding hot, after the shades of evening fell and darkness softened the colour of the mess. One must be thoroughly famished to appreciate it; but there is no doubt of the nourishing qualities of the black and glutinous mess, which is the standing dish of India's dusky millions.

While climbing the hillside opposite our camp next morning early, Jamála, the breakfast-carrier, saw an ibex across the valley, going up hill. I had four shots at him, at very long ranges, and missed. He was a small buck, and had evidently crossed over from our side a little ahead of us. The hill was so steep and slippery from the pine-needles which lay thickly on the ground, that I had not even firm foothold ground when I fired. The last spur dividing the Bóin and Hasharai streams are splendid places for márkhor below and for ibex above. I saw five small bucks of the latter, and had a long and tiresome stalk, but they disappeared by the time we neared the spot where they had been marked down.

We camped that night on the banks of the Hasharai stream, below a large and gloomy cave, the entrance of which was blocked by dense undergrowth. The small khaki tent was pitched under some grand pine-trees, not two yards from the brink of the stream, the deafening roar of which, echoing in the cave above, rendered hearing impossible, and required business to be carried on by signs. The coolies made a fire close to the tent against a fallen pine-tree; naturally, there was a conflagration in ten minutes, and the whole camp in danger of being roasted alive on one hand, or drowned and dashed to pieces in the raging torrent on the other. We had a battle-royal in subduing the fire with green branches and water, and I did without my log-fire.

We started at 5.15 next morning, and went up the Hasharai. After going a mile and crossing a goat-bridge over the stream, I sent back a coolie with some spare things, tent, bedding, etc., to lighten the loads and save the commissariat; the more coolies one has, the greater the quantity of flour it is necessary to carry. Carriage and commissariat are the two difficulties in all expeditions, great or small. Following the stream along an easy goat-path from the bridge, I reached the grazing grounds of the Ghór people; they would be here in ten days or less—so Mirza Khán said. The village of Ghór is on the other side of this range, a short distance from the water-parting above me. The Ghór people are beyond the border, and are rather turbulent, which was the reason why the Wazír was so anxious for me to leave this part. The Ghórians had no right to feed their flocks on this side, as the country up to the crest belongs to Damót; but they are the stronger party, and the people of Damót must keep on good terms with them. Ghór is, moreover, a convenient asylum for refugees from Kashmiri oppression, and a good many people from Damót and the surrounding villages have found refuge there. After breakfast we cooked two days' food, in order to make a dash for the head waters of the main stream. The Hasharai, I was told, was a good place for ibex, but the country is very open and undulating, and no fires could be made, as the head of the valley is a good distance beyond the limit of forest, and wood is not procurable.

We camped at the last birch-trees. With the help of Jáfar Báta, I was very successful in making a curry of ibex, seasoned with wild rhubarb. I must confess that the chief credit rested with Jáfar. One or two suggestions of mine were evidently so wild that he ignored them, hardly able to conceal his contempt. After this snub from a coolie, I subsided into the position of his assistant, fetching the water, peeling the rhubarb, etc. Jáfar had become invaluable since my regular chef's collapse, or rather inflation, for I heard he was "swelling visibly" every day. In the first days of my travels, Jáfar came to the front by sheer force of character, and was promoted from coolie to water-carrier; he made himself useful in the cooking-tent, and soon ruled the limp pseudo-Persian gentleman who presided there. When I cut loose from my regular camp, Jáfar again received promotion, being appointed general factotum in my rough shikári life—cook, water-carrier, and body-servant all in one. But I never discovered what a jewel he was in his first rôle until I tried to show him how to make a curry. I disdained his assistance when I essayed the chops; but Jáfar, having one attribute, at least, of genius,—sublime patience,—bided his time, and to-day he became master of the situation—and of his master. Only one drawback marred his utility—he was very dirty in his habits and clothes; it is the prominent characteristic of his countrymen. Twenty years of rough life in India and the Himalayas had somewhat blunted my senses, but I drew the line at Kashmiri dirt, and I refrained from asking Jáfar to display his culinary skill beyond cooking four chapátis every evening. However, nature could not be denied: warm food had become absolutely necessary, and I compromised by closely watching the operations of the accomplished *chef*, and made him conform to my ideas of cleanliness as closely as adverse circumstances allowed.

Our arrangements were completed in two hours, and, leaving the four coolies here, the two shikáris, myself, Jáfar Báta the indispensable, and Jamála (five in all), proceeded up the Hasharai as far as the watershed, to explore the country and hunt ibex. It would take us two or three days, and I hoped to have rare sport, as the upper portion of this valley had never yet been visited by any sportsman—in fact, it was rarely visited by anyone. The Damót people used to bring their sheep and goats here a few years before, but since their numbers had diminished they had abandoned these grazing grounds to the Ghórians, who seldom came so far. Mirza Khán said no sheep had been grazed here for three years at least.

At noon we set out along the stream, now a mere thread of water, which we followed for about two miles; the ground was gently undulating and clothed in tender young grass. The valley opened out considerably and the hillsides sloped gently down, denoting that the summit of the range was not far distant. I could see right round for about three-quarters of a circle: the sky-line bounding the valley is almost level all round, excepting at its head, where a steep wall of bare slatey rock rises against the sky. It began to rain and sleet as we neared our camping place, an old goat-shed very much in want of repair, and there was a heavy snowstorm during the close of the day.

QUARTERS IN A GOAT-SHED

The goat-shed was very uncomfortable; rain and snow came in through the roof, and the smoke from the damp wood fire nearly blinded me. The cold was so intense that we were driven to make a fire with wood pulled out from the goat-shed; but as it was made on the floor and a snowstorm was raging outside, it could not disturb the game. I managed pretty well under the umbrella, and the waterproof spread in a corner of the shed; but the rest, who were crouched round the fire, were not happy. The roof was no protection, as it was full of large holes, and half of it was quite gone. I preferred this uncovered corner, as I was quite protected by my umbrella and waterproof, though the space so protected was just enough to keep me dry standing or sitting. Having written up my journal and talked my companions dry, I fell back on an old *Pioneer* that happened to be in my blanket and read it through, sometimes sitting, sometimes standing. To sit down for any length of time in the pungent smoke, on a very hard stone, was impossible, so most of the time I stood, my head touching the ribs of the umbrella, and my eyes just on a level with the top of the hut wall.

The smoke conquered me at last, and I had to abandon my paper, shut my eyes, and think what a fool I was to endure such discomforts for the sake of a buck goat! Just before dusk, as the storm came to an end, I heard a bird piping joyously among the rocks close by—the only sound that broke the silence which had suddenly fallen upon us. It was a feeble note, and would have been inaudible fifty yards off; but the ring of joy in it was unmistakable, and mentally I joined in the little bird's song, for I knew he was the harbinger of fair weather. Before darkness fell I had time to get out and have a look round. My musical friend was on a rock close by—a very homely-looking, russet-coloured little bird. He sat beside his nest, and the partner of his joys kept the eggs warm within; my heart went out to that bird. No other living creature, beside my companions, was within miles, and the scene, though grand, was depressing in its desolation. I turned in for the night in the goat-hole, between the fire and the rocky wall—Africa on one side and Iceland on the other! I had a bad night, but luckily there was no rain or snow. Jáfar Báta slept next to me; then Sharafa and Jamála; Mirza Khán elected to sleep outside—there was no room for him; he had the shelter of some piled logs and a fire all to himself; but it went out during the night, and in the morning Mirza Khán looked cold and woe-begone.

At 5.15 we left camp, and went straight up hill to a point where Mirza Khán had seen some ibex (females) last evening. They had gone along the ridge down the valley, seeking shelter from the storm, so we followed their tracks. The slopes of this open valley were sheets of snow. From the top of the ridge we examined carefully with the glasses every inch of ground up to the rocky wall at the head of the valley; not a single living thing was visible, but it was not surprising. The violence of the recent storm had no doubt driven all the game away to shelter on the slopes of the Chilás valley, and they would not return to this side till the snow had melted. It was very bad luck to have such awful weather, as it lost me the best chance I was likely to have of bagging large ibex.

The upper Hasharai is of the usual saucer shape, level and undulating below, and gently sloping, grass-covered, in some places stony hills all round. The highest portion dividing it from the Chilás country is a rocky ridge, running round the head of the valley. Three streamlets run down to the bottom, and join to form the main stream.

A path runs along its bank to the top of the ridge, beyond which is the Chilás village of Khiner, about six miles distant from the goat-shed. According to Mirza Khán, Khiner is the village next in importance to Chilás itself. I horrified Mirza Khán when, in the extremity of despair in the goat-hole, I proposed walking across to visit Khiner. Bóin is divided by a ridge from Hasharai; the former looks much the more promising as ibex ground, and, as I was certain there were some good bucks there, I resolved to return to my former hunting quarters, and sent Jamála down to bring the coolies and traps round. I had time for only another week's shikár before my return tramp must begin, and I meant to make the most of it. After breakfast I went down the spur into Bóin valley. I had not gone far when a hurricane of wind, snow, and sleet came on, and I had to crouch behind a rock not much larger than myself on the bare hillside; there was no other cover except a few thin and scattered birch-trees. I stayed there till I became hopeless of the storm abating, and then made straight down for camp instead of going along the hillside towards the head of the valley; thus we were obliged to abandon the exploration of a most likely portion of ibex country. I had not gone far when the storm suddenly came to an end, and I regretted much having come down so soon; but a providence directs the movements of a solitary sportsman as well as the march of nations. Sitting on the hillside and scanning the central ridge of Bóin where I had shot the ibex, Mirza Khán saw three huge bucks towards the end of the spur, in the direction of camp! Had the shower not driven us down so low, we must have missed seeing them. Two of the ibex were grazing, and the third was lying near a large flat white stone, a capital mark to guide the stalker; he was a few yards above the other two, and had the largest horns. In a direct line they were not more than a mile away, but to get to them we should have to go double the distance, down to the bottom of the valley, across the stream, and up again over some precipices, which, from this side, looked utterly impracticable.

We soon rushed down to the bottom, but going up was much slower work, and we had some trouble getting across the cliffs. There was luckily a goat-path along the rocks; there were bad places in it, but with such game before us they were all crossed without hesitation. After this the going was easy enough, and I think we got into position above our quarry within an hour of starting. They had not moved from the spot where we had marked them down, and the best one was still taking his ease near the white rock. Creeping cautiously, we got within fifteen yards of him, and about thirty from the other two feeding below us. It was a most exciting position, but it was also a most uncomfortable and trying one for me who had to use the rifle. The slope of the hill was very abrupt, and I could not get firm footing on the crumbling earth. I was standing behind a rock, partially covered by the branches of a small tree, and standing on tiptoe I could see the ibex lying down, gazing steadily across the valley. There was a shallow water-channel between us. When I stooped down I could see him but indistinctly through the foliage. In neither position could I fire, and the excitement of such close quarters and uncertain footing was telling on my nerve. For at least two minutes I remained looking right into the eyes of the unconscious buck, and admiring the splendid sweep of his horns. There was a far-off look in his large liquid eyes, as if he were watching for danger on the hillside opposite, where we must have been under his view an hour ago—he certainly was not aware of the danger within fifteen yards of him, as he lazily shook his head and flapped his ears to drive off the flies. Once he looked straight into my eyes, but the thick screen of leaves and the rock saved me from discovery; the wind, I need not say, was favourable.

I found at length a small space among the leaves through which I thought I could bring the sights to bear on the buck's shoulder. I had to raise myself on my toes a little to level the rifle, and that is not a steady position for a shot. There was no other way, however—delay would be fatal, and I had to chance it. Motioning Sharafa to hold up my feet with his hands, I stood on tiptoe, took aim, and fired. I *missed!* The buck sprang to his feet and stood for a moment confounded. I gave him the second barrel, and *missed again!* The ibex vanished round the hill, and I thought seriously of suicide. Sharafa brought me to my senses by bidding me look out for the other two, and, turning round, I went down a few paces; no bucks could be seen, but a minute after, as we stood motionless watching, one dashed from under our position to my right about forty yards off; he was going fast, but I tumbled him over like a rabbit with a bullet through his neck. Sharafa gave a satisfied grunt, and I prepared for the third, but he never showed. We crossed his tracks afterwards on our return to camp; he had rushed down some distance before turning along the hillside.

Reason having returned, I could not bring myself to believe that I had missed the big buck twice at fifteen yards. Mirza Khán said I had hit at the second shot, but the ibex went off with such a rush that I was extremely doubtful. However, to make certain, Sharafa went off to follow up his tracks, Mirza Khán having gone down to halál the second ibex. After ten minutes Sharafa presently returned to report that he had found blood on the tracks; a hundred yards farther on he came to a place where the ibex had rolled, and, having followed the traces to the edge of the precipice, he looked over and saw the ibex lying dead in the Boin stream at the bottom of the valley. After a flight of a hundred yards, the animal must have collapsed and rolled down, shooting the precipice and falling plump into the water, two hundred and fifty yards below. Leaving Mirza Khán to cut off the second buck's head, Sharafa and I returned, climbed down to the stream, and followed it till we came to the carcase. What a smash there had been! The body was in two portions, the horns were in several pieces, the lower jaw was missing altogether, and the skin about the head was much torn. I was in despair at the loss of such a fine head, when Sharafa pointed out that the horns could be mended, as the cores had not been injured. He cut off the head, and, having picked up all the pieces of horn we could see, fitted them and found that none were missing. As the animal's throat had not been cut in the orthodox fashion, the meat was of no use, so we left the mutilated carcase, and waited for Mirza Khán with the other head.

I examined with the glasses the face of the precipice down which the ibex had fallen. A pair of large hill-crows were busy picking up bits of flesh from the ledges of rock, and by their movements I could judge exactly the line of descent. After falling over the edge, the unfortunate ibex must have twice struck rocky projections before the fearful and final smash, a short distance above the stream, whence it rolled into the water. The perpendicular height was not less than two hundred and fifty yards, as well as I could guess, but Sharafa said it was more. That the head and horns had not been utterly ruined by such a fall was a wonderful piece of luck. It was curious to watch the ravens flying from ledge to ledge to pick up the shreds of flesh. When we began our stalk,

"SHARAFA HELD UP MY FEET."

these birds appeared at once to divine our intentions. I was sure this was not the first time they had witnessed an ibex-stalk. They found our quarry at once, and sat close by the animals on a tree, croaking impatiently for the *dénouement*. After my first shot they disappeared, and I never saw them again till I came down to the stream.

This was not the first time I had noticed the intelligence of these birds; a pair of them always attended our camp, and followed us when we went off on our shooting excursions. I do not think they were the same pair, however. I fancy a pair locate themselves permanently in each valley. After we had left our breakfasting places, they invariably came down to them and made a thorough search for crumbs, etc. They were extremely cautious and cunning. I tried several times to tempt them down with pieces of chapáti, thrown to some distance. They would hover a few yards over the bread, or sit on a tree close by eyeing it intently, but never attempting to seize the morsels while I remained on the spot; but as soon as we left, they flew down, and had cleared away all the crumbs before we had gone many yards. They were present at almost every stalk I attempted, and, I am sure, were as much pleased with good shots as I was myself. On the other hand, I daresay I often heard their expressions of disgust at my failures. They were most amusing in their habits, which I watched closely, for hours together, when lying idle on the hillside. This must have been their pairing season, or connubial affection has been highly cultivated among hill-crows. When the female was any distance off from her lord, he would take up his position on the thick branch of a tree and begin a series of calls with every modulation of which his jarring voice was capable: first it was a wheedling caw of affection, accompanied by a gentle rustle of the wings; soon it changed into a querulous complaint of neglect; if this did not fetch her, he lost his temper, and, with a loud caw of rage, ordered her up. At this last stage he became most energetic; his head went down at every utterance, and his tail worked like a lever. All this meant that he wanted his head scratched. When the wife did turn up, she proceeded at once to rub his skull all over with her beak— an endearment which sent the old fellow into ecstacies, every feather in his body quivering with enjoyment; then he would launch himself in the air and, sailing in wide circles, scan the hilly slopes from side to side; then, with wings at an acute angle, he would flutter across the valley and back again, uttering self-satisfied cries. This, I suppose, to excite the admiration of his partner. The female was less demonstrative. She seemed always intent on household cares, and toil had evidently sobered her. She reminded me of the women of the country, whose whole life seemed one long drudgery. If these intelligent birds could be trained to mark down game, the sportsman would be saved many a weary trudge, and have many more chances of making a bag than he has now.

Mirza Khán came up after a long delay, which Sharafa attributed to his desire to hide the meat; but Mirza Khán said he had left it all on the hillside, bringing away the head and skin, and enough for his own dinner, that is, the liver, heart, kidneys, etc. The measurements of the two heads were as follows:—the larger 45 inches round the curve, the smaller $32\frac{1}{4}$ inches.

After breakfast next day, as we were discussing how I might best spend the three days I had left, a messenger, Manawar Khán, brought from the commandant of the Búnji fort a letter which put a summary end to our plans. This is a copy of the missive, which was written on a dirty half-sheet of letter-paper:

"Sir,—To-day received a written order on me that in Yásín enemies reached for battle. Therefore I begs that you kindly return in Boonjee. If you cannot come, then send me certification soonly.—Your servant,
"Farman Ali."

My friend, Bágh Singh, the commandant, had, it seems, gone in hot haste to Gilgit, so the letter was signed by the fort adjutant now in command. On the back of it was a Persian letter, more detailed and much more comprehensible

"From Farman Ali, Adjutant.—The General (at Gilgit) has informed me, by telegram, that Pehlwán Khán and Mulk Amán, the rebels, have created a disturbance in Yásín, and have collected an armed force. For this reason I request the favour of your at once leaving your shooting ground, which is close to foreign territory and most dangerous, and returning to Búnji. I have received very urgent orders from the General on this point. If you still remain after this intimation, kindly send me a certificate to the effect that you do so on your own responsibility.
"Farman Ali, of the Dhíraj Regiment."

It was obvious also that our supplies were stopped. I had sent down for a supply of flour to last three days more, and Manawar informed me that no flour was to be had; a sudden scarcity had fallen on the land! I was obliged, therefore, to give in, so packed up the skins and heads and marched for the main stream at once. My shooting in this valley was over. I had been thirty-one days here, and had gone through much rough and hard work, bagging two markhor and three ibex, not a large bag: but I had had a glorious time. The mountain air and vigorous exercise formed a splendid tonic, worth a donkey-load of doctor's stuff, and I felt as strong and healthy as I was when ten years younger.

It was a difficult business settling up with Mirza Khán. He had been with me a month, and I paid him twenty-five rupees, but he was not satisfied. He had certainly worked hard, and had served me right well. He asked for payment for the goats' milk that had been supplied to me. I paid him three rupees, about double its value, and he then demanded sugar for a sick child in some distant village (a palpable invention), and I gave him over a pound. At last, being at his wits' end, he demanded from Sharafa that he should be paid for the logs of wood that we had burned at our fires on the mountain side. I drew the line here, and the stream of my rupees dried up, but as a parting gift I gave him the largest skinning knife I had, remembering that several times I had seen him admiring it. He was gratified, but still seemed to regret his inability to frame pleas for further extortion. On the whole, I was pleased with Mirza Khán. He was every inch a mountaineer, and a true shikári. Without him my sport in this valley would have been very tame indeed, and my bag would have been about as large as that of my predecessor, who worked over the same ground for three weeks or more, and had to leave at last without a single head of game.

CHAPTER VII

BEAR SHOOTING

Return to Búnji—A nervous Kashmiri—The Indus and Kashmiri boatmen—My raw table-servant—Reach Astór—Settling with Rozi Khan and company—A bicoloured stream—The Kashmir army at drill—The commandant—The major—Attained his majority before he was born—Reach Chhagám—Bad weather and great discomfort—The Mír Malik valley—Flower-carpets—Another difficult dining performance—Power of the evil eye—Shoot a musk-deer—Effect of the ·450 hollow bullet—The voice of young Bruin betrays his mother—Maternal love—A long stalk—Bag my first bear—A beautiful evening—A bear escapes—Stalk two others—How they disported themselves—Bag only one through a mistake—A splendid trophy—Proceed farther up the valley—A magnified fox—Cross the pass—Sharafa slips, but saves the rifle—In Gúr's again.

EARLY the next morning I started for Búnji. After a short delay at the ferry, we crossed on the boat and got over safely. The Kashmiris are great cowards on water. One young man, a traveller, strong and sturdy, amused me greatly. He was in abject fear from the time he put his foot in the boat till he jumped out of it on the other bank. He began his prayers as he entered, mumbling them scarcely above his breath; when the boat was cast off, they became quite audible; by the time she was in the centre of the stream and buffeted by boisterous waves, his voice rose to a pitch loud enough to be heard on both banks; but as the boat neared the other side his voice fell in proportion as the danger lessened, and, by the time we came to, had subsided again to a murmur. The passage was somewhat rough, though short, and the boat used for crossing was very unsuitable for such a river. In shape it was exactly like the boats on the Jehlam, in the valley, but longer, without increase of beam. When the river is rougher than usual, all crossing is stopped, sometimes for two and three days. The boatmen are Kashmiris imported from the Jehlam, the timidest watermen in the world, and perhaps the worst for such a strong and boisterous river as the Indus at this ferry. The Búnji ferry was the most important point on the main route from Kashmir to the frontier post, Gilgit, for many years before I travelled in these parts, and certainly the weakest link of communication; but the Kashmir officials of that period never gave the matter a thought, though disasters had occurred more than once, owing to the breakdowns caused by rough weather. Of course these defects were promptly removed when the Gilgit Agency was established by the Indian Government. I reached Búnji at 10 P.M., and found here my invalid khidmatgár. A dirty sheet was his only garment; the middle portion of his body was perfectly raw; the blisters he had suffered from had burst, but would not heal; he was plastered over with a black, greasy ointment which, he said, had been given him by a wise man in the fort. I vowed on the spot that I would never eat anything from his hands again, and realisation of my dreams of warm and comforting food was delayed. It was extremely hot down in the plain, and the flies in the apricot garden were a perfect plague. I sent my traps on ahead and started again in the evening, camped on the road for a few hours, and moved on at midnight. This night march was absolutely necessary at this time of the year, as the heat made day travel most dangerous, most risky.

We reached the crest of the Huttú Pír Pass at seven, thus saving myself and the men a very trying ordeal. The porters from Damót dreaded the sun and heat as much as I did myself, and came along in the dark very willingly. The first rays of the sun caught us as we were topping the pass, but fifty yards down the other side we were in the shade of the mountain, and we pushed on without being touched by the sun at all. We reached Doín fort at 9.30 A.M.; the sun was hot enough then, and I was glad enough to seek shelter in the small travellers' bungalow. I returned by the upper or mule road; the heat on the lower road by which I had gone up would have been quite unendurable, and, in that portion of it where those terrible ups and downs occur, heat apoplexy after ten o'clock would have been a certainty. The higher road, though it is longer and the ascent of the Huttú Pír is very stiff, is much the pleasanter route.

On the second day, at 1 P.M., I reached Astór. Rozi Khán, Wazír, called in the evening, and the silver stream had to flow again. I had promised the Wazír a double-barrelled gun if he got me sport to my satisfaction, but, as my bag was by no means large, I considered that he had not earned the present, and gave him, instead, twenty rupees in cash and my best double blanket: he was well pleased. Fancy "squaring" the chief official in a district in the plains with a similar gift! But then the Magistrate and Collector in a British district maintains the dignity of his position on forty rupees per mensem. I bought four maunds of flour, ten days' supply for a ten days' expedition after brown bears. I had just that time to spare, and intended making the most of it. I found the old postman here, twenty-one days from the date he last left me. He was the only man of my party who had not given satisfaction. I degraded him and made him a baggage-porter.

My next march was to Gúrikót, which I reached at 8.30; we halted under the shade of leafy walnuts, surrounded by fields of green wheat—a most unusual sight for the traveller from the scorched plains of Hindústan in June. The country about here strongly reminded one of a home farm. It was difficult to tear myself away from this pleasant spot when the coolies came up—especially as I knew that the road ahead was a hot one for several miles. We crossed the river by a bridge, and followed the right bank for a couple of miles, then recrossed by another bridge, and halted under a tree for breakfast. The sun was extremely powerful, and I was forced to seek shelter for a couple of hours. There was a striking contrast between the two streams that join below this road, a short way from the first bridge. The larger, the one that rises in the Búrzil Pass on the Gúrés route to Kashmir, was pea-soupy in colour, while the other was bright and sparkling. The contrast was very noticeable for some distance below the junction, the bright stream seeming to shrink from its muddy companion as long as possible. At Chhagám I met the gentleman who had occupied the Búldar nálá. He obtained two pairs of nice márkhor heads with horns of 39 and 37 inches: they were not long, but very broad and massive, and curved gracefully outwards.

In the morning, at the *Idgáh* (praying-place), the polo ground of the village, about two miles on this side of Astór, I had an opportunity of seeing half of that garrison at drill. The sepoys flocked down the path like so many sheep, the men of various regiments mixed up anyhow, and in every variety of uniform and equipment. I could hardly get along for the crowd. Young and old, sick and lame, were all turning out. It seemed necessary for every one to put in an appearance on the parade-ground, if he could crawl so far carrying a musket. I met some veterans carrying a rifle in one hand, while a stout stick in the other supported their steps. Undress uniform was evidently the order of the day: no two sepoys, even of the same regiment, were clothed alike, and the accoutrements displayed rich variety of colour and pattern. This particoloured mass of "soldiers" resolved itself into three separate groups on the polo (Púlú is the indigenous name) ground—a large piece of oblong greensward, with pools of water standing in many places, and surrounded by rough stone walls. Drill was in full swing, though parties of men were joining the various groups at each word of command. Each regiment seemed to have its own peculiar words of command in its own particular language. The commandant and drill-sergeant took separate portions of their regiment, and drilled them alongside of each other, each bawling different orders at the same time. The manual and platoon exercises were first got through, then the men did it themselves, going through the motions with great energy to a sing-song tune, marking the time of "*ek, do, tin*" (one, two, three). At the end of each exercise the commandant shouted out his "*Shábásh*" (well done), and told his "children" to rest. The Balbhadr regiment went through the bayonet exercise at the English words of command. This was really a dangerous exercise, for as the men made their points, several bayonets were thrown off their muskets to long distances, and fell about promiscuously. When this fatiguing business was over, and all the lost bayonets recovered, the commandant ordered his regiment to rest—and they all squatted. He then came over to me and had a chat. A strange dog turned up during this conversation; the regiment at once broke ranks and chivied it down the hillside with the aid of their own mongrels, which had turned out in great force. The commandant is a pure Púrbiah (Southerner) from the

Cawnpore district, and is a pleasant, gentlemanly man. He introduced me to the major, a gentleman from Akhnúr, a hill-town not far from Jamú, who attained his majority before he was born, according to the commandant's statement. The major's uncle, an officer of the same rank in the Maharájah's army, was killed before Chilás when that stronghold was stormed many years ago. The deceased left no son, the greatest misfortune, both in this world and the next, that could befall a Hindú. The thoughtful ruler of Kashmir was grieved. He made the slain major's brother marry, and ordained that when a son was born he should receive his deceased uncle's commission. Thus this gentleman attained his majority. Each regiment had its band on the ground, which struck up whenever they saw a favourable opportunity. The musket stocks of the different regiments were dyed different colours.

Up to Chhagám I had followed again the route by which I went up to my shooting. I now left this track to have a few days' úrin (*Ovis vignei*) and brown bear shooting, sending on my extra luggage by the Guais route to Bandpúra in charge of the khidmatgár, taking only the usual kit for a ten days' outing at the higher elevations.

It rained during the night. There was no sign of it clearing up at 5 A.M., so I started, as we had some distance to go before reaching the nearest úrin ground. We went up the right side of the valley, and got to the ridge after some wet climbing: up here a cold wind was blowing furiously from the higher slopes. We took a peep into the Mír Malik valley, and had a glimpse of splendid ground for úrin just below us; but the wind was blowing with such fury, shaking the rain to and fro, like a vast sheet of dirty-coloured cloth, that we were glad to bolt down hill and get under shelter of the biggest birch-tree we could find. Here we made a fire of wet birch logs, and sat and stood over it for three mortal hours. The trunk of the tree was just large enough to protect one person, and that was myself; but even I, after a short time, gave up the position in favour of the rifles, which were getting frightfully wet, notwithstanding all the care of the shikári; their best dodge was leaning them against the tree trunk and covering them with sheets of birch bark. There were eight of us, and most miserable objects we were to look at. I had to eat my breakfast standing, and, under the circumstances, it was one of the most difficult performances I went through during this trip. The coolies ate their cakes as best they could, with the help of lumps of snow from the neighbouring snow-field. At eleven o'clock the rain held off a little, and we made another start and crossed the ridge. We had not gone a hundred yards when the flood-gates were again opened, and we were again driven to seek shelter under trees and rocks. This time we had the full force of the cutting wind right in our faces, and ten minutes of it was enough; we rushed down the slope to a clump of firs, about a quarter of a mile below, and made another huge fire, regardless of any game that might be above looking at us. The weather cleared gradually from two o'clock, and once more we started up the slope and went along the hillside—first-rate places for úrin—but saw nothing. We camped in the evening in a very tight place under a rock; luckily it cleared up at night.

In the morning the sun peeped over the opposite range for ten minutes, and then the clouds hid him again. We started early and went along the hillside, slanting upwards for a good distance, disturbing a half-grown ibex not one hundred yards from the place where we had camped. I saw some others shortly afterwards on the ridge, high up, but there were only two small males in the flock. We

came to the spur running down to the village of Mír
Malik, but there were no úrin to be seen anywhere—it
was too early for them on this ground, and we ought to
have tried above Chhagám; they had not yet come as far
as the valley. I came down to the village at noon,
collected all the coolies, getting a couple of extra men to
carry supplies and show the road, and started again up
the Mír Malik stream. This is a most charming valley—
broad and open, the hillsides sloping gently down to the
stream; the vegetation is luxuriant and water abundant;
the ground was carpeted with thick grass, and had a turfy
spring under the foot. Hardly half a mile of the path
but we crossed a stream of sparkling water from the
snowy slopes above. Flowers of many hues jostled each
other in the grass, to get a peep at the sun, especially the
yellow crocus, which was in full flower. These grew in
large beds here and there on the hillside, and from a
distance glowed like a field of cloth of gold. The main
stream runs at the foot of the range bounding the right of
the valley, thus giving the mountains on the left a gentler
slope down to the water's edge. Our path led over this
gently undulating ground, and we marched up steadily for
five miles, crossing the main stream by a snow-bridge to
the right bank, leaving the usual path up the valley which
leads to the Shótar Pass, and on to the village of Kél in
the Krishganga valley.

Rain, with a cutting wind from up the valley, set in as we
stopped to camp under a rock. It had been drizzling off
and on since we left the village, but now it began to come
down steadily. The wind increased to a gale, and the cold
grew more intense as night came on. I ate my dinner
again under difficulties, being obliged to leave the warmth
of the fire, and seek shelter under the rock where my
blankets were spread; here, covered by waterproof and

umbrella, I crouched under the rock with a pot of rice between my legs. However, I made a good meal of warm rice and fine ox-tongue, finished a pot of jam with the help of a thick chapáti, finishing off with two stiff "goes" of whisky. My blankets were laid right under the rock, which protected me from the wind but not from the rain. I got into my "Dutch oven,"[1] then between two blankets and two waterproof sheets, one above and one below, and was asleep in no time. It must have cleared up soon after, for I was up in the morning dry and fit for anything.

We started up the Dabin valley on the right at half-past five. It is broad and open, very grassy, but bare of trees save for a few stunted bushes along the streams. The waters of these upper valleys unite about six miles above the village, and form the main stream lower down. There is a path to Phúlwáin up the Dabin; we took this direction, as it is a short cut back to the Krishganga valley. The Chambíl valley, which is on the right, takes its name from a large split rock. It is said that in ancient times a passing traveller, as he stood before this immense rock, admiring its grand proportions, said, "What a fine rock!" As he uttered the words, it split in two! This was told to me as an instance of the power of the "evil eye"—the most striking effect on record, I should say. We had not gone a mile when Jamála, behind me, spied a musk-deer in a clump of dwarf birch-trees above us, about forty yards off: Sharafa at the time was ahead, making steps in the snow. The snow-bed sloped very sharply down to the river, thirty yards below us, which rushed along at a frightful pace. The deer did not seem at all alarmed; I had a shot at him, and missed; he was looking down straight at me, and in that position did not

---

[1] An ulster of lambs' wool cloth, a quarter of an inch thick, and lined; impervious to the greatest cold. Its weight was its only drawback.

offer a large mark, and my footing on the steep incline was very uncertain. The animal rushed up twenty yards farther, and stood again—this time giving a fair chance at his right side. I hit him in the root of the neck, and nearly severed his head from his body! Jamála rushed up, made a gash in the wound, and said the animal had been properly halálcd. Fresh meat, after a month of tinned beef, was my first thought. The deer was a young male, and had small musk pod; his tusks were not long. We then recrossed the Dabin stream, and camped at the end of the spur that separates the upper valleys, then went up the Chambíl nullah, crossed the stream, and toiled up the left hillside for a long way, but could find no trace even of bears in any direction. It was half-past nine, and I was thinking tenderly of breakfast, when the voice of young Bruin was borne to us on the morning breeze, from the far-off mountain slope in front and above. We all cocked our ears and laid them to the welcome sound, like so many hounds. We heard it distinctly three times, but the faintness of the cry told us we had a long and toilsome stalk before us. Young Bruin had, no doubt, lost sight of his worthy mother, and by thus raising his voice betrayed her. Sharafa searched the mountain sides in every direction with the glasses, but it was a long time before he spied the mother and her young hopeful, very far away, and very high up indeed. The stalk began at once, first straight up hill for half a mile, then faster along the hillside, often a run, for a mile, and we were at last above the family party, who were still over two hundred yards from us. The wind was in the right quarter, and I had time to recover breath, for the ground was so open that we could not approach nearer without the certainty of being seen at once, and we had to lie and watch them for a long time. Mother Bruin sauntered off to a shady rock and lay down, as the sun was getting warm; young Bruin at once tried to improve the opportunity, and attempted to suckle—a hulking beast nearly half-grown! He got a clip on the side of his head from his mother's paw, that sent him howling down to the grass, when he again began his search for roots. As soon as he wandered out of sight, his mother, anxious for her precious child, got up, and both gradually worked down the ridge, grubbing up roots and eating the tender young grass in damp places. We worked down parallel to their course along our ridge, and so gradually approached them. At last they crossed over to our side, and we slipped down at once, getting within fifty yards. The bear had her right side to me, looking down hill. I fired, and hit her just behind the shoulder: she rushed down the slope of the hill for a few yards, and stood for a moment; the second shot missed her, and off she went again. I missed again, but she went very groggily now for a short distance, and stood on a rock, giving me a fair chance. The fourth shot took her in the small ribs on the right side again, and she fell over dead into a split in the rock. I could have bagged young hopeful too, but spared the rascal in the hope that he might give good sport another day. The shikáris were very anxious that I should shoot him too; he deserved punishment for betraying his mother, but I stayed my hand. The dead bear was sitting bolt upright in the crack, which was just the size to hold her body in that position. She looked so natural that for a moment I thought she was still alive. The stalk took us exactly two and a half hours, and it was hard going most of the time—not bad work, I felt, for a hungry man, who was just on the point of attacking his breakfast. It was a beautiful day— bright sun, intensely blue sky, with fleecy clouds and a delicious breeze—such a contrast to the last three days!

A lark began his melodious even-song a few yards from the leafy hut that had been prepared for me, and kept it up long after the sun had imprinted his last kiss on the highest hilltop. The evening star, a blaze of light in the west, illumined the valley, casting distinct shadows on the sward. The lark would make believe to drop to his nest like a stone from the blue sky, but, when a few yards from it, would mount again on quivering wings, till out of sight once more, splitting his throat with melody. It was glorious, and gave to the scene around a finishing touch that nothing could surpass.

Next day we went farther up the Dabin valley, the coolies following some distance behind. The road was blocked by bears. We had not gone half a mile when one was seen on the hillside on the right bank of the stream, obliging us to go back and cross by a snow-bridge. We began the stalk, but just as we were within range something disturbed the bear, and he bolted in our direction, but a little above us; he was not more than fifty yards from me at one point, running as hard as he could go. I waited for him to stop to make sure of him—a fatal mistake, for he never stopped, but went rushing on as if the devil were after him! At one hundred yards or so I had two snap-shots at him, and of course missed; a third shot at much longer range was also unsuccessful; and altogether this stalk was fairly bungled. We never discovered what alarmed the bear, but probably he saw the coolies on the path across the stream, though the distance was more than half a mile and the men were lying still, not moving about. We went along the right side of the valley and crossed a narrow gorge running down to the main stream, and had not gone half a mile beyond this gorge when *two* large bears were sighted on the hillside opposite, across the stream, about half a mile above the path along

"THEY CAME SLOWLY TOWARDS THE ROCK ON WHICH WE LAY."

which the coolies would presently be coming. One was a splendid animal with very bright-coloured fur, and I set my heart on him at once. I watched them for some time through the large telescope: they were very hungry and also very playful; after industrious grubbing for a time, they would set to and have a friendly wrestle, then, as the sun was getting high and hot, they would rush off to the shade of a rock and sit there panting; I could see their lolling tongues quite distinctly through the telescope. After getting cool, they would come out again and have another feed until they could bear the sun no longer; their winter coats were certainly heavy wear for this weather. We had to retrace our steps before we could cross the stream safely. I went over on a coolie's back, and then began a very trying ascent up the hillside to get above the bears before attempting the stalk. I had to go half a mile straight up with the sun blazing on my back, and I did not wonder that the bears should feel it. After going high enough, we went along the hillside till we were above the place where our game had been marked down, when we had some anxious moments, as we could not make certain of their exact whereabouts after losing sight of them for so long; but we knew they had not left the spot, as the coolie left below to watch them signalled that they were still there. We crawled on to a large rock that jutted out of the hillside in a sharp point, giving us a capital look-out station, which commanded the ground all round, and determined to remain here till we had again sighted our game; and after some anxious watching, both the bears turned a swell in the hillside and came slowly towards the rock on which we lay. This was luck, for once. They were grubbing up roots and feeding on the grass, and took their time over it, so I had ample time to examine their coats and admire their fine proportions.

8

They were less than a hundred yards off, and still came on. The light-coloured bear was by far the largest, and had the best fur; I would have him first. They were now not fifty yards off, and Sharafa, who was lying close to me, became so excited and insistent that I covered this bright-coloured one, and hit him fairly behind the right shoulder. At the crack of the rifle both the bears rushed up to my right, turned and stood, and I again hit one in the left shoulder. The light-coloured bear now rushed round the slope out of sight, and the other bolted across my front and then down the hillside to my left, standing for a moment about two hundred yards off. I missed him with No. 2, and he disappeared. The wounded bear, after going about thirty yards, had collapsed and rolled down the hill. After examining him I discovered I had made a most stupid mistake: I had determined to plug the light-furred one with the first barrel and the other with the second, and thought I had done so; but when the slain bear was skinned I found two bullet holes, one behind each shoulder, exactly opposite each other—I had fired twice at the same animal! After the first shot they mixed in the rush, and in the confusion I mistook the one already hit for the unwounded one. As the holes appeared, it seemed as if one bullet had gone right through. But this was impossible, for the Henry bullet always smashes up; and in this instance, both shots having been fired at rather an acute angle from above, one bullet could not have gone horizontally through the bear's shoulders. The broad head, handsome fur, and immense size of the animal made a splendid trophy. I was loth to have him skinned. His head was the finest I had ever seen, and I was greatly tempted to preserve it for setting up; but to cut it off would have been to spoil the skin. From the neck to the point of the nose taped fourteen inches; between the ears eight and a half inches; length of hind foot seven inches. The two bullets had made a terrible smash inside him. These bears take a lot of killing. This stalk began at 9 o'clock and ended at 10.30.

Having come down to the main stream, we stretched the skin, and presently moved on, camping at sunset where the valley turns sharp to the right and the last of the vegetation is found: this was the foot of the pass that we were to cross to regain the Krishganga valley. Its turn to the right is so sudden and unexpected that, as one comes up the valley, a semicircular wall of rocks, with a glacier peeping over it, appears to close the end of it. A splendid waterfall, just opposite our camping-place on the other side of the valley, thundered down to the stream below, the only sound audible. I saw a quantity of trout in the stream as we marched up; the coolies caught some with their hands.

Starting early for the pass, we went up a gentle ascent for two miles, then had a very stiff scramble up to the ridge; it took us over three hours, and there was snow on the ground every inch of the way. When we were about half-way up I saw ahead of us a fox gambolling about and evidently enjoying himself, though it was a cold and dreary place for a solitary lark. There was absolutely nothing to be seen for miles round but snow and glacier, and the fox must have been travelling across the pass like ourselves. We tried to stalk him, but he was above and ahead of us, and was master of the situation. The last I saw of him was through thick mist, his head peeping over a rock; it looked as large and exactly the same shape as the head of the bear I shot yesterday, so greatly did the mist magnify. The descent on the other side of the pass was very difficult and dangerous for a short distance. The coolies from the village led the way, followed by

Sharafa, who had not gone many yards before he slipped on a snow-hidden rock, and went head over heels, bumping on rocks and rolling over the snowy slope. I made up my mind that the stock at least of the rifle he carried had been smashed; but Sharafa, like a true sportsman, took the bumps and knocks himself and saved the weapon: he was not hurt, but very much shaken. We passed a frozen lake, about half a mile below the crest. We had been warned at the village not to walk on it, so we gave it a wide berth. There was snow on the ground all the way down. At noon we reached the first birch-trees. There were two bears' tracks along the path on the snow almost all the way from last camp; the tracks were quite fresh, and must have been made late in the evening—no sun had shone or snow fallen on them, and the impressions were very distinct. I concluded that we must have disturbed the pair on the previous night. There was splendid-looking ibex ground on both sides of the pass, but we saw no sign of ibex anywhere. We camped at one o'clock under a large rock, having reached the Gúrés district, on the watershed of the Krishganga, and in the valley of Phúlwáin.

CHAPTER VIII

BEAR SHOOTING—(continued)

The beautiful Phúlwáin valley—Good for stags in the season—A dangerous pathway—Reach Bagtour—Beautiful Krishganga valley—Anticipating a bogus thunderstorm—Waiting for an unpunctual bear—Sharafa's imaginary ailments—Shoot a musk-deer—Tremendous power of Henry's ·450 Express—Musk-deer numerous—How they are slaughtered—The Hánt valley—Nanga Parbat—Legends about it—How the "naked mountain" was named—The nomenclature of Himalayan peaks—Ibex not at home—A snow-cock's family—The power of maternal love—Delude a coolie—Waiting for a bear—A friendly hill-crow turns him out of cover—A painful stalk—Ends in failure—Wounded bear escapes—Two graceful hinds—Little flies cause great irritation—Hill-crows drive a musk-deer over me—A bear's bed-chamber—He is out—My shooting-trip comes to an end—The last notes in my journal—Return journey.

THERE was rain towards morning, but the large rock under which my blankets were spread kept me dry. We went up a side valley, but saw nothing, and came back to try the main valley, which opened out with lovely views on every side. It was impossible to go ten steps without stopping to enjoy the scenery: such a change from the bare rocks and precipices I had been contemplating for the last two months! I wanted to camp and rest in every pleasant spot I passed, and progress in consequence was very slow indeed. Far away, on the sky-line, rocky peaks pierced the sky, their bases muffled in fresh green grass; below, on the steep hillsides, hung forests of dark pine and light birch, in beautiful contrast. Lower still, the slopes fell in green undulations to level meadows, glowing with the hues of a thousand flowers, while sparkling rivulets cut up the plain into variegated parterres. These little streams hasten down the sloping hill to join the roaring monster below, but, frightened by his increasing roar, shrink from the contact, and stray murmuring among the flowers of the meadows. From seven until noon I revelled in the scenery of this valley, and found the time all too short. We reached the village of Phúlwáin at last; it stands on the right bank of the Krishganga, and consists of four log-huts and two fields.

We had seen no trace of game all the way. Sharafa informed me that this was a good valley for stags when they first begin to call; I did come across fresh tracks of hinds in the upper portion. Even now, had we spent a week here, wandering along the higher slopes, brown bear could be found, and perhaps ibex among the rocky peaks and ridges that bound the valley on the right; but I had no time to spare, and, after changing a couple of coolies, we went on again. The path led up the right bank of the river; it was slow and very fatiguing work, pushing our way through rank vegetation and over the trunks of fallen trees. There was said to be a goat-track, but it was never visible, and we had to feel for it in the thick grass at every step, and were continually losing it. We camped, in the evening, next the stream—a very cramped place, but the only clear and dry spot we could find. The Machhal valley was just across the range in front, and from where I lay I fancied I could see the very spot where I smashed my knee-cap two years before, rushing down hill after a bear that I did not bag.

We were on the move early in the morning, and found the going as bad as last evening, or worse. This tramp was most disagreeable, and often most dangerous: we had to cross sheets of rock, often high above the water, sometimes actually below it; at one point we had to walk for a few yards along a rocky ledge, a couple of feet below the water—there was no other practicable path. A slip in any of these places would have lodged me in the stream without possibility of escape. The steep grassy slopes, too, were awkward places, being very greasy and slippery. I was glad to get to the first village, Sirdári, where these troubles ended. Krishganga is one of the most beautiful tracts in Kashmir, and outrivals the valley itself in its combination of forest, fell, and flood. At Halmatto I heard that a gentleman and his wife had spent ten days here; he shot two bears and four musk-deer, and they left for Kashmir six days ago.

A mile and a half from the village of Bagtour we camped on a beautiful spot a few paces from the river. I had still a few days, and determined to spend them on the range above this village, where brown bears were said to be plentiful; so sent for my friend, the head-man, to arrange for flour and coolies. Looking up towards Bagtour, three graceful curves of the river could be traced. Its bed seeming to be a perfect level, it flows without a sound, except where an obstructing rock wakes it to complaint. On either side, the hills, clothed in green, slope gently to the water's edge, the pine forest on the right bank having its very roots in the water. Upwards, the jungle-clad hills swell in green undulations—an island knoll rising here and there to break the monotony of the wave. High above all was a stony ridge crested with snow.

During the night there was a thunderstorm. It came right over the valley, north to south; and as I lay on the hillside, without even a tree for shelter, I watched it from the very beginning, when the black and threatening cloud topped the range and swallowed up the stars one by one. The gradual approach of the storm appeared to me like a nightmare, as I lay in a half-dreamy state watching. The big drops came at last, hitting hard and viciously the waterproof under which I was tucked, my faithful umbrella over my head—and lo! it was over in five minutes, leaving me snug and dry between my blankets. The storm had passed on, and the stars were again peeping out at its lower edge, slyly winking at the blustering monster that had roared so loudly and done so little.

A man I secured in the village to show me "bearish" places told me of a bear which had been rolling in the shallow of the stream the day before, and I hoped he would not intermit his tub to-day; but he came not, though I dozed in the forest for four hours waiting for his arrival. At last I started up and climbed beyond the limit of forest, to the undulating grassy slopes below the crest of the range; I saw nothing, though better ground for bears could not be imagined. Camped in a grove of pines and birches, Sharafa was slow, sluggish, and dull; he said that last night, when the thunder and lightning came, he started out of bed, thinking the rifles were getting wet, and so caught a chill. He always posed as a very delicate creature, racked with pains and aches in every limb and organ. The condition of his head, his ears, eyes, back, and legs were all brought to my unsympathetic notice at various times during the trip, but he received little comfort and less medicine. He was getting a bad fever once, and my quinine bottle would have been soon emptied but that the happy thought struck me to make him take his dose in my presence: two doses cured him! Though his ailments failed to touch my heart, the coolies were thereby greatly moved; and their sympathy, displayed in little kind acts, was very soothing to him. To give

Sharafa his due, these little indispositions never interfered with his work, and, when game was in sight or he was stalking, his affections were dropped, and he was the keen shikári, every inch of him. He had the real hunting instinct, and worked with me in the most pleasant and satisfactory manner throughout. I considered myself lucky in having secured his services, and excused his mannerisms as a phase of the complicated Kashmiri character.

Next day we reached the crest dividing the Hánt valley from Bagtour. Shortly after leaving camp, and while going through a birch forest, I put up a musk-deer, and missed him like a man at thirty yards, with the left barrel of No. 1. The rifle kicked disagreeably, and the bullet went high. I think its base could not have been seated on the powder, as I had not crimped it in. This is a detail which should never be forgotten, as cartridges get a good deal of shaking about in this kind of shooting, and if the bullets are not properly secured over the powder, they work out a little: the consequence is, a disagreeable blow on the shoulder and a bad shot at the closest range. Going on a few yards, I saw the deer again. I hit him this time with the right of No. 2 at twenty yards: the bullet blew the poor creature nearly in half. The hair and meat were blown about the place, but we were all keen on fresh meat, and the halál was of course successful. The striking power of Henry's ·450 Express, with five drams of powder, could not have been better exemplified, though the effect was not pleasant to see. We went to the crest of the range, and climbed the Lósar peak, where ibex were known to be, but saw nothing, save, on the Hánt side, five musk-deer feeding, for which we did not try lest we might disturb ibex. Musk-deer were plentiful. The local shikári from Bagtour, whom I had with me, said that this year, so far, he had shot only twenty males and *about* twenty females, and they were still numerous. He shot two stags last October. Since the Mahárájah stopped his yearly demand of stags' heads, the slaughter has decreased, and only a few are now shot here and there for sale to the skin-cleaners in Srinagar at five rupees a-head. Musk pods are sold to traders at two and five rupees each, according to size. From the crest I had a good view of the Hánt valley; it is very beautiful, wide and open, and the left side very level, with a gentle ascent to the ridge that divides it from the Machhal valley—my old shooting ground ten years ago. The right side of the valley has less gentle slopes, and is more densely clothed with forest: it must be a good place for bears and stags at the proper season.

From the ridge I had a fine side view of Nanga Parbat straight in front of me. The proper name of this glorious peak is Daia Mar—the name of a village, I was told, at its base on the Chilás side. People say Daia Mar is inhabited by *Déos* and *Paris* (genii and fairies), and the mountain has a sacred character even among the Mahomedan population. Every Friday the Chilásis wash themselves, put on clean blue clothes, and go out to the mountain to watch the fairies and genii disporting themselves on the crags and precipices above. This tradition and custom must be survivals of the old heathen time, before the sword of Islam gathered these people under its flag. "Nanga Parbat" cannot be an ancient name: probably it was named by a Hindustáni Hindú, camp follower with the survey party that first took the bearings of the peak. Kinchinjanga is a fine name for the highest mountain in the world; but "Nanga Parbat" for the third highest is certainly bathos. The second highest, too, was badly treated; it blushed every morning at the indignity put upon it by the G. T. Survey, who labelled it "K^2" in their maps. The *amende*, however, has since been made by re-christening it with an Englishman's name — Godwin Austen. I went up the stony ridge to Lósar peak, where a survey cairn had been erected—a bare pole sticking out of it. This is where the ibex should have been, but were not—bad luck to them! Their tracks in the snow, droppings and hair about the rocks, were plentiful enough; but they were not at home, and at seven o'clock we came down to camp. No bear was anywhere within sight, and we overlooked a good many miles of country from our points of vantage. I found the camp in a most awkward spot on the steep hillside just below the ridge, and a thin stream of water running past my blankets. The ground was so steep that I found it difficult to eat my dinner in any position.

Up at 5 A.M., and off to the ridge again, along which I went towards the head of the valley, carefully searching both the Hánt and Bagtour nálás. It was a splendid morning; a bracing cold breeze swept along the open downs, which were carpeted with flowers, especially a yellow kind like the marigold; they were so plentiful and grew so thickly that I crushed a dozen of them at every step. I enjoyed this morning's walk exceedingly, though we saw nothing. The beauty of the scene so impressed me, that a bear, had he come in sight, *might* have been allowed to pass. Such surroundings are not conducive to bloodthirsty thoughts. Suddenly we walked nearly over a hen rám-chakór (the hen of the snow-cock) and her brood of six chickens nestling among the flowers. The chicks were fluffy, and half the size of my fist, but they could run; they ran a few yards, crouched, and disappeared among the flowers. The mother, too, ran, but limped and fluttered along in such helpless fashion that Jamála, the breakfast coolie, bolted after her with outstretched hand, expecting to catch her at every step; but she kept just beyond his reach, and, after a run of a hundred yards, Jamála came up panting and looking very foolish—for the hen mother was now following him! Her stratagem, however, was unsuccessful, for our party was still standing a few yards from her brood. A finer illustration of maternal love overcoming natural timidity could not be imagined. The hen came within five yards and circled round us with drooping wings and ruffled feathers, and limping, the very picture of decrepitude, inviting capture by a display of utter helplessness. Jamála this time was not taken in, and we all stood motionless in sympathetic admiration, my companions exclaiming, "*Subhán Allah! Subhán Allah!*" (Praise to God! Praise to God!) When these manœuvres failed to move us, the hen settled on the ground, raked up a cloud of dust, fluttered her wings, and clucked for her chicks to come under protection; but by this time the chickens had run farther down the hillside and were out of hearing. We left her still calling for them. Farther on we came across the tracks of an enormous stag that must have passed over the bed of snow on the previous evening; his head would be a splendid trophy four months hence. Sharafa then spied, on the opposite side of the Hánt valley, a bear coming down to the forest for his mid-day rest. We determined to visit him in the evening, so turned down into that valley, and waited for him to show up on the opposite slopes; but the bear never appeared, so we walked down to the Hánt stream to camp for the night.

When a short distance from our camping-place, a bear suddenly rushed down the opposite hillside out of a clump of birches, hunted by a hill-crow, just as though the crow, seeing our approach, hunted the bear out to have him shot. This was certainly the bear we had been

"HUNTED BY A HILL CROW."

watching for all day, but he had kept under cover until long after the usual hour. The crow had been hovering about the birch clump and cawing for some time: suddenly he made a dash down among the trees, and out rushed the bear, the crow almost touching his back. A pair of these hill-crows were, as usual, attending on us. This bird must have reasoned that until the bear showed himself there would be no meat, so drove him out! The coolies at once squatted, and the stalk began. The first thing to do was to get under cover, and this could be effected only by going down to the bed of the stream below the bear. So we went slowly and cautiously, for we were within full sight of the game—he could not have been more than five hundred yards away. Every time he put his head down to eat or dig, we dashed along a few paces, falling flat the moment he looked up. The hill was steep and stony, and slushy from melted snow, but we got safely to the bank, and soon crossed. Then began a most exciting stalk: the bear was a short distance up the hillside, but could not be seen till we were within a couple of hundred yards of him. Our movements had to be slow and cautious, and when he was sighted we had to crawl on our stomachs, watching the bear, and stretching ourselves flat whenever he raised his head. At last we reached a rock about seventy yards from him, and were in position, but I was thoroughly done and my nerves completely upset. In this state I had to fire, and at once: of course I made a bad shot, wounding the bear low down in the fore leg. He rushed to our left front and then straight up hill—three snap-shots at long ranges were misses also. We gave chase, and had a rough climb for some distance up and along the hillside for half a mile, through forest, rocks, and rank vegetation, but had to give up at last, as the bear was going fast and it was getting dark. We returned and examined the place where he had been feeding. The bullet must have broken his fore leg a little above the paw. I was disgusted with myself—less because I had lost the bear than because I had wounded the poor beast and allowed him to escape. No doubt he would recover from the wound, but it was an uncomfortable thought that he had been put to unnecessary pain. He was a small animal, little more than half-grown.

Off at five o'clock next morning, with Ghaffár, the local man, and down the stream for some distance, across a snow-bridge and up the left side of the valley. I saw many fresh traces of bears when we got above the forest-line and on the grassy hill slopes, and I made certain of sighting Bruin as we topped each swell of the undulating mountain side, but met disappointment instead. As we emerged from the forest and came on to the flowery meads, two hinds rushed out from amongst the trees and passed in front of us, not more than a hundred yards away. Two crows had been cawing and flying about the forest in the direction from which these animals came; I suspected they were driven out by these very sporting birds, as the bear had been last evening. The hinds went up the slope for a bit, and then stopped on our left front and a little above us; they were not more than a hundred yards off, but had not seen us as we crouched in the long grass. One was smaller than the other, and seemed inclined to romp with her companion, but the latter was too intent on her morning meal to join in the game. Their grey sides, groomed by nature's hand, shone again in the morning sun, and flashed back his rays like a mirror at every movement. They did not see us for some time, and were entirely at their ease: it was a pretty sight. Ghaffár Bat said, "Shoot one for meat"—the beast!—when I could see their sides heaving with each breath and the sunlight rippling on the glossy flanks. Ghaffár got so excited at last that he pointed his stick like a gun at them, and the movement caught the eye of the larger hind at once. She threw up her slender neck, gazed at us intently for a moment, then dashed away, her companion following.

We went along the meadows for some distance, but saw nothing, and at length put up for the day in the highest clump of pines and birches, on a grassy slope, with a deep watercourse close by. The flies here were an intolerable nuisance; in a short time I had several wounds on my hands, drops of blood oozed from them, and they became very itchy. The fly was a very tiny one as to body, but he had a large head. I was driven at last to shut up my pocket-book and put on my woollen gloves. While I was lying with my eyes closed, I heard a pitter-patter close behind; turning round, I discovered that I had been nearly run over by a musk-deer. He came from below, and must have been disturbed by something, as it was the hottest hour of the day, and game never move at this time. I made sure it was the crows who were beating up the forest again for my (and their) benefit. The two had been flying about all the morning in our vicinity, and, when we came to a halt, posted themselves below us, and kept up a loud and disagreeable cawing for several hours. The musk-deer having arrived, the crows followed immediately after. This is the third time in this valley that I have noticed the strange conduct of these birds; it surely could not be mere coincidence. I could plainly see design in their manœuvres, and that design was to have animals shot. How disgusted they must have been at my failure!

In the evening, on the way back, we discovered a bear's lair at the foot of an enormous pine; there was a large round depression in the ground, where he had evidently slept for several nights; his droppings round about were plentiful, but he himself was not at home. Probably he had winded or heard us in the morning.

I had fired my last shot on this trip, and what a sad miss I had made of my last bear-stalk! Wounding that bear still lay heavy on my conscience; I felt it more than any other mishap that had befallen me during this tramp.

We camped next night near a bed of snow that had a tiny lake at its lower edge. The green grassy slopes about this bit of water were the favourite napping-places of vultures; we disturbed numbers of them lying about when we came up, and their feathers were scattered in every direction. It was a delightfully green little spot; a bracing breeze was blowing over it, and the omnipresent hill-crow was sailing around as I sat writing my notes.

This was our last evening at these altitudes, 10,000 feet—I had not been lower for nearly two months.

In three days I was back again in Bandpúra, and was received with salvoes of thunder and brilliant flashes of lightning.

PART II

SPORT IN CHANG-CHEN-MO, TIBET

CHAPTER IX

THE PROVINCE OF LADAKH, AND THE WAY THITHER

The happy hunting ground of the Englishman—How he takes his sport—General description of the country—Start from Lahore—Road as far as Sultanpúr—The transport difficulty—My travelling kit—Details of arrangements—Chamúrti, my Tibetan pony—Fifteen coolie-loads for a six months' trip—The Kúlú valley—Englishmen settled there—Flying-foxes—Destruction caused by them—Game in Kúlú almost entirely destroyed—A sporting tour round the Kúlú valley—The Ralah bungalow—Crossing the Rotang—Native servants—Chamúrti's pranks—My spirits rise with the elevation—Koksar bungalow—Reach Kailang.

LADAKH has been the happy hunting ground of the Englishman for nearly half a century. From the time when Gerard and Cunningham first explored its virgin valleys to the present day, our fellow-countrymen have year after year sought the various routes to those high table-lands. They have searched its remotest corners in pursuit of the large game of the country, and have shot them at elevations which far exceed that of the monarch of European mountains. To obtain six months' release from his duties for a sporting tour in Ladakh is the summit of the big-game hunter's ambition. Until he has shot his tiger in the hot and steaming forests of the plains, and his *Ovis ammon* at 15,000 feet above sea level, he considers that he has not accomplished his manifest destiny.

The natural boundaries of the province of Ladakh are the Karakoram and Kuen-Lun on the north, with Chinese Turkestan beyond; the political frontier dividing it from Tibet on the east; the British districts of Spiti-Lahour and the independent States of Chumba on the south; Kashmir and its sub-province, Baltistán, on the west. Roughly speaking, within these limits is contained an extent of country two hundred miles in length and the same in breadth, at an average valley elevation of 14,000 feet above the sea. The Indus, for nearly three hundred miles of its course from S.E. to N.E., cuts the province exactly in halves. Its principal tributary is the Shyok river, which, after a most devious course of nearly two hundred and fifty miles, falls into the Indus on the western border. The Zanskar and Dras are minor tributaries.

The mountain ranges drained by the above water system are the Karakoram barrier as to its southern slopes, whose waters are collected by the Shyok; the Gangri or Kailas range, which starts from the Mansarowar lake in Tibet, and ends in the angle which is formed by the junction of the Shyok with the Indus. This remarkable range has a length of four hundred miles, the greater portion of which, almost in a straight line, runs along the right bank of the Indus, dividing the Shyok and its tributaries from the former. On the left bank of the river there is no well-defined or continuous range comparable to the Kailas. On the south-east are the great plateaux of Rúpshú and their lakes; farther west are the steep and lofty mountains of Zanskar; and beyond them the ranges enclosing the Sorú and Dras valleys. These are the north-eastern spurs of the great Himálayan buttress facing the Indian plains.

Let the traveller or sportsman take his stand at Leh, the capital of the province, and the only town within its borders, and face north. Before him, across the high ridges of the Kailas that overtop his standpoint, is the district of Nubra; to the north-east is the Chang-chen-mo valley; and beyond them, again, the elevated and dreary Lingzi *thang*, or Lingzi plains; to the west he has the great Pangong lake—the longest stretch of still water in Tibet; south-east flows the Indus; directly south are the high plateaux of Rúpshú—the highest inhabited portion of the globe; north-west is rugged Zanskar—the exact antithesis of its neighbour Rúpshú; west are the valleys of Sorú and Dras. The circle is complete: Leh is, as nearly as possible, in the centre, with a radius of one hundred miles all round.

This condensed description of the country I was about to visit, and in whose eastern extremity I intended to shoot, will give a sufficiently detailed view of the outlying province of Kashmir. Reference can be made to standard authors for further details.

The first stage of my present journey is so well known and is so frequented a route, that the sooner we get over it the better. I went from Lahore to Pathankot by rail; thence it is twelve marches to Sultanpúr, the headquarters of the Kúlú subdivision of the Kángra district. There is a cart-road as far as Pálampúr (six marches), and a good riding-road for the remaining six. A tonga dak runs as far as the latter place, and there are staging bungalows along the whole route, some pleasant and comfortable, others just the reverse. The pleasantest is the Jhatingri bungalow (ninth stage), and the worst Karaun (beyond the Babbú Pass). This pass is 10,000 feet above sea level, between the tenth and eleventh marches. At Shâhpúr the traveller enters the tea country, and his road leads him through miles of gardens. From Dharamsala to a point several miles beyond Baijnath, a distance of thirty miles, he can hardly travel half a mile without skirting tea-gardens—trim and well cared for if under European management; the reverse if under the control of the son of the soil. The soothing effect of these pleasant surroundings is mightily enhanced by the sighing of the wind through the pines and the delicious rose-scented air, for the bridle-path is hedged in by rose-bushes in full bloom. Pálampúr (sixth stage) is the headquarters of the tea industry in the Kángra district.

I found my travelling kit and servants awaiting me at Pálampúr, and after a halt of two days made my first onward march. Before going any farther, it may be as well to give some particulars of my arrangements for so long a journey, for the benefit of those who may follow in my footsteps. Be it known, then, that the difficulty of procuring carriage at all stages on the roads in the Kángra district is the most temper-trying obstacle one encounters. The authorities, in their wisdom, have decreed that no carriage of any description shall be available without due notice at each stage, and the responsible suppliers of the same have passed another decree that it shall never be available at the time fixed. Former experience had acquainted me with the innumerable difficulties connected with transport, and I was resolved on this occasion to be entirely independent of local carriage. I therefore hired six mules at Amritsar, and sent them on with my travelling kit to Pálampúr. I entered into a formal agreement with the owners to carry me right through, from the beginning to the end of my journey; and in trying, by this arrangement, to avoid one set of difficulties, I fell into another, which nearly wrecked my expedition before I had been a month on the road. But it answered admirably while I was within the limits of the Kángra district, and I enjoyed a most independent, free, and easy life. I would recommend all tourists who contemplate a tramp in these parts to follow my example in this matter of carriage; it will relieve them of all the petty troubles which would otherwise await them at each stage of the journey—irritating annoyances that entirely mar the pleasure of the outing. My caravan consisted of six mules, two muleteers, three servants, and myself. For the mules I had three pairs of leather trunks made up out of blue bull-hides, from animals I had shot at various times in the plains. This was an excellent arrangement; the trunks were light and strong, most capacious, and withstood admirably the roughest usage. Two of them were a light load for a mule, and between them, on the mule's back, another load of bedding, etc., could be secured. A mule could be loaded up, ready for a start, in five minutes. Each box was a fair load for a coolie. I had several pairs of boots and shoes made after a pattern of my own from other blue bull-hides. This supply lasted me and my servants for the whole trip, and for some time afterwards. With a liberal application of " dubbin " now and then, they were thoroughly waterproof, and, with screws in the soles, gave firm footing on the hill slopes : the cost of making up was trifling. I also used my black buckskins to make up a dozen bags—one bag out of each skin—in the shape of the usual canvas clothes bag, but narrower. Some were used for carrying the servants' things ; and when supplies had to be carried for several days, they answered admirably for carrying flour, rice, sugar, etc. Three other skins I had made into rucksacks, after the Swiss pattern; these were most useful when away from camp after game. They can be filled up to any extent, and were comfortably carried in the usual way by a coolie over the worst ground. In this manner I used up the skins and hides I had collected during many expeditions in the plains. Good shoemakers, to make up these things, can be found in any large station; they are very handy in turning out anything required, if properly instructed. I obtained some manilla rope and cords from Calcutta; they are practically indestructible, and are most handy for tying up mule loads. The want of a stout cord in the mountains is a most serious hindrance, and sometimes causes the greatest inconvenience and delay. A small supply will always be useful, but a sharp look-out must be kept on the porters who carry it, for they will invariably walk off with cords when relieved by a fresh set. My tents were two patent "ridgeless" from Cawnpore, made of tan waterproof drill. This is a most handy pattern; they were thoroughly waterproof, and withstood the furious gales of the Tibetan plateaux most efficiently; they were exceedingly light, just a coolie-load each. I must not forget my Chamúrti pony—a handy little grey under thirteen hands, and as sure-footed as a goat. I bought him at the Rampúr fair, beyond Simla, for 150 rupees. He was at first almost as shy as the wild sheep of his mountain home, but after a time became tame as a spaniel, and followed me during my long tramp like the most faithful of dogs. The only drawback about him was that he had to be shod, and shoeing could not be done in most of the places I visited. In consequence, his hoofs got worn when he lost his shoes, and he walked very gingerly along the stony valleys of Tibet. But he saved me many a weary trudge in the long stages of my journey, and his tricks and friskiness made him a most amusing companion.

The six mules and Chamúrti, as I called my purchase,

were the only animals I took. My traps, including stores, gun-cases, etc., were easily taken by the mules; I should say that there were about fifteen coolie-loads—the calculation was made for a six months' trip. I need not go into further detail: the excellent advice given in *The Sportsman's Vade Mecum for the Himalayas* cannot be improved upon. That compact book should be in the baggage of every Himalayan traveller, whether sportsman or not.

I reached Sultanpúr on the 28th May. The Kúlú valley is well known to tourists, as during the season it is constantly visited by parties from Simla, though the inconveniences placed in the way of travellers, not only in this portion of the Kángra district, but every other part, are enough to choke off any less enterprising individual than the travelling Englishman. Three marches (thirty-two miles) from Sultanpúr, along a good road very much frequented by tourists, brought me to Ralah, a small rest-house at the foot of the Rotang Pass. Between these two places, one passes the estates of several gentlemen, who have settled permanently in this most pleasant valley. For many years they have been engaged in tea-planting; but Kúlú is so much out of the way, and so distant from the markets, that the occupation has not been profitable. Though the tea produced is of the most delicious flavour, its yield is not abundant, owing to the altitude of the valley and the severe winters. During the last few years a new departure has been made in the growing of fruit, which gives a much better return than tea, though this occupation also has its drawbacks, the markets being too far distant for such a perishable commodity; and flying-foxes, which commit great devastation during the nights, cannot be kept off the trees when the fruit is ripening. They probably destroy more than fifty per cent. of the crop. These pests come every evening in thousands, remain in the gardens during the night, and return before morning to their retreats in the lower parts of the Kángra district—at least fifty miles in a direct line of flight. Human ingenuity has not yet invented means of protecting the fruit from them. It is well known that flying-foxes travel enormous distances in search of food, and this is a case in point. Sterndale, in his *Mammalia of India* (p. 39), says that these bats are exceedingly strong on the wing. One of these animals boarded the steamer he was on when it was more than two hundred miles from land. Their depredations seriously affect the planters' profits. If nothing can be done to prevent them, the flying-foxes may, in the end, ruin the industry entirely. Another serious drawback is the uncertain climate during the fruit season, when severe storms are frequent. The principal market is in Simla, where Kúlú pears, apples, and peaches have established a good reputation for themselves; but the cost of, and accidents during, carriage over so many miles of mountain road, on the backs of coolies, are grave considerations. In addition to these must be added the very probable contingency, that fruit-gardens in and about Simla will so undersell the Kúlú fruits that the latter, in the end, will lose its most paying market. If a manufactory of jams and jellies could be started in the valley, a good trade might result, but sugar cannot be produced on the spot. The experiment of growing sugar-cane is, I believe, being tried, but the inevitable heavy cost of carriage would again probably swallow up the profits. Though Kúlú may not be a money-making country, it is, without doubt, a perfect paradise for the European with a small competency, who wants a quiet place, with a perfect climate, beautiful surroundings, and cheap living, in which to end his days. Probably, with very few exceptions, this was the intention of those who settled here and made Kúlú their home.

The valley has a great reputation as a game country. I have had some experience of it, but cannot say that it now affords that return to the enterprising sportsman which he obtained some years ago. The native of the country is sportively inclined,—in more senses than one,—and licences for owning and using a gun can be had from the resident Civil Official for the asking. A former Lieutenant-Governor of the Panjáb spent his hot youth on these pleasant slopes, and did not forget his protégés when he came back, after several years as governor of the province. During his rule they were specially favoured; they were freed from the oppression of the bégár (forced labour) system of supplying carriage, and were allowed to have as many sporting firearms as they liked. The result, as regards game, was disastrous: game birds and animals are persecuted all the year round. In severe winters, when the snowfall is heavy and animals cannot escape, they are surrounded by gangs of villagers, driven into deep snow, and then clubbed to death: a few years ago, when there was an unusually severe winter, the slaughter was immense. It is not possible that the game of Kúlú will ever recover from this blow, and the reputation of the valley as a game country may be considered at an end. Bears, of course, can still be had in a few valleys, but that is a kind of sport that soon palls. The Himalayan hunter now passes along the road by double marches; he makes no halt, but presses on to the grounds beyond the Rotang Pass.

Though the shooting in the valley is practically *nil*, good sport may yet be had in the huge ranges of mountains that surround it—always provided that the sportsman does not expect to make " record " bags.

The small, dirty, uncomfortable little bungalow at Ralah is well situated to give one the blues. It is a lath-and-plaster affair, built in the roughest manner; the furniture is of the most primitive kind, and filthy to a degree, while evil smells have a permanent residence. The Beas river roars a short distance below, though only a couple of miles from its source—a very lusty infant indeed.

The hanging forests in view are the only redeeming feature, but they are not an *annexe* of the bungalow. A few hundred yards up the stream is a fine waterfall, spanned by a glorious rainbow when the sun gets a chance to light up the spray. This is not a frequent occurrence, as Ralah is a dreadfully rainy place; all my recollections of it are damped by deluges of rain. On the present occasion I was obliged to wait here two days till the weather cleared up sufficiently to allow us to cross the pass. The mule men made the request for a halt, and during the day went up to see how the snow was lying and whether the road was passable for their animals: it appeared that the usual annual repairs to the road had not yet been begun, though it was the first of June. There were several camps about the bungalow during my stay, and sheep, donkeys, and ponies were straying all over the place; they too had been stopped by the bad weather.

The mule men, after making a survey, came back and reported the road passable; so we started at four o'clock in the morning of the 3rd June for the passage of the Rotang. The first accident occurred when we had been on the road an hour: one of the mules went over the side of the road and fell down a steep slope. His load—two of the leather trunks—went down much farther than he did, but no damage whatever was done either to the mule or the contents of the boxes. As we ascended higher, the patches of snow became more frequent, and the mules slipped about a good deal, but no accident happened, only great delay. We reached the crest of the pass at nine, had breakfast, and started again. The snow-bed on the Lahoul side was continuous, and by this time had become softened by the sun's rays; the mules were continually sinking and falling, and we came to a standstill at last in a bad place. All the loads had to be taken off and carried down a few hundred yards by the five coolies whom I had fortunately brought with me to assist. The made road could not be seen anywhere; it was entirely obliterated by the snow. Most of the packages had to be pushed down the snowy slopes. To add to our misfortunes, sleet came on, and a piercingly cold wind. The syce in charge of the pony, a Panjábi Mahomedan, had never seen snow before, and this was his first experience of a snowy pass. He had been toiling up the ascent in a very sad frame of mind, invoking "*Shekhji*" at every step. He had served as an attendant on the tonga dak in the plains, and was a stout lump of a man, and, as he was used to horses, I was induced to take him on in preference to the usual class of Hindú syce, as all my marching establishment were of the other religion. This is another tip for travellers and sportsmen: your servants should all be of one caste or religion. They will pull better together, and their impedimenta will not be so awkward to carry.

Kallú, the groom, had followed me down the slide with the pony, the latter having cleverly negotiated the passage by sliding down on his haunches. The syce, being now on the right side of the difficulty, took advantage of his position to poke fun at his companion, the cook, who usually made the dull-witted Kallú the butt of his caustic remarks. The latter now had his revenge; he invited his friend to have a ride free, gratis, all for nothing, and was immensely delighted to see him come down the slide wrong side up, for the unfortunate man lost his balance before he had gone two yards. Chamúrti was quite at home as soon as his hoofs touched the familiar snow. He had been on the level plains for more than six months, and now greeted his old surroundings with exuberant joy: I am sure he was the only one of the party who felt at home during the passage of the Rotang. His first performance was to grab mouthfuls of snow and munch it with evident relish, to the horror of his keeper. When he reached the top he capered about like a goat, escaped from Kallú's control, and had a most enjoyable roll, saddle and all, in the snow—a freak which resulted in the loss of his curb-chain. He was altogether too frisky to be led on the way down, and I was obliged at last to free him from the syce's leading-rope, after which he generally kept with the mules when I was not on his back. He would follow me or his attendant like a dog, but became quite disagreeable when an attempt was made to lead him. On the present occasion, as the pony skipped about on the snowy slopes of the Rotang, and Kallú stood on the path (the only place where he could keep his feet), they put me in mind of the mother-hen when her ducklings first disport in the water: Kallú, doubtless thinking the pony would break his neck during some of his capers, shouted the most endearing terms to coax him back, but he never ventured off the pathway himself.

We reached the Koksar bungalow at two, the journey across the broad back of the mountain having taken five hours for the ascent, and the same for the descent! The blue devils of Ralah had such a tight hold of me when I left that place, that I really was on the point of giving up my expedition and retracing my steps. I was thoroughly convinced that I was not equal to the task of crossing the pass, though I had done so more than once before; but I had not gone half-way up the ascent when my spirits began to rise at every step, and I felt as lively almost as the pony, and thoroughly enjoyed the rough work: there could be no more striking proof of the wonderfully exhilarating effect of mountain air and surroundings at an elevation of 13,000 feet. The Koksar bungalow is a windy place. A regular Tibetan gale was blowing down the valley, and the cold was much too bracing. The building itself was a wooden one, very roughly put together, and the furniture was in the same style. It is three marches from Koksar to Kailang. The road winds along the foot of the Lahoul mountains on the traveller's right hand, while on his left the mud-coloured Chandra river, at varying distances from the road, rushes down to its junction with the Bhaga at the village of Tanda. There is nothing for the sportsman to do along this portion of the route but admire small bits of scenery here and there, and push along as fast as possible. The distance to Kailang is about thirty-two miles, divided into three marches; there are no bungalows. Mules can do the distance easily in two days. The mountain range across the Chandra is the one mentioned before, along which good bear and ibex shooting can be obtained; a good length of it can be viewed from this road.

The Lahoul mountains on the right contain ibex; but they are difficult to find, and it is not worth wasting time after them when the sportsman is bound for more distant hunting grounds. Thirty years ago ibex were shot from the road by the infrequent traveller; but the beasts have now been educated into a better appreciation of the Express rifle. In the winter months, however, they can still be found close by; but I should say very few men would undertake a six months' sojourn in such a (literally) howling wilderness as this valley must be at that time of the year.

CHAPTER X

THE JOURNEY TO LADAKH

Kailang—Unavoidable delay—A difference in temperature—The Moravian Mission—Thakur Hari Singh—His travels—Lahouli Buddhists—The district of Lahoul—A sporting trip recommended—Resume the march—The last villages—A pass into Zanskar—The fall of a mountain on a village—Patsio annual fair and market—Filthy surroundings—Put up a bridge—Rather unsuccessfully—Zingzingbar—Halt at Chotenrong-jéún—A cold camping-place—Bad weather begins—Collapse of Indian servants—Alter my plans—Mules and servants dispensed with—Two Lámas turn up.

KAILANG is the headquarters of the subordinate magistrate in charge of Lahoul, and of the Moravian Mission to the Tibetans. A halt must be made here for the coolies, supplies and fuel, for nothing can be procured between Kailang and Rokchen in Rúpshú, ten marches away. I was consequently delayed here for three days. Thakur Hari Chand, the Magistrate and Tehsíldár (sub-collector) of Lahoul, a very respectful little man with a cough, was most obliging, and did his best to please me; but the people of the country have their own way of doing things which involves, according to my experience, a terrible waste of time. The weather also was unpropitious. It began to snow on the morning of the 6th June, and then to rain. The bad weather continued till the evening of the 7th. During this day the thermometer recorded 48°

inside the house and 38° outside—a temperature to which one is not accustomed in the month of June; a hundred miles away, down in the plains, these figures would have to be multiplied by three to get the proper feel of the weather. The 8th was a clear dry day, and fresh snow could be seen on all the hills around. This bit of bad weather luckily came when I was comfortably housed; it would have been awful in a tent. No coolies or supplies arrived on the 9th. The Thakur had collected some from the villages adjacent, and promised to hurry up the rest after me, so I made a start, and marched to Kúlang.

Before going any farther, I had better finish my say about Lahoul, and give some details of the shooting to be obtained there. The Moravian Mission has been established here, I believe, for more than forty years; it is in a most flourishing condition now, and, under the charge of its present head, the venerable and amiable pastor, Mr. Heyde, will continue to flourish in years to come. Venerable is a misleading term to apply to this gentleman, whose fresh face and robust frame, full of the energy of strong vitality, belie the word entirely; but I should be sorry to make a guess at his age.

Thakur Hari Singh, the local magistrate, was very communicative. He knows a great deal of the geography of Tibet, and gave me a very interesting account of his travels. He has been all over Ladakh with Philip Egerton, a former Deputy Commissioner of Kángra, who sent him on a mission to Gartokh in Tibet to open trade communication between the two countries. When he arrived there he got the stereotyped answer: "It was a new custom, and they could not allow entry into their country; it was against orders," etc. The Thakur accompanied Sir Douglas Forsyth in his mission to Yarkand, and was a great help to him during that trying journey. The inhabitants of Lahoul, he says, are Kanaits—the same people who are found in the Kúlú valley: there are no true Tibetans here. These Kanaits are Buddhists now, and their priests, even, belong to the same caste as the people. Many centuries ago the Rajah of Gugé in Tibet conquered Lahoul, and converted the people to Buddhism. The Tibetan Lámas remained in the country some time, but gradually died out, and now not one real Tibetan Buddhist priest is to be found in the country. Gúrú Gantál, at the confluence ("Preág" in Hindi, "Súmdo" in Tibetan) of the Chandra and Bhága rivers, some distance below Kailang, is the largest monastery in Lahoul. On Hari Chand's recommendation I engaged a man named Saráp, belonging to a village across the Bhága, as interpreter, guide, and general help. He was well acquainted with the country and routes in Ladakh, and had accompanied Sir Douglas Forsyth and Mr. Russell during their journey to Yarkand; he had also frequently accompanied sportsmen through various parts of the country. I did not discover what a thorough-paced rascal this man was till I was well beyond the passes that divide Lahoul from Ladakh, but his character was revealed to me as I got on.

A few hints, now, regarding the shooting in Lahoul. This district may be described as a triangular piece of country, with two sides, fifty miles in length each, and the third about thirty. At the three angles are situated, (1) the Baralácha Pass; (2) Shigri "camp" on the Chandra, where this river takes a sharp bend; (3) the large village of Tánda at the junction of the two rivers. Within these boundaries rises a tremendous knot of snowy mountains, round the bases of which the sportsman can spend a couple of pleasant months, though he must not be too sure of making a satisfactory bag. The best plan would be to proceed straight to the Barakicha Pass and thence begin operations, travelling down slowly from the sources of that stream as far as the angle at Shigri—a distance of, say, fifty miles. Sheep-tracks will be found all along the stream, but it will depend upon the time of the year whether he can shoot along the ground on *both* sides of the river, as in many places it may not be fordable. Proceeding down, he will have the whole of Tibet on his left,—the Tso Morari lake about one hundred miles off as the crow flies; but he should not be tempted to make an excursion in that direction: he should stick to the matter in hand, and thoroughly explore the Lahoul mountains. About fifteen miles above Shigri he will reach the Chandradal, a lake just below the Kangzam Pass leading into Spiti. At Shigri itself he will be confronted with the well-known glacier of that name. All along his line of march he will find ibex and, perhaps, barhal on his left, if he can get off the beaten track a little, and if the time of the year is favourable. At the end of his tramp, above and below Shigri, he will meet brown bear. After turning the corner, he will have Koksar, about twenty-five miles, before him, under the Rotang and the Hamta Pass leading into Kúlú, on his left. Ibex and bear will be found on the slopes. From Shigri to old Koksar is a well-known shooting ground; but it is so close to the main road that it is pretty well shot over, especially by local sportsmen: if this has been done lately, no time should be wasted searching for game.

The above is the longest shooting tour that can be made in Lahoul: it is well worth trying. The other two sides of the triangle are traversed by the commercial road to Leh, and game has been driven away from it for years past—that is to say, during the season open to the sportsmen. The extent of the bag will depend a good deal on the time of year: early in the season or late in the season are the only periods that he should choose. That means June to July, or September to October. The reason is that thousands and thousands of sheep, with their shepherds and watch-dogs, work their way gradually up the slopes of the valleys leading from the lower ranges of Mandi, Kángra, and Chamba to the highest spurs of the Himálayan buttress, and cross it. As these innumerable flocks graze upwards, the game recedes before them, and is driven and scattered gradually into such inaccessible ground that following them up there is not worth the trouble. The sheep reach their farthest points in July and August, and then begin their return journey. This is the course that is followed year after year. The sportsman must take note of it, and so arrange the trip as to keep in front of the flocks in the beginning of the season, or reach the grounds towards the end, after they have left. One of the farthest points reached by these nomads is the knot of mountains in Lahoul.

The road to Kúlang, the first march from Kailang, is a gradual ascent, but near the former village descends to the river level, where the Bhága is yet a considerable stream. The hills on either side are barren and rocky, capped with snow here and there, with a little vegetation fringing their feet, which are washed by the river. A couple of small glaciers are in sight above the village of Tinnú on the left bank. Cypress-trees are frequent on the slopes, and willows in the cultivated parts: the latter are planted, and are, I suppose, private property; it is a valuable timber-tree in this treeless country, and is used in a variety of ways for domestic purposes. The valley narrows gradually, and the view is greatly contracted by dark and frowning mountains on every side: this stage is uninteresting. Travellers generally make a double march

A PASS INTO ZANSKAR

from Kailang, and get over as great a distance as possible after the enforced halt of several days; but I was hampered by the non-arrival of my coolies and supplies, and had to go slowly to let them come up. Next day I made Dárcha, eight miles. The village is on the opposite side of the river. The streams that flow in on either side of the Bhága were considerable in volume, showing that the snows now felt the power of the sun. A path into Zanskar (Jaskar, according to local usage) leads up it by the Shingo-la (wood-pass), at its head. The pass derives its name from the fact that wood for fuel can be obtained along that route: such a rare occurrence in this woodless country is fuel! A sportsman went up this way a month ago because the Baralácha was not then passable; so the Shingo-la must be a lower pass. It is a four days' journey from this point to the first village in Zanskar beyond the pass. If the traveller cannot cross back by the Morang-la, he has no alternative but to march down the Zanskar river until he strikes the high road from Kashmir to Leh. The Zanskar mountains, when you are once in the valley of its main stream, present such a formidable barrier all around that there is no exit at all on the right towards Ladakh; and only a couple of very difficult passes on the left towards Chamba and Kashmir. The early traveller is therefore liable to be led into a trap if he tries to double round the passes on the regular route: it all depends upon the snowfall of the previous winter. The gentleman who took this route I met subsequently at Rokchen; he found no insuperable difficulties, and had a good time among the Zanskar ibex. Perhaps the man who attempts the same journey next year may have an experience just the reverse.

The stream which joins the Bhága on its left bank drains the knot of Lahoul mountains on that side. All

the nalás in this direction have been shot out long ago,
and the sportsman should not be tempted to waste his
time among them, whatever stories local shikáris may
tell him. Just at this confluence, by my camp, a part of
the mountain on the right bank of the Bhága had fallen
upon the angle formed by the two streams. The vast
masses fell and spread out all over that part of the land,
and were scattered about in the wildest confusion. A
small village which occupied the site was completely
overwhelmed, and not a soul escaped; even all the fields
belonging to the place were blotted out. This disaster
must have occurred centuries ago, as the existing face of
the mountain now shows no signs of the disruption, nature
and weather having effaced all traces of it. There is a
huge gap in the mountain side (now covered up with soil
and grass), out of which this mass of rock must have fallen.
The coolies and supplies having arrived at last, I was free
to move onward. The next stage is Patsio (11 miles).
Darcha is the largest village, that is, human habitation
with walls and a roof, I shall see till I get to Shúshal,
three weeks hence; and no supplies will be procurable
till Rokchen is reached—eight marches ahead. I laid in
supplies for twenty days—also fuel; we were therefore on
the safe side. The road was in very bad repair; for the
latter half of the stage it had been carried away by the
melting snow. It took us five and a half hours to do the
distance. Patsio is the place where the great annual fair
is held: traders from both directions meet here and
exchange their goods. The trade begins in July, and lasts
for a couple of months. The Tibetans bring their flocks
down here in thousands, carrying salt in little woollen
bags across the sheep's back; the fleece is then sold and
sheared off on the spot; the salt is disposed of at the
same time. Grain principally is taken in exchange, and

carried back in the same way. Ponies come from Zanskar and parts of Tibet, and nice little animals can be picked up by anyone who chooses to stay and await his chance. The grain and other goods are brought by Lahoulis from below on their tattoos ; so, in the season, the surrounding hills swarm with ponies, sheep, and goats. The pasturage is splendid and sufficient, and the animals are soon in condition after their enforced starvation during the winter months. There are some huts here, but they were filthy in the extreme, and the surrounding areas of level ground were in the same condition. The whole place reeked with sheep's dung, which lay several inches deep, wherever there was a level spot. The turf was still very wet from the melting snow; no good camping ground could be found anywhere, and my tent, perforce, had to be pitched next the huts, in the midst of the dirt. As the usual Lahouli gale of wind was blowing, everything was smothered in the malodorous dust, which I breathed from the moment I arrived, and of which I certainly ate a fair quantity with my dinner. I amused myself in the evening by putting up the bridge over the Bhága at this place ; we found the boards lying under the rocks close by, and the coolies helped very willingly. The bridge has to be dismantled every year, to prevent the snow from smashing it and the river from carrying away the materials. In the afternoon clouds came up, and the wind reached a furious gale before evening. Ugly rocky hills surround this place, and patches of snow lie in the clefts. There are flats along the river as far as one could see, and a flush of rich grass was visible just above the surface, making these little plains very refreshing to the eyes tired of rugged mountains. Sheets of flowers relieve the sameness of the tender green ; but as yet they hardly showed above the surface.

Our engineering of the bridge was not of the best, for

next morning, as the third mule was coming over, one of
the boards fell through, and the poor animal nearly followed.
The board was carried away by the river, and the rest of
the caravan had to ford the stream above the bridge—a
very cold and disagreeable job in the early morning. The
road as far as Zingzingbár (11 miles) was good and level :
we were now on the left bank of the stream. This place
is a collection of stone walls and a few roofless houses a
little distance above the river, and just under some striking
rocky peaks partly covered with snow. We halted here
till 4 P.M., as the weather looked threatening. The road
ascended to Choten-rong-jéún with a gentle slope ; we
crossed by a bridge to the right bank again, and reached
the above place at 5.30 P.M. ; distance about three miles.
This is considered the foot of the pass, that is to say, the
highest point where camp can be made, for the snow from
here is continuous to the foot of the pass on the other
side. We had no protection of any kind, neither rocks,
walls, nor anything else, and no tents were pitched, as I
wished to make an early start before the sun softened the
snow. I slept in the open, under the lee of the grass
bundles that were brought up for the animals; my
quarters were rather cold, but no fire could be made, as fuel
was precious and had to be husbanded carefully. The
thermometer marked about 40° at sundown, 34° shortly
after, and 32° before it got too dark to read it ; then
everything began to freeze, and I turned in. Our troubles
began now—the biggest disaster that befell me on this
trip. When we started in the morning from Patsio, the
sun shone, and we were all light-hearted enough, notwithstanding the cold dip in the river; but before we had
finished half the journey the clouds gathered, and bad
weather omens met us at every turn. The Lahoulis, who
knew what was coming, began to murmur; they first

wished to return, then they clung lovingly about the roofless walls of Zingzingbár, and had certainly very sad hearts when they were driven onwards. The mule men, too, were unwilling; but my liver was in its right place at the foot of *this* pass; I felt no qualms, and no malingering was allowed; everyone had to make the best of a bad job. My bed was laid on a patch of bare ground under cover of the grass bundles, and my followers had similar quarters; I was better off as far as the bundles went—nothing more. I was too anxious for an early start to sleep, and my companions were too cold; so I had everyone up at 2 A.M., and we prepared for the ascent: the weather, however, was too threatening, and, instead of starting, we all sat still, and in the end had to put the tents up to protect ourselves. Heavy snow came on shortly afterwards, and continued for six hours; the sun came out strong at noon, and the tents were dry in an hour. But at 4 P.M. it began to snow again, and shortly after sun again for another hour. This alternation of snow and sun was most tantalising, and kept my hopes going up and down like the thermometer. My three Indian servants collapsed during the day: the bitter cold wind and snowy surroundings were too much for them—they simply lay down in their tents and became torpid. Nothing would rouse them: threats, coaxing, even hunger had no effect, no sound escaped their lips: their faces had become as black as charcoal, and their eyes were fixed in a meaningless stare.

It snowed during the whole night, and up to 9 A.M. next day (14th June). The fall was very heavy, and in the pass itself must have accumulated to a great depth. The mules and ponies bolted during the night and sheltered themselves under the roofless walls of Zingzingbár, and some of the men followed their example. There was snow again during most of the day. Under these circumstances the firewood began to disappear rapidly, and I at once sent men off to Dárcha for a fresh supply. The servants were so utterly helpless that they could not cook for me, and, after existing on tea and biscuits as long as nature permitted, I was driven to cook for myself. The men themselves had not energy enough to take any nourishment; they lay like logs under all the blankets and warm things they could put their hands on. I must say my appetite did not suffer, and my spirits rose as the thermometer fell. The condition of my followers, however, caused me anxiety, and I long debated in my mind the wisdom of a backward move.

The next day was clear, and the crisis came: the servants were manifestly unequal to any exertion whatever; they had had no food for three days, and looked most miserable—black, shrivelled-up, shivering bits of humanity. I made up my mind at last, and decided to send back my Indian servants and mules, and push forward with the coolies and ponies I had brought up from Kailang. I reduced my traps to eighteen light loads, and there were twenty-five coolies: the tattoos would carry the grass and fuel. The mules, too, were in bad condition; it was too early in the season to cross these passes with them, and they would certainly collapse farther on, in a situation perhaps beyond help. I therefore made up my mind to free myself from these encumbrances. I should certainly have a bad time without any servants; but I depended upon Saráp, who said servants could be procured from Leh. When I announced my intention, the countenances of the cook and syce lit up with joy, but the third man, Yákúb, the smallest and weakest of the three, but a Pathán and with the Pathán grit in him, objected as strongly as his weak condition would allow. He had suffered the worst, and was certainly the least fit of the three; but he flatly refused to return.

"You can carry me like a bundle on a tattoo until I am well again, or bury me on the roadside if I die, but I won't go back," he said, and began to blubber. So I kept him, certainly to my own great relief, and afterwards, through the rest of my rough journey, to my great comfort. But the other two were thorough Hindústani curs, as spiritless as the pie-dogs of their country; they were only too eager for the return journey. While busily engaged in making these arrangements, two Lámas came down the pass, and I entertained them at four-o'clock tea. They had had a very bad time on the other side of the pass, where they were obliged to curl up in a cave for three days, and they had not yet thawed sufficiently to be very intelligent—I could not get much information out of them. They belonged to Rodokh, and were going on a pilgrimage to Tilóknáth, below the junction of the Chandrabhága. The evening was fine and clear, but the icy wind from the snows blowing down the valley doubled one up: no amount of warm clothing could keep it away from the body; shelter was the only remedy.

CHAPTER XI

THE JOURNEY TO LADAKH—(continued)

We force the pass at last—Yákúb in a bad way—Height of Tibetan passes—A frozen lake—A grand snowy panorama—Water-parting of the Indus and Chináb—Nasman-Nisman camp—Saichú camp—Meet the first Tibetan traders to Patsio—Their sheep—Salt trade—Kiám camp—Enter Kashmir territory—Súmdo camp—More sheep—Láchálang Pass crossed—Effect of rarefied atmosphere—First game animal seen—Pangta camp—Two young kiangs take stock of us—Ponies stray—Reach Rúpshú plains—A long march—Rokchen camp—Examine a sportsman's bag—Picked-up heads—Test of made-up trophies—Great cold at Rokchen—Coolies paid up—Yaks engaged—Plateau of Rúpshú—Meet a sportsman from Calcutta—Leave Rokchen—Tso-kar salt-lake—Sheldrakes—Their nests—Polokónka Pass—Tibetan cairns adorned with horns—The Púga valley—Rakdong camp—Varying temperatures—Reach the river Indus—Delay in crossing—Yaha-Jaha camp—Lámas' encampment—Shoot a black wolf—Description of him—First hunt after nyan—The valley of frozen lakes—Get on the wrong side of the pass—A Tibetan beggar—See some nyan—Reach the Mirpa-tso—Three impressions of Ladakh—Cross the Thaota-la—Reach Shúshal at last.

ON the 16th of June at five o'clock we were at last able to face the pass, after lying at its foot, in the worst possible weather, for nearly three days—an experience to which the Tibetan traveller must accustom himself. In such circumstances he should follow the example of the aborigines, whose marvellous capacity for surviving such misfortunes proves them the hardiest of mountaineers. He must have patience and endure the monotony of inaction, remembering that with fuel, food, and warm clothing no harm can come. As we started, a man with twenty sheep came up from

HEIGHT OF TIBETAN PASSES

Dárcha on his way to Rokchen, whither he was going for wool. He was the first trader of the season, and would buy his wool on the sheep's backs and take delivery at Patsio. The sheep he had with him would carry his supplies. Yákúb had to be hoisted on to Chamúrti and held on, as he had not strength to keep his seat in the saddle; he had had nothing to eat, and could not possibly take food till he had thawed a little. Probably a human being could exist in this condition, like the hibernating bear, for a length of time, provided no bodily exertion was exacted. Chamúrti kept with the two Lahouli ponies carrying the fuel, and became quite sociable with them; he had sobered down somewhat now; the three days of cold had taken some of the friskiness out of him.

We crossed the pass without the least difficulty, and reached the second frozen lake on the other side at a quarter past nine; the coolies took two hours more. This was a very small performance indeed compared with the passage of the Rotang. The fact is, the first pass over the buttress of the Himálayas is always the most difficult and trying: most of those which come afterwards, on the Ladakh side, are across ridges at the heads of valleys—not solid, upstanding ranges of mountains with bases twenty and thirty miles in breadth. The height of Tibetan passes (fifteen to nineteen thousand feet) sound very awe-inspiring, but, with a very few exceptions, they are passes only in name. It is to be remembered that the average altitude of Tibet is not less than 14,000 feet. The ascent of the Barahácha is very gradual, and presented no difficulties except sloping patches of snow here and there. After going up some distance, level tracts are found where the snow lies thickly; in one of these is a small frozen lake, the road running round its margin. This portion of the road is considered the most dangerous on the pass, as animals are liable to slip if there is much snow, and, if laden, are certain to be lost. A trader lost a pony here last season, and it was still lying, load and all, in the lake. There was, however, not the slightest danger when we passed, as this part of the road was quite free from snow, notwithstanding the recent heavy falls. A little way beyond the first frozen lake is a ridge, looking back from the summit of which a grand snowy panorama lies spread before you—a splendid stretch of mountains along the entire line of sight from right to left, a glorious tent-shaped peak of pure white arresting the eye over minor elevations. The view was bounded on both sides by two snowy wings, the slopes of the narrow valley by which I had just ascended. It was a study in white: neither rocks, earth, nor vegetation were visible anywhere, from the white carpet at my feet to the horizon far away in the south—an unbroken white expanse unequalled on any other mountains on the globe. The next hardly perceptible undulation I walked over was the top of the pass, where are two stone huts and the usual Tibetan cairn with ragged flags stuck about it. To the right as I passed north, a short distance off, was the source of the Chandra; at my feet rose the Bhága—a few yards only divided them. The Lingti stream, down which my path dipped, begins its course at this point also; so that I now stood on the water-parting between the Indus and the Chináb. The snow melting on this slight elevation feeds these three rivers here, and, after hundreds of miles of widely independent wandering, meet again in the turbid water of the "Panjnad" below Múltan. What a contrast between the scenes of separation and reunion! Descending the other slope, the road winds among overturned rocks as far as Kinlang, the usual halting-place. There are two double huts in a stone enclosure here, and below is the bridge crossing the stream. The baggage animals had to go by the old road, as the bridge was out of repair while I took the new road, which, still descending, passes along curious little patches of flat ground —sometimes covered with young grass and surrounded by disrupted rocks.

We camped on reaching the level of the stony valley, through which the stream runs. The name of the place is Nasman-Nisman. On the right edge of this valley are peculiar-looking small hills, which decrease in size as they descend along the slope; my camp was under the first and largest. Were these brought here by glacial action? That is, are they moraines brought down and deposited at the bottom of the valley, afterwards cut through into hillocks by the action of streams, and then moulded into rounded and conical mounds by the action of weather? The disrupted rocks along the road above may have been placed in their present position by the same means. Marmot burrows were plentiful after passing the second lake, and several of the animals were sitting about.

The next camp was at Saichú near the bridge, distance about nine miles, over a plain on which marmots were numerous. The alluvial soil here has been cut down to a great depth by the action of several streams, whose waters all flow towards Zanskar and join that river. The Zanskar valley can be easily reached in two marches by following this stream. I met here more traders for the Patsio market, with their laden sheep. The latter wore their fleeces, and were fine large animals, very strong and active, in splendid condition, and noticeable for their small, well-shaped heads. The salt which the traders had was bitter (fit only for cattle), collected at the numerous salt lakes in Tibet. The good salt comes from Chakchaka, near the Thok-jalúng gold mines, far away in the Chang-thang —the great plain of Tibet. It is sold with profit as far south as Kúlú.

Kiám, the next stage, was a very cramped place, between a rocky ridge and the steep bank of the river; a regular sun-trap. This stage took the coolies seven hours: the old and the new roads were so mixed up that sometimes one was followed and sometimes the other—the latter was much the longer of the two, and seemed to be rarely used. Besides, the whole extent of country during the stage is cut up by streams; they all flow into the Tsarap river, which carries them to the Zanskar. The waters have eaten down through the soil to a great depth, and high perpendicular banks had to be negotiated more than once. I started late, at the request of the men, as they had to wade through the water frequently, and it would be cold work early in the morning. This was all very well for *them*, but, by starting later, I suffered from the sun cruelly. Two boundary pillars on either side of the road, shortly after leaving camp, mark the point where Kashmir territory begins. I was now in the Ladakh province of that kingdom. As there was no grass near Kiám, the baggage animals had to be sent across the Tsarap to graze, and the start in the morning was delayed in consequence. There were several disagreeable ascents during the next march; the first one from Kiám was the longest and most tiresome. In fact, the distance from Kiám to the top of the Láchálang is one long ascent to that pass.

The next camp was Súmdo, at the foot of the Láchálang crest, distance about nine miles, nearly all up-hill: the coolies did it in seven hours. Súmdo camp was a most dreary place; the surrounding mountains are stony and black, and shut in the view on all sides. There was no grass whatever, only a few dáma plants (furze) and the curious knobby, smooth, and rounded moss-like lumps that are found at high elevations. Flocks of Rúpshú sheep passed my tent at all hours; they travel day and night across this grassless tract, taking a good rest and a good feed at either end. The sheep are too thin and tough to make mutton, and the shepherds always take with them a few goats for food. The sheep are merely beasts of burden, and as such are indispensable to the people, for no other animal would suit them so well. Death does not close their career of utility—their skins are made into garments, and their carcases feed the watchdogs. For every two sheep shorn at Patsio one rupee is given for the wool; then there is the load they carry—altogether a very profitable business, I should say. Two journeys are made during the open season; but sometimes great loss is suffered by snowstorms in the Tsarap valley. It is said that on one occasion 3000 sheep were lost in one storm.

The ascent from Súmdo camp to the Láchálang crest did not take long. My breath came very short as I went up. The rarity of the atmosphere was making itself felt. On the Baralácha, which is 16,060 feet above sea level, I did not experience any inconvenience at all, though of course I had to halt more frequently than usual to recover breath. On the Láchálang, which is 16,630 feet high, or 570 feet higher than the last pass, the feeling that I could not inhale sufficient air at each breath was very present with me. I am not subject to any of the other symptoms which attack people at high elevations, such as nausea and headache, though I have spent several days, at various times, at elevations of eighteen and nineteen thousand feet. We left Súmdo at six, and reached Pang camp at 3.15 P.M.; the distance could not be less than eighteen miles a gradual descent all the way after crossing the pass. The snow on the north side of the pass was much more frequent than on the Súmdo side. At one point in the valley, the mountain side on the left has fallen bodily down into the valley, and blocked up the course of a stream which enters it on the left, and which for some distance runs under the débris, and the road zigzags down among these ruins in a very rough fashion. There were some sweet-smelling plants at this place: at a distance the faint odour was delicious; but when I went down and plucked a few stalks, the smell was very strong and decidedly disagreeable—something like the strong-smelling sacred Hindú plant called the tulsi. Perhaps these strong odours, at such high elevations, have given rise to the native idea that the traveller becomes faint and ill through inhaling them when crossing passes. A little farther on we came to a green patch by the side of the stream, overhung by a conspicuous and peculiarly-pointed hill, called Gagnájal. The valley gradually opens out from this point, and is bounded by huge rounded mountain sides with fantastic points, towers, etc., standing out in true Tibetan style. But it is only after crossing the Láchálang that the characteristic Tibetan scenery meets one's eyes; and the country on this side of the Baralácha is only the prelude to the topsy-turviness with which one gets familiar in the land of the Lámas. On the left of the road, on a projection commanding a view up and down the valley, I saw a burhel ram watching us—the first game I had seen; he was about six hundred yards off, and, though he had small horns, was a welcome sight. When we reached the camping-place, a short distance from the stream, a tearing wind was blowing, and there was no protection from it but rough stone fences, evidently put up to break the force of the wind. When the traps arrived, the ponies were let loose, and started off at once for the green grass fringing the stream—the first food they had had since their feed on the Tsarap river. Poor Chamúrti was much reduced by these privations, and having lost his shoes, his feet had become very tender. As I was lying on the bank, encouraging the kettle to boil, two kiangs (wild horses) came running down the valley—evidently attracted by the ponies. They trotted round in a circle, stood about a hundred yards off, had a good look at me, and then raced back neck and neck, kicking up their heels, and disappeared in the distance—a very pretty sight. They were the size of small donkeys, and looked very much like them.

The next stage brought us to Rokchen, a long and wearing march. We started at 6 A.M., having been somewhat delayed by the disappearance of Chamúrti and another pony, who had wandered away during the night in search of grass. We had to encounter at once the stiff ascent from Pang camp to the level above, which landed us at last on the Rúpshú plateau. Kiangs were everywhere and marmots were plentiful, but both these animals are uncommonly wide-awake, and kept at a respectful distance, while they indulged their irrepressible curiosity by staring at us (out of rifle-range) as we passed along. The road is along a broad open valley, with extensive plains on either hand and level all the way, winding about the turns of the hills, first on the right and afterwards on the left slope. We did not get into Rokchen till 4 P.M.—a ten hours' journey. The distance must be twenty miles. The truant ponies caught us up some hours after starting. They had gone up the valley some distance, and were comfortably grazing about among kiangs; the men had some difficulty in persuading them into the right path. There were about thirty-five black tents, of all sizes, scattered about the level ground near the camp, and close to a small stream, which comes down from the snow-topped hills on the left; the water is evidently the attraction which makes this valley a favourite camping-place for the people

of the country. The gentleman shooting about Kardok
sent in some heads and skins during my stay at Rokchen;
there were two nyan heads (*O. Hodgsoni ammon*) and
some nápú heads (*O. nahoor* or barhal). The former were
evidently picked up or bought: one was bleached by the
weather, and very old; the other seemed a skull of last
winter; there were no nyan skins. The horns of the
largest head measured forty-two inches, or about two inches
above the average size. These picked-up heads are often
passed off in the plains, by the sportsman who uses the
silver bullet, as trophies that have been acquired by him
after going through unheard-of hardships. The old heads
are even set up, sometimes with the skins of smaller
animals that have really fallen to his rifle, and thus a
greater air of verisimilitude is given to the story. The
cunning taxidermists of Srinagar city are unapproachable
in this kind of forgery. Who has not heard the rotund
warrior holding forth after dinner to an attentive and
admiring group of youngsters, filling them up with the
wonderful incidents of that difficult stalk on the stony
plain beyond Hanlé, where he had to crawl *ventre à terre*
for half a mile, while a scorching sun blistered his back?
No; the real Tibetan sportsman is tall, lean, and most
exasperatingly silent as to his adventures. He is met
now and then in his favourite haunts, clad in an old suit
of khaki, weather-worn and ragged at many points, a
battered old felt on his head, and a pair of worn-out
ammunition boots on his feet. His face is the colour of
brick dust, where it is not hidden by the hairy growth of
many days. He has lived on chapátis, cooked by his
faithful Gúrkha orderly, and jam made by his careful wife,
for the last three weeks; but he is now walking away
with the three biggest trophies of the season—and he has
done it all within three months' leave! This is the style

of man who bags the largest head in the flock of nyan, 19,000 feet above sea level, or a Victoria Cross in storming a stockade at the level of the seashore. Forgive me, General, should this rough pencil-sketch meet your eye! To revert for a moment to the picked-up trophies: these may always be known too by a sign which inevitably betrays them; the tips of the horns will always be found to have been gnawed—either by the Tibetan wolf, who pulled down the original owner during some severe winter, or by the Tibetan shepherd's watch-dog, who has amused himself by chewing the points during his moments of leisure.

It took me thirteen days to reach this place from Kailang, in ten marches. The calculation I made was to reach Rokchen on the 19th, but I got in on the 21st June; I therefore lost two days over this portion of my journey. I halted here on the 22nd. The thermometer in the tent at night went down to 26°. At Rokchen I paid off the Kailang coolies (their wages amounting to sixty rupees), and arranged for yaks to take me on. Yaks are cheap—three annas a stage for each load—not animal. The yakmen take along as many animals as they please, but get paid for the number of loads only. Three coolie loads equal one yak load. Eighteen men brought my things here, so that I had only six yak loads.

A few words about Rúpshú, or Rúkshú, and its people will not be out of place here. The altitude of the valley or plateau is between fourteen and fifteen thousand feet high, or about double that of Simla, and it is surrounded by mountain ranges from two to five thousand feet higher; the climate is therefore rather rigorous. But the people live in tents all the year round, and apparently thrive under these conditions. Water freezes here every night of the year. Though the cold is so intense, the air is extremely dry, and the snow limit is in consequence 20,000 feet. The snowfall is said to be very small, so that below that level it always disappears during the summer. Vegetation is scanty: a little grass may be found near a spring or along the banks of streams. The population is nothing to speak of—about five hundred souls in the 4000 square miles of the tract. They have about a hundred tents, one for each family, and are divided into two camps. The people are called "Champas," or tent-dwellers. The tents are made of yak's or goat's hair, and are very roughly put together. They have numerous flocks; sheep and goats in large numbers can be seen returning in the evening to camp from all points of the compass. The people I saw at Rokchen seemed a lively lot, though they must have a rough time of it in their tents all the year round. Rúpshú pays a revenue of 2400 rupees. The people told me it was oppressive, but their numerous flocks and yaks, and the trade they carry on so profitably, did not bear out the statement; they certainly did not look badly off. They were all comfortably clothed, well-fed, and light-hearted. Their costume is a *choga* (long cloak), two or more according to the temperature, pájámahs, and a waist-belt. They wear a cap with ear-flaps made of black lambskin, the wool next the head. This headgear is carried with a very jaunty air by the young men; the cap is placed on the side of the head, and one of the ear-flaps is brought over the forehead like a peak. With the cap at a proper angle, and a certain swagger, the youthful Champa looks quite a dandy, though a dirty one. The men are tall, well-made, and good-looking; the women small, ill-formed, and hard-worked; they are unceasingly employed in collecting fuel, carrying water, and in other domestic duties; some go with the flocks, and remain out all the day. Most of the men seemed to spend their time lounging about, but many were absent on trading business. I met here the gentleman who had come over the Shingola and through part of Zanskar. He got some ibex and burhel. He said the Zanskar country he passed through was full of ibex—he counted more than sixty on one hillside. This secluded valley seems to be rarely visited by sportsmen. This gentleman came all the way from a cantonment near Calcutta only on four months' leave; he marched in by Kúlú and Lahoul, intended shooting about Hanlé, and would return by Spiti and Simla to Calcutta—a good round journey. Next morning we started together with our traps, but soon parted; my friend went off to the right front, while I continued down to Tso-kar, or salt-lake, and camped at the farther end, where there was a little fresh water and some grass. This was a very short march, but I was greatly exhausted, as most of the walking was over a dead sandy plain. The lake at this time was in the form of a crescent. It must have been enormous at some time, the shores being the edges of the surrounding hills, along which the water-line is visible in many places. It was now shrunk to the lowest level of the valley. Numbers of sheldrakes frequented the lake; these ducks spent a great deal of their time on the ridge overhanging the west margin of the lake. As this was their breeding-time, they had evidently built their nests high up on the hillside. I was not aware that this was their habit, and I have not seen it mentioned in any book on natural history: to verify my conjecture demanded more climbing than I was equal to; but all appearances were in favour of it. These birds were more noisy than usual. There were also a few geese on the lake; these must have been weak or sickly birds, which were unable to continue their flight to Central Asia. The prospect from my tent door was a blank sandy plain;

fifteen kiangs were disporting themselves within my view.
A high wind began to blow from the west, and there was
a great rise in the temperature at once; at 5 P.M. the
thermometer was 68° in the tent.

Next day I crossed the Polokónka Pass, 16,500 feet
high; but the ascent was so gradual, and the actual
dividing line so invisible, that I should certainly not have
noticed it but for the usual large mané, or cairn, by the
path. Many horns and skulls of nyan and napu in
addition to the flag on this cairn, but no large horns. It
is much more profitable to sell them to the wandering
sportsman than offer them to the local deity. I was
told that the *Ovis ammon* horns came from the Tin valley
to the right of my route. They were all votive offerings
by successful local shikáris—a sure sign that game was
near. The sun was very hot during this portion of my
march—in fact, it was unendurable, and I had to take
refuge under a rock, where luckily I found some water,
and therefore stayed for breakfast. This descent from
Polokónka-la in the direction of Púga is much more
marked, and a stony pathway winds down to the plain.
The Púga valley is the place where sulphur is collected
for the Mahárájah of Kashmir. The people of the adjacent
country are impressed to do this work, and each person
is paid one anna per day for the four months during
which the operations last. The Púga valley is an ugly
bit of country, shut in by high mountains. We camped
about a mile and a half below the sulphur works, at a
stream of sweet water. The distance from last camping-
place was not less than eighteen miles, I should say.
During this march I met at three different points men
returning from Sáhibs who were out shooting in various
directions. Sáhibs were getting pretty thick as I
approached the game ground—the usual thing.

At Tso-kar the thermometer at seven o'clock in the evening in the tent was 46°; at 5 A.M. it was 12° below freezing point, but the cold was not disagreeable. At this latter camp, Raldong by name, it was 60° inside the tent at 8.30 P.M., and 38° when I started in the morning. These figures will give some idea of the climate in these parts at this season.

I continued down valley along the Púga stream. At 8 A.M. I came to a tent belonging to an R.E. from Roorkee, who had arrived here two days before. He was out after game, but left a note " for the two gentlemen coming from Púga," asking them to stop at his tent and have breakfast, or anything else. I had some tea, and stayed half an hour. Yakúb, my servant, found a fellow-townsman in the gentleman's body-servant, and the cook recognised me as his quondam master in the plains. The Sapper, in his note, mentioned that he was going to Hanlé; and that, as far as he knew, three men were on the road to Chang-chen-mo; this was not a promising prospect for me. I am sorry I missed seeing the hospitable sportsman. I now thank him again for his kind note and the information it contained.

Went on along the stream and reached the Indus in an hour—old Aba-Sín, " the father of waters," as the Patháns call him. A few years before I had crossed his deep, sullen, and altogether too wrathful stream at Búnji, on the road to Gilgit—how different was his aspect here! This is his innocent boyhood—small, mild, and gently playful; his infancy is passed higher up, in the pure bosom of the Kailas. We all know his lusty manhood when he rolls his accumulated strength, tearing away the land in the season of his temporary madness, along the level plains of the Panjáb and of Sind. The path turns up along the left bank of the stream, and after a short walk the village of Maya, on the opposite bank, came into view; that is to say, three donkeys in a patch of green field—I saw no houses. The ferry-boat and the yaks from Neuma were to have been ready here for me, as I had sent on a man from Rokchen to arrange, and had sent Saráp with the messenger whom I met returning, to see the matter *was* arranged; but we continued our journey till we came to the ford opposite Neuma, and no yaks or men were yet in sight—in fact, not a living creature of any kind. We therefore pitched camp and awaited developments. Saráp arrived at eight o'clock with the animals and men, and reported that the messenger had never gone to Neuma, nor given the order for carriage. The people of Rúkshú are said to be the highest dwellers in the world, and, in my experience, also the tallest liars, as witness this instance. Query—What has made these gentle and elevated shepherds what they are? It cannot be the degenerating influences of the outer world—their bleak country effectually protects them from such contamination—it must be natural.

We crossed the stream next morning, the men taking the things over on their backs through water up to their thighs; on the other side we repacked the yaks and went down the right bank, reversing yesterday's journey, and so losing a day. I shot a kiang on this march: he was hit in the right shoulder at 225 yards, and took the shot without flinching, but rolled over before he had gone twenty-five yards. My shooting him was partly due to my wish to examine one of these animals at close quarters, and partly to try the range of the rifle—a double Express—which I bought in a hurry just before starting. It is a pity to shoot them, and no sportsman should bag more than a single specimen. I never fired at them again, though the aggravating creatures spoiled many a stalk after nyan.

"FERRY ACROSS THE INDUS AT NEL MAI."

The kiang I shot was an enormous brute, a very old stallion, sturdy in limb and build, with hoofs as large as those of a horse, beautifully shaped, and as hard as iron. The rest of the herd stood about two hundred yards away, looking on, and Yákúb was tempted to have a shot with the smooth bore: the bullet fell at least a hundred yards too short, much to his astonishment and disgust. Distances, of course, are very deceptive in this clear atmosphere. Yákúb had a glorious spill off the small (very small) Tibetan tattoo he was riding; after having his shot, he mounted and galloped off to the dead kiang to get the skin. The carcase was lying in a hollow, and the little pony did not see it till he nearly ran over it; the consequence was a tremendous shy, and when I came up I found a struggling mass of man, tattoo, dead kiang, and my precious gun. It took some time to separate the component parts, and I was anxious about the gun, but no damage was done, luckily. I used only the first sight on the rifle for the long shot I had made. The conclusion I came to was that the range is just doubled at these high elevations: the 100 yards sight will do for 200 yards.

We left the Indus near the village of Maya, and turned up to the right, commencing at once a dreadfully stiff ascent. I found the heat of the sun intolerable, though I was riding. We made camp at half-past three in a singular-looking valley named Yaha-jaha; it is circular in shape, and has only one narrow entrance, by which a small stream flows to a lake at the farther end of the valley; there is no outlet; bare and steep rocky hills are all round, and the level of the valley is turfy and boggy where not covered by water. The wind during the night was most boisterous, and kept me much awake, in dread of the tent coming down. We started early next morning in a very cold and most disagreeable wind. The valley along which our path lay was at first very narrow, but soon opened out into a wide plain, with large snow-beds in many places. Farther on we came to three tents, surrounded by stone enclosures, closely packed with sheep and cattle. There were several Lamas here. All this country belongs to the village of Chumathang, which belongs to the Lamas of the Hemis monastery; that is to say, they receive the revenues, and these flocks and herds belonged to them. Lamas manage all the business. We camped a mile farther up the stream, which, next morning, I found completely frozen. The thermometer, in the warm tent, was 32°, but the sun was not out an hour before all signs of ice had disappeared, and at ten o'clock the heat was unbearable!

I tried the hill-range on my right for nyan next day, but saw only nápú (the Tibetan name for barhal), and returned to the valley to move camp a few miles higher up. I shot a wolf on the way. I was lying down near the stream late in the evening, resting, when a marmot spied me and began piping. I was watching his jerky movements through the glasses, when, presently, a dirty-looking animal came trotting along the edge of the valley towards the marmot, who disappeared. When the wolf got between me and the marmot, I called, and he stood to look. I hit him in the head with the ·500 Express, and he fell dead. To me the dead beast looked more like a hyæna than a wolf. He was very old; the teeth were ground down to the gums, and were hardly distinguishable. The pelage on the back and sides was blackish on top, bluish below next the skin, and whitish under the belly. The hair behind was three inches long, under belly four and a half inches, on the neck four inches, and under the neck five inches. The tail was bushy, and seventeen inches long. The bullet entered the right eye, and so smashed his head that I could not preserve the skull; but I kept the skin, and sent it afterwards to Mr. Sclater of the Calcutta Museum, who informed me that the animal was the black wolf of Tibet (*Canis niger*). This valley is called Phia-lúng (marmot valley).

On the 1st of July I started for my first regular hunt after nyan, leaving most of my traps in the main valley. I spent five days to the west of the Phia-lúng across the dividing ridge, but had no success whatever. There are a number of frozen lakes in the valley I visited, joined by tiny streamlets. The lakes, from all appearances, seemed to be constantly frozen. A few feet of ice along the margin thaws for a few hours during the day, but hardens again towards evening: I could not see any outlet to the waters. These curious mountain tarns are frequently found among these ranges. Are they the remains of glaciers? I examined the grassy plains about these pieces of water and the surrounding hillsides with the glasses for an hour; they were the most likely places for game, but I could discover only two kiangs. The guide with me made an awkward discovery here: after topping a ridge, he looked about, and then announced the fact that we were on the wrong side, that is to say, on the Shúshal side of the pass—we had crossed the dividing range when going down to the frozen lakes. My heart misgave me when I saw the stream running north, and could view the country right down to Shúshal, not more than fifteen miles off. I sent the coolie off at once to bring the little tent, and went down to the foot of the pass to await its arrival. This saved us a long and useless trudge to the shooting in front of us. On the level plain, near the foot of the pass, we found a Tibetan tent and a few goats. The wandering shepherd was very kind, and we soon had a roaring fire of yak's dung and turf. This lonely shepherd had a deaf wife and thirty shawl goats. He was by profession a beggar, and belonged to the province of Kham in Tibet. He ran away from home when he was quite a young man—probably with the woman who was now with him. He was a strong, good-looking fellow, who had a very lively way of talking. Nothing betrayed his profession, except his profuse thanks and salutes with both hands to his forehead. The tent arrived at nine o'clock, and soon we were all snug. During the whole day I must have been wandering at a very high level, as I found breathing very laboured and difficult. Next morning, as I was having tea, Sarúp announced a flock of nyan behind the tent! I rushed out and counted six ewes and one small ram; they were not worth following, and I watched them till they disappeared over the ridge at their leisure, grazing as they went, not more than six hundred yards from the tent. The weather was abominable, and prevented us from making a start till eleven; we then resumed our hunt, or rather search, but snow came down again soon after we started, and the wind was terrific; we saw nothing all day, and made camp lower down in the same valley. Next day we ascended the range on the right of the valley, by a well-worn kiang path, and on the way I discovered in the centre of the path a neatly-made stone-pit for trapping animals in the winter, when they come down to drink at the main stream. We went down the other slope of the range facing the lake on the regular road, by the Thaota-la pass to Shúshal; and having seen nothing, camped in a nálá leading down to the lake—the Mirpa-tso. We had great difficulty about water—a load of snow had to be brought down as a substitute. The surrounding hills are black-looking, barren, and most forbidding, and the dead lake, whose water is saline and smells abominably, lies in the midst; there is a total absence of animal life of any kind. Thus a hunt of five days was an utter failure : not a ram good enough to follow had been seen, nor a shot fired. For the benefit of those who may follow me, I here put on record that in Ladakh (1) the wind is lord paramount; (2) that the only beautiful thing in the country is the sky; and (3) that everything *looks* near, but is very distant. This was the outcome of my experiences, and it relieves my mind to say so.

The things left behind in the Phia-lúng having arrived, we made a start next morning, and, skirting the lake shore, proceeded to the Thaota-la (17,000 feet). Saráp had dismal stories about the *búti* (plant) on this pass, the smell of which takes away the traveller's breath. I asked him to procure me a specimen of it, but he could find none; neither did anyone suffer from the rarefaction of the air. Saráp had come out in his true colours within the last few days; he was a cunning malingerer, a first-class bully, and a monumental liar. The ascent of this pass is nothing to speak of from the lake side, but the descent of the other (Shúshal) side is considerable. In the route map of the Himálayas, published by the Great Trigonometrical Survey, the pass is shown on the south-west of the Mirpa-tso; its real position is just in the opposite direction, that is, to the *north* of the lake. As we went down to the plain below, I met a gentleman coming up in my direction; he was going up the nálá leading to the Décé-la (pass), the very ground over which I had just hunted. He had come from Simla *via* Kashmir and Leh, had been to the Changchen-mo valley, and was now on his way back. He had passed through the Phia-lúng in May, and had bagged five *Ovis ammon* in the valleys I had found so empty! Three of the heads were thirty-eight, forty, and forty-two inches. He had left eight rams behind, and was now going to look them up. When I told him my experience, he seemed rather disappointed, but said he would still make the attempt—at anyrate, this was his way back. He had not had much luck in Chang-chen-mo, having bagged only ten Tibetan antelope; there were four sportsmen still there. The information he gave me proved again what thorough-going liars these Tibetans are. I made every inquiry in the Phia-lung regarding game, and whether the country had been shot over lately, and had been met by denials on every side: there was no game, no Sahib had been here, no nyan had been shot at, etc. It seems a rooted conviction in the minds of these people that a consistent course of denials, when questioned on any subject, is the easiest way out of all difficulties. The traveller or sportsman must bear this constantly in mind. Had I known that this bit of country had been shot over, of course I should not have wasted a week knocking about those desolate and frozen valleys.

CHAPTER XII

NYAN (OVIS AMMON) SHOOTING

The village of Shúshal—Its mud *bangla*—Arrange for the shooting—Old Tashi—Treatment of native shikáris—Hardiness of Tibetan ponies—Start for shooting ground—Saráp again—No post—One of the hardships of Tibetan travelling—Saráp deposed—My boy head shikári—The regular Kashmir shikár establishment—First sight of nyan—My first stalk—My boy shikári does splendidly—Bag my first *Ovis ammon*—Camp out—The Pangúr-tso—On the border—Some more nyan—The old ram's cautious generalship—A successful stalk—Habits of the nyan—The valleys near the Pangúr-tso—Cloudy weather—Another nyan hunt—Six hours in a shallow trench—A trying ordeal—The nyan score this time—A desperate rush—Sight the nyan again—A long shot—Bag one—Return to camp—After nyan again—Nonplussed by idiotic kiangs—The hunting ground—An excursion suggested—Big heads are getting scarce—Causes of their disappearance—Old rams are adepts at concealment—Return to Shúshal.

THE habitation in Shúshal, dignified by the name *bangla*, was certainly a roomy place, but built in the most primitive style, with mud walls, mud roof, and mud floor. The dust resultant from these materials was pre-eminently obtrusive, owing to the genial blasts of Tibetan wind that could not be denied entrance. The doors, windows, and chinks were not on the dust-proof principle like my watch, and when the rain came down (which it did frequently), copious douches of liquid mud bespattered myself and my belongings. The village of Shúshal is a collection of miserable mud huts straggling over the green fields, round a hill which, of course, is crowned by the inevitable gonpa, or monastery. An open valley comes in from the west, another from the south,—the road by which I came,—another on the east. All these open flat valleys combine to form an extensive plain, with the gonpa on the hill in the centre. Sprinkled over the plain were sheep, goats, and ponies, with darkly-clad figures moving among them. Nearer, in the fields, women were working; and lounging about the houses were dirty mangy dogs mixed up with children in the same condition. The incomparable Tibetan sky above, and Tibetan winds, also incomparable, tore over the plain. The prospect had charms of its own for a weary traveller just arrived from the dreary mountains in the south—principally because it offers the opportunity of a good rest. Supplies also were procurable, and it was the nearest point to my first shooting ground. I halted here for two days, and arranged for a trip eastwards up the Tsaka valley for *Ovis ammon*. I discovered in the village a very old man, who had been a good shikári in his time, and who knew all the haunts of game in these parts; he was too old for active work now, but I took him with me on a pony, and got a deal of information from him while he sat in camp drinking my tea. Some men have a reprehensible habit of ill-treating those who go out with them to show game, when, as frequently happens, no animals are found at the spot or at the time when or where game was promised. The sportsman who follows this short-tempered gentleman is the real sufferer. The man who has been roughly handled goes into hiding when he hears of the advent of the next Sahib, feigns illness, or swears roundly that no game has existed in his neighbourhood for years, and thus the unoffending new-comer loses the help of, perhaps, the only man who can show game. Old Tashi, I am sure, had had some experience of this kind; it was

with difficulty that I could get hold of him. And when
he did put in an appearance, he was most reluctant to have
anything to do with me. I left most of my things at
Shúshal, taking only a light camp for the shooting.
Chamúrti, too, was left behind for a rest, to get his feet in
order. The grass of these highlands has undoubtedly most
nourishing qualities. This hardy little beast went off and
on several times during this expedition, but never knocked
up. The important point is to know when to give them
rest. Their starvation experiences during the long winters
of their native land must be a good training. I hired for
riding a little Tibetan pony, which proved the most difficult
animal to ride that I ever crossed—there was so little of
him! But he carried my twelve stone bravely, when a
steep climb had to be negotiated, or a long plain crossed
under the burning sun. My hunting ground lay on the
road from Shúshal to Hanlé, and the road passes up a
broad and level valley, inclined to be swampy in its lower
parts. Droves of kiangs were numerous to the left of the
road, on the grassy flats, seeming quite at home, though only
a short distance from Shúshal. I saw quite two hundred
of them during the first march.

When nearing Thinné-gongma (that is, Lower Thinné), I
made out three *Ovis ammon* at the mouth of a gorge on
my right. They were grazing on the slope of the hill just
over the edge of the plain, so I took Saráp with me for
the stalk. He made a mess of it. He had bad eyesight,
and was a bad climber as well as a cunning malingerer.
The game soon spied us, and were off at once. We were in
full view on the plain, and could not get cover enough all
the way, so the result could have been hardly otherwise.
At Thinné-gongma we found a spring of good water, and
pitched tent close to it. I felt rather out of temper this
evening: the principal cause was the non-arrival of my

post. At Rokchen I had paid three rupees to a man, and started him off (as I thought) to Leh for my letters; he solemnly promised to meet me at Shúshal, but he never came, and I had to send another man from the latter place. I found out afterwards that the Rokchen man pocketed my money and remained at home. To be deprived of one's letters and papers for weeks at a time is another of the disagreeables of travel in these wild parts. This is a hardship which the over-civilised Englishman feels acutely. There was only one post office in the whole of Ladakh (at Leh), so far as I was aware, but with the improved means of carriage as far as Srinagar a letter from any part of India should reach Leh in ten days, and in another ten days find the sportsman in the most distant shooting grounds. But I was again the victim of the unsophisticated nomad: that he should never be trusted under any circumstances was my conclusion.

Continuing my journey up the Tsaka valley, I saw some animals on the hillside, which Saráp insisted were nyan, but after close inspection they were found to be barhal. This man was not worth a coolie's wages, so I deposed him. I had a Shúshal boy with me to carry tiffin, etc., and he was much more useful than Saráp. As he was unusually intelligent, I kept him with me as head shikári. Communication between us was somewhat limited, but he was less aggravating than the fraud I had brought from Lahoul; keen as mustard, and a capital worker; also he knew the country well. His eyesight, of course, was equal to a pair of good binoculars. He was a short, stumpy little fellow, hardly fourteen years of age. This was a smaller establishment than the usual Kashmir shikár outfit: head shikári at thirty rupees a month, tea and all the luxuries thrown in; second shikári at fifteen rupees a month; tiffin coolie at ten rupees a month, etc. etc. How the inexperienced Englishman sheds his rupees while he is gaining experience! The premier scoundrel is always the English-speaking servant he brings up with him from the plains; his able assistant is the "head shikári," than whom no more scientific swindler exists on the earth. When they two fall out, their "master" comes by his own. These experienced gentlemen, however, are too wise to cut their throats in that fashion. They scrupulously observe the secret pact between themselves, and loot the common enemy.

We crossed the Tsaka-la (15,500 feet), and camped at Dong-lúng or De-chang, as marked on the route map. The traveller should note another mistake here in this useful map. The Tsaka-la is not, as marked, on the Indus side of this camping-place, Dong-lúng; it is on the Shúshal side. The distance between these two places is about twenty-two miles. The Dong-lúng camp is about 14,500 feet above sea level, so that in reality the height of the Tsaka-la is only about 1000 feet above the level of the valley—a slight rise only, very typical of Tibetan passes with five figures attached to them on the maps. Nevertheless, the sun was all there, especially in the close places where the winds could not find free play. Just after topping the pass we disturbed a flock of seven nyan. They ran down, in the direction of camp, along the hillside, and stopped behind another hill; I tried for them in the evening, but they had moved. I saw on the hillside numerous tracks, certainly not a day old, of large rams. I had viewed my game at last, and felt that I was really among them. Old Tashi had kept his word.

I began my regular *Ovis ammon* hunt on the 9th July. Myself and the boy, with another man to carry lunch, started at 5 A.M., went back to the foot of the pass, and turned up to the ridge where we had seen the nyan. We found them on the plain on the other side of the range, after a long hunt. There was no cover, and we could not manage to get down even to the plain; the mountain slopes were perfectly smooth, without a single friendly undulation, and the plain below was like the palm of one's hand. The game became suspicious—probably they saw us on the sky-line—at anyrate, they crossed the valley to the opposite hills, without the least hurry. This seems a characteristic of all wild sheep: unless very hard pressed, they are dignified and slow. As regards nyan, they always have such an extensive view over the country they frequent, that they have ample time to get out of the way, without over-exerting themselves. Even after they have been fired at, though they will go off at a hard gallop they soon slow down; and, as long as they have the danger in view, will not mend their pace, though they may go long distances before lying up again. The seven I was after having crossed the crest of the opposite range, we descended into the plain and followed their tracks. They were not visible when we reached the sky-line, but their tracks showed that they had gone towards the left, across a low spur, into a dip where they had evidently come to a stand. A troop of kiangs was just below us; we waited some time for them to get out of the way, but they showed no intention of doing so, and, as I was not inclined to lose much time on their account, we attempted to pass them. The moment we came within their view there was a great commotion; they threw up their heads, cocked their ears, and trotted round us in true asinine fashion, most irritating to behold, and then they went straight up along the track of the wild sheep. The inevitable happened. When we reached the crest of the spur, the nyan were on the next sky-line, right ahead of us, and the rascally kiangs were galloping down to our left, making for the large plain we had crossed a while ago. This was my first introduction to kiangs and nyans at close quarters. The boy with me, however, was not beaten. I understood him to mean that the game had crossed over to a valley, and he proposed to follow them; so we bent our backs for the sky-line again, the noonday sun punishing me most unmercifully. We saw the nyan again, far down below us, going in as leisurely a fashion as usual, four a good distance ahead, and the other three lagging behind. The flock had evidently separated: the first four were making for some distant place of safety, while the three laggards showed signs of soon lying up. So I had something to eat, and resumed the hunt. The three were now out of sight, having entered one of the numerous side nalas on the left of the main valley; the other four, still travelling easily, were now about two miles off. Getting off the hillside into the bed of the dry watercourse at the bottom, we proceeded downwards very slowly and with great caution. We passed many side valleys on the left—regular pockets—opening into the main line of drainage, and were always disappointed when we peeped cautiously in and found each one empty. This sustained suspense, with the sun pouring into the close valley, was beginning to tell on me, when the boy, who was picking out the way, two paces in front, dropped as if he had been shot. He was a born stalker; he had got a glimpse of one nyan in one of the small valleys on the hillside. He dropped so quickly that the animal did not see him, though he was on the hill above us. We drew back, went up the back of the hill, and within ten minutes of sighting him I was in position.

When I looked over, only one sheep was to be seen. The distance was certainly over 150 yards when I fired at the sitting nyan, but the bullet struck over him, though the hundred yards sight was used. The sheep bolted away without waiting to find out what had happened; but the other two, who had been lying upon the slope of the hill on *my* side, rushed out from below, and came to a stand on the hill facing me, about 200 yards off—not looking, but intently listening; they had evidently been sound asleep when the crack of the rifle roused them. The bullet from the second barrel went true this time, and the largest ram of the two came rolling down the hill with a broken back. I used the standard sight again for the second shot—another instance of the difference in sighting in these elevated regions. When we got up to the dead animal, both the boy and myself were on the best of terms with ourselves. It was my first *Ovis ammon*, and his too, probably. The boy's excitement knew no bounds; he was quite "above himself." But when I patted him on the back and put a rupee into his hand, he was calm in an instant; this meant business. It was now 3 P.M., and I felt that I had done enough for one and the first day: I had been tramping since five o'clock, and for a great portion of the time had been under intense excitement—kept up pretty well at boiling point by the too vigorous sun; so I rested until the things came up. When I made up my mind to follow the game down this valley I knew that I could not return to Dong-lúng by evening, and therefore sent the extra man who accompanied us back for the small tent, bedding, and food, intending to sleep that night as near the game as possible. This precaution saved me the awful trudge back to camp, which tells so fearfully on the returning sportsman spent with the exertions of the day. When the things arrived, I went down the valley and camped by a trickle of water: Pangúr-tso was within sight, about two miles lower down. Camp was a shorter distance beyond the border; the men with me were in consequence uneasy, fearing discovery by the trans-

"NOT LOOKING, BUT INTENTLY LISTENING."

frontier Tibetans of the villages a few miles to the right of the lake. For some reason or another, Ladakhis are always nervous about going any distance beyond this imaginary line, though the people on the other side are closely related to them, and are the same in manners, customs, and language. In this ugly stony valley, where the steep hillsides were not more than a couple of hundred yards from each other, there was no sign of the presence of human beings, and I was sure it was rarely visited except by nyans, who seemed to make it a place of refuge when hunted away from better grazing grounds. After making camp, a yak was taken back, and the ovis brought down. The horns measured thirty-two inches, and were massive at the base. They were below the average, but when I first beheld the animal I imagined him to be of enormous size. The two yakmen and my sporting boy had some difficulty in breaking him up, but they rewarded themselves afterwards by fids of meat warmed at the fire, and eaten with every sign of satisfaction. In the evening eight nyan were discovered grazing on the slopes above the camp on the right, less than half a mile away, but I left them undisturbed for next morning.

I was up at five, and ascended the slope with the boy only, on the tracks of the four rams we had hunted the previous day. We reached the crest of the range without seeing anything. But after a long search the boy descried the flock of last evening, feeding in the bottom of the main valley, between the tent and the lake. We had to wait their further movements, as in our respective positions it was not possible to get within a mile of them without being detected; but as the sun grew warmer, they moved up the slope on our side—a piece of luck for which I was thankful. We lay and watched them quietly; they came along very slowly, snatching a mouthful of grass at each step, till they reached the entrance of a side valley just below us, about eight hundred yards away. We could plainly see their every movement: there were seven—two fine large rams, the rest of no account. They kept steadily to the bottom of the nála, along the dry bed of the watercourse, seeming inclined to spare themselves as much climbing as possible. After getting well up into the side valley, they turned up a short ravine, evidently for their mid-day sleep. They gave themselves away by making this selection, and were completely in my power. It was most amusing to watch the generalship of the leader, the oldest ram, as he led his comrades into this trap; he was most cautious and deliberate in his movements, using both eyes and nose while he picked his way slowly along—wholly unconscious, poor beast, of the two pairs of eager eyes that were watching him from above. It was mid-day now, and the sun had thoroughly warmed this open-air sleeping chamber. As soon as the ovis reached it, each selected his bed, smelt it, and lay down, stretching out his limbs, and laying his head on the slope of the hill with every appearance of settling down to a comfortable sleep. The old ram was the last to make himself comfortable; he evidently felt the responsibility of his position, and the *abandon* of his companions showed clearly their confidence in him. I admired this picture through my glasses for some time: the peacefulness of the scene would have disarmed anyone but the bloodthirsty hunter.

When my sense of admiration had been appeased, I made my dispositions, laying out in my mind all the points I was to make, the exact place from which I was to fire, the position of the old ram, and the distance from my firing point. We then began our stalk, going straight down the slope, and getting into the dry watercourse in ten minutes. We followed up the tracks till they turned to the right, when we ascended the slope, and reached the firing point without a hitch. I used the ·450 Winchester Express for the first shot, distance about one hundred yards, and broke the neck of the old ram as he lay in the warm sun, in a most comfortable sleep. Poor beast, he passed from ovine dreams to the sheep's paradise (wherever it may be) without knowing it. These cold-blooded proceedings cause a certain amount of revulsion, but such are the fortunes of sport; and when one marches for a month over the roughest country in the world, it is lawful to take advantage of all the luck that falls in one's way, when hunting a wild animal credited by all authorities with the wiliness of the prince of darkness. After the shot he just stretched himself out a little more and lay still, but the others were over the crest of the slope in a second, and in a short time they were on the higher range in front of me, going slowly as usual, and making frequent halts to watch us: our positions were reversed. The horns of this ram were a handsome pair, measuring thirty-eight inches.

It seems to be the habit of nyan, in these mountains at anyrate, to sleep high up on the open hillside in the night; in the morning to graze down to the level of the valley, and remain about there till noon; then slowly graze up a side valley; select a warm, secluded ravine, concealed on all sides, and lie up for a couple of hours enjoying the sun; then to graze up again by evening to their night quarters on the steep and open hillside, where they are most secure from prowling animals. The proper time to catch them is when they are napping at noon—the hottest time of the day. The approach must always be made from above; if the sun is bright and hot, the wind is sure to be blowing from below. This is my experience.

Next morning we struck camp and crossed the range on the right into the next valley. A small thin stream runs down the bottom from a patch of snow above, and we camped here, only on account of the convenience of this water, but at noon it suddenly dried up as some dark and heavy clouds shut off the sun from the snow-field! This was rather a sell, and I thought our water supply was cut off, till to-morrow's sun warmed up the snow again. There were small patches of coarse grass visible, but not a living thing, though we came across some fresh nyan tracks after passing over the crest; probably those of the animals that had been disturbed by my shooting on the other side.

Heavy clouds were hanging about, but there was not much wind. They must have brought their moisture from the Indian Ocean and have come a long way. How did they escape the great barrier of the Himálayas? The accepted notion is that the clouds which pass over the plains of Hindústan impinge on the sides of this huge range, and are precipitated in rain, the waters of which flow back through the plains to the sea. I watched these clouds for some days; they all seemed to come from the south-west; great masses of them were constantly passing over and going farther north: probably they are finally used up in the "Chang-thang," or great plain, which forms such a large portion of Tibet. This was the warmest camp I had been in since I have been travelling in Ladakh; it was quite hot during the day in the tent, and at night very pleasant. We went out in the evening and found the tracks of two nyan, evidently the companions of the one I bagged; they appeared to have crossed this valley and made an attempt to get into the next, but the black, rocky mountain sides in every direction discouraged them, and, their fears having subsided, they apparently went back to their favourite grazing ground, whence they had been ejected by the kiangs.

The little stream began to flow again at about four o'clock

when the sun reappeared, and kept running all night.
Again we struck camp, which the yaks brought after me.
They could follow us easily by our tracks, and when they
failed, a yakman had no difficulty in finding us in any
direction, as all he had to do was to climb a convenient hill
After looking about the neighbourhood for some hours,
and finding no encouraging signs, my boy shikári said it
would be best to turn back into the valley where we had
first met the ovis on the morning when we started from the
permanent camp. He called it "Nyan-lúng," or the nyan
valley. He said it was a certain find for them at this
season, and no doubt it was a favourite grazing ground;
so we turned and crossed the range, again coming
across the tracks of the nyan, and after a time passed the
sleeping-places of five, who had spent the night here not
long ago. After an hour's tracking, the boy spied four
dark spots and a white one on the opposite range, beyond
the Nyan-lúng, which divides it from the Dong-lúng, where
the main camp was. We left the tracks and crept painfully along the plain, in full view, as far as we dared, and
then lay down in a shallow nálá, where we remained
for six mortal hours, from nine o'clock till three. We
could not move a step, as we were in full view of the game,
which was nearly at the top of the range, and kept there,
grazing about and lying down. A regular gale began
to blow shortly after, and heavy clouds came up; but the
wind was steady from the east, and in my favour. Presently
drizzling rain came on, beating straight in our faces. Our
situation was not a comfortable one, but I waited patiently,
as every look through the glass told me that the nyan
with the light-coloured coat was a beauty, and would repay
even six hours' exposure. There was another darker
ram, larger in the body, but I came to the conclusion,
after careful comparison, that the first had the better

horns. The sterns of these animals were white, and when they turned from us they became almost invisible against the light-coloured hillside. The two big nyan remained feeding about on one spot, occasionally lying down, the younger and smaller ones ranging farther and lower. By three o'clock my patience was exhausted, for evening was coming on, and the game showed no signs of coming to graze on the plain. A move had to be made, and, thinking I saw a chance, I made a rush, and got four of the beasts under the crest of a lower range just in front, which concealed us from their view; it was lung-splitting work, and pumped me completely. I heard the boy behind blowing like a grampus and murmuring "Ami-na, Ami-na" under his breath—that is, invoking his mother. The largest nyan, the dark-coloured one, was highest on the hill, and the only animal left uncovered; he no doubt was the senior, and kept careful watch over his younger friends below him—a habit just the reverse of that I noticed in the ibex. One rush more would have brought him too under the crest of the closer range, but as we made it he detected us, and when I looked up again he was standing like a statue with head erect, in full gaze—a splendid picture. We dropped as if shot, but the old ram was not to be deceived. Our movements caught his eye for perhaps a second; he knew it meant danger; and after a steady look of a couple of minutes, during which he could not have discovered anything, he ran down to his companions —and it was all over, as far as that stalk was concerned.

We went slowly up the hillside, and, reaching the crest, discovered the rams in full but slow retreat. They crossed over to the Dong-lúng side, and we followed them as soon as they were out of sight, the boy taking up the tracks, which could be plainly recognised fifty yards ahead, on the crumbling slope. We went a long distance, crossing the crest of the range and ascending the other side among the spurs leading down to the Dong-lúng, where the tracks of the sheep were lost in a rocky, steep side valley, covered in places with clumps of the dama plant.

The contrariness of sporting luck was now fully illustrated. All day the wind had been blowing a gale from the east, entirely in my favour, and now, as soon as I was within striking distance of the game, it veered quite round, and went down the valley directly from us to the nyan! We were too close to retreat, and before we had gone a hundred yards the boy sighted the rams: they were huddled together in the bottom of one of the small side ravines, apparently concealing themselves among some dama bushes. It was impossible to say whether they were seeking protection from the weather, or trying to keep out of our sight. At anyrate, they were fully aware of our proximity, and were looking in our direction, for a regular Tibetan gale was blowing towards them from us. We crossed over to the next ravine on our left and rushed along its bottom to get within range, but the rams guessed our tactics, and when we topped the ridge they were retreating down the main channel. Instead of following the windings of the nálá, where they would have been out of sight and perfectly safe, they went down it a short distance, and turning up the opposite side, huddled together on a knoll watching us, about 300 yards distant from our position on another hillock. It was my only chance, I thought, and I took the shot at the dark-coloured beast that had been the sentinel. Putting up the second sight of the Winchester Express, I caught him just behind the left shoulder, and he rolled down, while the others disappeared. As I fired, the thunder rolled, and there were several successive claps, quite close above us, which came in very dramatically at the right moment, but were nevertheless very alarming. A brisk shower followed, and I was quite drenched, even through my greatcoat, before I could reach the dead ram. The stalk thus ended in very grand style indeed, and amid characteristic Tibetan surroundings: wild ravines on all sides, the heavens dark with thunder-clouds. The ram was a splendid fellow, with horns of thirty-nine inches. My gratification was complete when the boy informed me that the big camp in the Dong-lŭng was not far off! It was, in fact, hardly a mile away, and we reached it within half an hour of firing the only shot of the day. I tipped that boy every time we stood together over a slain ram, and he was now the proud possessor of three rupees—more money than had ever rested on his palm before. His enthusiasm was boundless, and he seemed ready to lead me after nyan to the farthermost limits of Tibet. Everyone in camp that evening was happy. The postman had arrived a short time before me, and nyan-mutton was boiling in the brass pots of the yakmen before the sun had set, so we were all suited according to our several tastes. It was a brilliant evening: the clouds had cleared away, only a gentle breeze was blowing, and the air was just cold enough to be bracing.

I remained in these shooting grounds for one week, and during that time had very bad luck indeed. On three occasions, after long and painful stalks, my labour was lost, owing to the utter perversity of kiangs, who were fifty times more numerous than the *Ovis ammon*, and were always turning up at the critical moment. Once I was just getting within range of two fine rams, when a solitary kiang lunatic turned up on my right front, got well above me, and began to snort and trot to and fro, with his ears cocked and his tail in the air, cutting a most ludicrous figure. We had to lie flat for an hour while this wild jackass was satisfying his curiosity. He was evidently in abject terror, yet curiosity chained him to the spot. He did not cease his attentions till the two nyans were fleeing for their lives, frightened out of their wits by his carryings-on. Then the kiang, having discovered that we were harmless so far as he was concerned, trotted peacefully away over a slope, in the opposite direction, with, I trust, his mind at rest. But for the fear of disturbing other game, that brute would certainly have had a bullet through his hide. Another time we came on a herd of kiangs in the course of a long stalk, and had to roll and crawl for several hundred yards over a very stony hillside to avoid them, but were in the end detected, after my elbows, knees, and hands seemed worn down to the very bone, and I was breathless to boot. On another occasion I was in position, getting my wind to take the shot, when a shout arose from the plain, and a party of Tibetans came into full view. They were travellers on ponies, proceeding towards Rudók. There had been a faint tinkling of bells borne on the air for some time, which had puzzled me greatly, and the mystery was solved when the cavalcade came in sight—and the nyan disappeared before I could get my shot. During the whole of this week I bagged only one ovis; he was the smallest of the four I got, and gave me most trouble. I stalked two nyan up to within three hundred yards, and could get no nearer; they went to bed on the bare hillside for their mid-day nap, and I had to await their pleasure for an hour. I hit the larger of the two in the left leg, high up in the fleshy part, but he went off as if untouched. A long chase followed, which was brought to an end for that day by a storm of sleet and rain; the former punished me dreadfully on the face, neck, and hands—the sensation was like that of a charge of small shot at long range. The sleet lay so thick that the tracks were lost, and we had to give up. Next morning we took up the hunt again, and followed the frozen tracks till we discovered them lying down in a hollow. The unwounded one vanished like a ghost, but the one I had hit was stiff and was not quick enough; as he topped the ridge I fired and hit him in the shoulder. The smaller animal remained faithful to his elder friend till the moment of his death; he even lingered on the hillside a short distance off, after the latter fell, and did not take his final departure till he saw us start again for the valley ahead of us, in which direction he was evidently bound himself; he then disappeared. It is said that the young rams always show this sympathy when an older one—the leader, I suppose —is hurt, but the older ones do not reciprocate the attention when a junior is the victim.

It will be observed that I did not see any phenomenal heads during my stalks: the four I bagged were all below the average—only one could be said to be really good; but if a sportsman went along the border-line, and made trips beyond it, after procuring information regarding likely and unfrequented localities, I think he would come across nyan the heads of which would bear comparison with any that have been obtained. I am afraid, however, that heads having forty-five or fifty-inch horns have become extremely rare. The nyan is an animal that sticks, it would seem, to the bit of country where he "growed." Big heads become matured in certain places: the sportsman comes along and lays himself out to get as many as he can. After that there will be no desirable heads in that locality for years—not, in fact, until the young rams of the place have had time to grow them. Severe winters, the rapacious wolf, and the local shikári, are also causes which militate against really good trophies. The old ram with a heavy head is naturally slow, and he soon falls a victim to the wolf after a heavy snowfall, or to the Tibetan with his pronged matchlock—especially towards the border. I do not think nyan migrate—that is, to any distance. Of course they must follow the course of the seasons, and seek places where grass is obtainable; but I should say a distance of twenty miles would cover the extent of their migration. Wherever they are, the old rams seem to have the peculiar faculty of concealing themselves from human view, and it requires an immense amount of travel, and a pair of good Tibetan eyes, besides a first-class pair of binoculars, to spot them. General Kinloch has had a good deal of experience in hunting these gigantic wild sheep, and he possesses more than the ordinary faculty of observation; his opinion, therefore, should be received with respect. He writes: "After a lengthened experience, I can unhesitatingly affirm that there is no animal so difficult to stalk as a male nyan." Colonel Ward, in his *Sportsman's Guide*, says: "The difficulty of obtaining specimens of this fine sheep is made the most of by many writers, nor is it as rare, nor as difficult to obtain, as some sportsmen would have us believe." The latter, too, is a man of observation and experience, and I incline to his opinion. The nyan to me seemed rather wanting in intelligence, and endowed with his full share of ovine stupidity. Once found, the ram can easily be circumvented with patience and perseverance.

I returned to Shúshal on the 20th July, and proceeeded next to my shooting ground in the Chang-chen-mo.

CHAPTER XIII

SPORT IN CHANG-CHEN-MO

Paljour, the old shikári—Saráp is "run in"—His iniquities—Leave Shúshal—The Pangong lake—Its absent beauties—Reverend Mr. Redslob—Dalgleish's murderer—Reverend Dr. Lansdell—Commissariat and transport for a month's trip—The "Great River"—Kiám camp—Bag my first Tibetan antelope—Description of the Chang-chen-mo country—Gograng camp—Madmar camp—Explore the Chang-lúng—Nyan at last—A fatiguing stalk—Another tramp—Miss chánkú (wolf)—Servants from Leh arrive—Yákúb's hard work comes to an end—A rare servant—A final exploration—Curious glaciers in Gograng—A weird and oppressive scene—Inaccurate maps—Return to Kiám—Correct name of Gograng—A change in the weather for the worse.

AT Shúshal I found that Saráp had returned from Lukúng, where I had sent him to make arrangements for my trip to Chang-chen-mo while I was nyan-hunting in the Donglúng: he reported everything ready, and had brought with him old Paljour, Colonel Ward's shikári. This was a stroke of luck, as he knew the ground thoroughly, and had great experience in yak-hunting in the Chang-chen-mo. Though he was old and blear-eyed, and his sight none of the best, I found him of great use to me; there was some go in him yet. To my astonishment I also found waiting a warrant for the arrest of Saráp, issued by the Joint Commissioner of Ladakh, and a sepoy to take him into custody. There was, further, a letter addressed to the "Master of Saráp," explaining that this individual was wanted on several criminal charges which had been pending since his last visit, two years ago! It appeared that he had been plundering the people wholesale, beating head-men, etc., and, when he was reported to the authorities, deserted his former employer and ran away, leaving the latter to bear the brunt. He harried the country again when I entered Ladakh, and I heard many tales of his lawlessness while he was away from me at Lukúng and other villages. He was a well-known character in these parts. As soon as the head-man of Shúshal recognised Saráp, he sent information to headquarters, and the warrant came down for him at once. This is the sort of rascal who, with profit to himself, earns an evil reputation for his employer in these out-of-the-way countries: such scamps are seldom if ever caught, but their masters have to answer for their iniquities, and compensate the aggrieved parties as best they can.

Heavy rain was continuous from the time I ceased shooting in the Dong-lúng: the "bangla" at Shúshal was no protection, and I had to sleep under my umbrella and waterproof in the best room to keep dry. My little tent was certainly more comfortable, and I was glad to make a start; wet though the weather was, it was pleasanter to be out in the clean open country than suffer blue devils in a leaky and evil-smelling mud hut. I had breakfast on the road in wind and rain, and made camp at Khaktat village, only a few miles from Shúshal; but before I could get under the shelter of the tent, the sun was pouring down; it was fearfully hot—such are the varieties of climate in these regions! In the evening it was stormy again, dark clouds hanging all round, while the howling wind lashed the broad Pangong lake into white-crested waves. I had seen nothing of the beauties of this lake yet. The descriptions I read had raised my expectations; but

I was greatly disappointed with my first view of the largest sheet of water known to exist at such a great elevation, and which also has a name that no other country in the world could match. Here it is—Tso-mo-nang-lari, or Pangong! It is said to be forty miles in length and, in some parts, four miles broad, and it is nearly 14,000 feet above sea level; the waters are saline. I did not notice their "lovely colours," nor the "richest blue," nor the "sapphire tint" of the waves when disturbed by wind, about which other tourists had raved. Under the conditions which prevailed when I travelled along its shore, it appeared most uninteresting. Its waters are so salt that every living thing avoids them; there are no fish, I never saw a bird, and nothing green grows on its margin. At the village of Man, on the way to Lukúng, an old woman offered me for one rupee the skull of an *Ovis ammon*, picked up near the Pangúr-tso, in a valley near Rishan, where I had been shooting; the horns were thirty-six inches in length: I did not buy. I met on the way a gentleman who was called by the people "Kilang Sahib," a name that puzzled me, until I discovered that the owner was the late Rev. Mr. Redslob, thus called by the Ladakhis, because he came from the Moravian Mission at Kailang. We had tea together, and he gave me the news from Leh. One of Dalgleish's murderers, said to be a Panjábi fakír, had been caught; the Rev. Dr. Lansdell, the great traveller, was expected in a couple of months, on his way to the Grand Láma at Lahsa, and Mr. Redslob was preparing a letter in the Tibetan language for him. This journey never came off. I reached the valley of Paobrang at noon, and found one returned sportsman there from Chang-chen-mo. I had dinner with him, and heard with sympathy his grievances connected with a hardly-averted disaster in the Egyptian campaign, of which he seemed to

PANGONG LAKE.

have been made the scapegoat. Though this occurred some time ago, he was still brooding over his troubles, and was wearing his heart out in these lonely regions, because he could find no means to vindicate himself from the aspersions cast on him and his regiment by an incompetent general. I heard from him that only one man was now in my prospective shooting ground—a colonel, who was not likely to do much damage to the game, but who would certainly disturb them a good deal by indiscriminate firing.

Supplies and carriage must be procured from Lukúng and Tanksé for the trip into the uninhabited country beyond the Marsemik-la. Nothing whatever is procurable there; even grass and fuel are rarely found, and camping-places have to be arranged accordingly. I took with me eight yaks, two ponies, and a small flock of milch goats, and supplies sufficient for a month's tramp for myself and my followers. To avoid delay, a reliable servant should be sent on in advance, for necessaries to Tanksé, and for transport animals to Lukúng. Everything should be ready for the sportsman on his arrival at the latter place. In my case I sent on the scoundrel Saráp, who certainly did make all arrangements, but doubtless at a profit. By so managing, I avoided the necessity of halting anywhere on the road from Shúshal till I was well within my shooting ground, thus saving a lot of time and trouble. Nearing Kiám, after two days' march through desolate country, we saw signs of a camp, which turned out to be the colonel's last coolies just leaving; he himself had departed an hour before, and was going on to Ning-rhi up the valley. He was evidently leaving this shooting ground, so I could not have timed my entry better. I sent a note to the colonel asking about his movements; he replied that he was now on his way back to Ladakh, and was kind enough to send me a most welcome parcel of papers. He also volunteered the information that he had left an antelope at Kiám with a fine pair of antlers; and he advised me to go after it—the buck had eluded him. This must have been the animal I bagged the same evening: he had a fine pair of horns. As soon as we reached Kiám, Paljour started on the game-path at once; he saw two antelope up the valley, and we went for a stalk in the evening. We got within two hundred yards, and I had a steady shot with the Winchester off Paljour's back. The buck was hit a little too far back in the small ribs, and gave us a long chase; I hit him twice again before he could be brought to bay. I remained two days at Kiám, resting, making up cartridges, and preparing for a hunt in the Gograng valley. Kiám is well situated for a main camp whence to make excursions into the various valleys where game is found. There is a good deal of grass along the river, and the baggage animals can get grazing.

The principal valley of Chang-chen-mo runs directly east and west, and the length of the river, which runs along it from near the Lanak-la in the north-west to its junction with the Shyok, is, perhaps, seventy-five miles. The level does not extend more than four miles in its broadest part, and its total breadth, from crest to crest of the highest enclosing ranges, north and south, is about thirty miles. From Pamzal to the mouth of the river, a distance of about thirty miles, it is said to run very rapidly in a narrow rocky channel. This lower portion of the valley has been rarely visited, and no game is to be found there. The part which will most interest sportsmen is from Pamzal to the eastern border of the valley—a distance, say, of forty-five miles. The principal valleys which drain into the Chang-chen-mo (great river), and where all the varieties of game are found, I give below.

(1) Gograng (the most northerly), about twenty-eight miles in length. Its side valleys on the left (as you go up) are the most likely to contain game. If there are any wild yaks in Gograng, they will be found in Longnak-gongma, one of these side valleys, or the smaller ones above. In the lower will be found *Ovis ammon*, barhal, also antelope, on the slopes between the mouths of the valleys and the course of the stream. The highest point of the main valley, called Phú-Gograng, is blocked with glaciers and débris, and holds no game, as no grass grows there. The right of the Gograng stream, as you look up, is bounded by an almost straight mountain range, pierced by only one opening, by which the waters of Chang-lúng-gongma are drained into the Gograng stream. I would here observe that there is a serious mistake in the G. T. Survey Map $\left(\text{Quarter sheet, No. } \frac{63\text{A}}{\text{N.W.}}\right)$ at this point. The opening I have mentioned is not given; the mountain range being shown in one solid length, from the head of the valley to Gogra. The mistake is misleading, as Chang-lúng-gongma is a long valley, and of some importance—to sportsmen, at anyrate—because it generally holds nyan and wild yak, when they are travelling to and from Gograng. They cross over into Chang-lúng-gongma, and enter the former by the said opening. If the hunter is in Gograng looking for yaks, he should keep a constant watch on this gap. He will either find the animals themselves near it, or their tracks, if they have had time to pass up into the upper part of the larger valley.

(2) Changlúng. (*a*) Kongma is the valley mentioned above, for which no exit is allowed in the map; it is about fifteen miles in length, and narrow, and there is a considerable stream. The slopes on the left bank, as you go up, are grassy; on the right, the mountain sides are

steep, abrupt, stony, and difficult to climb. It is a good find for *Ovis ammon*, and, at certain times, for wild yak. (*b*) Yokma, the next valley, almost a half-moon in shape, is barren and open, with little water and less grass; game is consequently rarely found here.

(3) Keipsang, the next, is a narrow side valley. There is a little grass along the course of the stream, above the camping-place, for a couple of miles, where a travelling wild yak may be found by the lucky sportsman, as these animals pass along this path on their journey to Gograng. I got my first yak at Keipsang. Antelope may be found on the grassy plots and hillsides in the lower part of the valley. Kiamgo Traggar is about twenty-five miles in length. On the north the valley is bounded by a range of mountains. Some of the short side valleys running down south from this range contain grass along their bottoms and on the slopes. A travelling-path of wild yak runs along these slopes; the grass is, of course, the attraction. The southern slopes of the range are therefore very good places for wild yak, at the proper season. I got two here, and could, no doubt, have shot more by staying on.

(4) Tatta-Hor. The survey map before referred to is at fault with regard to this valley also, and the mistake is a greater one than that last mentioned. The name "Tatta-Hor" does not appear at all, the valley seems to be wrongly sketched in, and the watershed of this portion of Chang-chen-mo has certainly been incorrectly laid down. The sportsman will do well not to place too much reliance on the map as regards this end of the valley, but, as there is not much game in that direction, the error probably will not affect him. With the exception of antelope, which were in large numbers, game was scarce. I saw only old traces of wild yak, and none at all of *Ovis*

ammon. Exploring these valleys would take some days, and I do not think the sport would repay the time and trouble.

(5) There are several small valleys running into the main valley from the range of mountains on the south. None of these is more than five miles in length nor one mile in breadth, and are good finds for *Ovis ammon,* provided they have not been too much disturbed. These *nalás* are so small that the animals are soon frightened away when there has been any shooting. In former years, wild yaks, too, were found here, and a few were shot, but now these animals appear to have given up visiting this portion of the valley, owing probably to the increasing number of sportsmen, who seem to visit the Silungs more frequently than other parts. Between Kiám and Pamzal there is no shooting ground to speak of; the last is the valley leading down the Chang-chen-mo Pass (Marsemik-la) to Pamzal, about twenty miles. *Ovis ammon* will be found along this route early or late in the season, when there is good grass.

The mountains which surround the valley of the "Great River" have a nearly uniform height of 20,000 feet; near the head of Gogrung only do they exceed that figure by a few hundreds. The passes range from 18,000 to 19,000 feet, and, as the level of the valley may be between 15,000 and 16,000 feet, the sportsman has no great heights to climb. Experience will soon teach him, nevertheless, that going up hill at these altitudes entails uncommonly hard work on the lungs. His Ladakhi followers will set a good example, for they take things easily. What sport one obtains depends, as I think you have discovered now, on the weather. Few situations more cruelly tax one's patience than having to sit or lie in the small tent, and listen to the Tibetan gale tearing at the ropes, while the snow or sleet creeps in through every crevice, and all the while you know for certain that game is on the hillside not a mile away.

On the 27th July I made my camp in Gograng, with the intention of first doing that valley; but when I reached Gogra I was met by some coolies belonging to my predecessor's camp carrying away the last of his traps; he had them apparently scattered in many places. I at first thought myself lucky, being under the impression that the gallant sportsman had come into this ground very early, and had remained stationary for two months, so keeping out all subsequent prospectors; but I soon found that I had deceived myself. It was the custom of this sportsman to enjoy the luxury of his bed (a very strong temptation, indeed, I must confess) during the early hours of the morning, while his shikáris scoured the valleys. When game was found, information was sent to him, and he then proceeded to the stalk,—if it was not a very difficult one, —and, getting within a comfortably long range, he would open fire and keep it up while the animals were in sight. In this way he managed to bag a couple of cow yak and some antelope. But the consequences to myself were disastrous. The men knocking about all day, and the indiscriminate firing, had driven all the game to the skyline, while all the good heads had disappeared entirely. I remained twelve days in Gograng, explored every corner of it, and got seven shots! True, my predecessor was good enough to leave at the best season, and I replaced him just in the nick of time for wild yak; but his reprehensible way of loosing off emptied the valley with little profit to himself, and less to his successor. My camp was pitched a short distance above Gogra. It was not cold, but during the night rain came on, and continued till morning. At noon I moved again, and made camp two and a half miles

PANGONG LAKE, LOOKING WEST.

farther up. Paljour advised me not to take the tent any higher, as the fires would disturb the game. I started out next day to view the country and decide upon my course. We went as far as Longnek, but saw nothing excepting a few nápú (barhal) high up on the range to our left. We tried to stalk, but they were much too wide-awake, and went up to the sky-line at once and disappeared on the other side; they evidently knew all about us. The Longnek was the first place, Paljour said, where wild yak were likely to be found; but we saw no sign of dong (wild yak) anywhere. I was told afterwards that my predecessor had shot his two small animals in this place. After breakfast, Paljour went on three miles farther round the bend, to the other side of the Gograng stream, but came across no traces of game; and we got back to camp, pretty well fagged out, at nine o'clock. The going was very slow after dark. I was very much disappointed, and my thoughts of the preceding occupant were uncharitable. Next day we took the camp on to Madmar, two hours' travel, on the opposite side of the valley, just below the entrance of the Chang-lúng stream, and, after making things snug, sent all the baggage yaks, ponies, and extra men down to Pangúr, to remain there till wanted. Early next morning we started for a day in the Chang-lúng, the only valley on the north side of the Gograng. After travelling steadily for about eight miles, we spotted five nyan just in front, grazing along up the valley. When first seen they were nearly a mile ahead, and the wind was blowing right towards them from our direction; but they did not wind us, and shortly after they went about fifty yards up the hillside and lay up for their mid-day sleep. Then we began the stalk, straight up hill for two hours, to get out of their sight. After a very long and rough scramble, we at last got round and above them—the most important object in a stalk, and the one which must be accomplished at any cost, if success is to be achieved. We could not, however, from the open nature of the slope below us, get closer than two hundred yards. The nyan were all lying down at their ease; and the largest ram was the closest. We had to remain watching them for more than an hour before they stirred. Two then got up and began smelling about, and, grazing down towards the bottom of the valley, they disappeared; the rest, except the big fellow, the laziest of the lot, soon followed; he never stirred till the others were out of sight. He was evidently very stiff, for he made two or three attempts before he stood up. His horns were a fine pair, full sized and beautifully curved, and the tips had the outward curve which gives the finishing touch to a perfect head. Paljour was lying motionless on his stomach in front of me; I put the Winchester across his back and took a steady aim—one inch behind the animal's tail!—this after mature deliberation, and with all my faculties in good working order. It was a beautiful shot, for the bullet hit exactly the point aimed at. A miss is a mystery to outsiders, and the above must seem the most extraordinary of them all; but the rifle placed the bullet where it was aimed, so it could hardly be called a miss. The third nyan and the antelope I shot near Kiám camp were both hit by the first shot in the hind leg. This was caused, I imagined, by the strong wind which deflected the bullet. I had had several days to consider this matter, which exercised me a good deal, and having determined to make good allowance for wind next time, I did so, with the result described. I must confess that, although a wind was blowing, I discovered, after the shot was fired, that it was not coming from the right, but from the game and towards me. I cannot explain my failure to notice this important detail: the wind may have changed suddenly, or it was simply a stupid oversight. Whatever the cause, the lamentable result was brought home quite clearly to my understanding when I saw the white rump of the big sheep vanish over the nearest mountain swell. I had two random shots as he was crossing the stream below among the boulders; but the splashing of the bullets about him served only to take the stiffness out of his limbs. The whole lot ran up the opposite range, and when near the crest went along what seemed a path, and crossed into the Gograng valley, evidently by a pass well known and well used by them. If ovines think, it may be presumed that the old ram, as he worked his stiff legs up the steep, must have said to himself, "That pottering old colonel again; he rattled me out of Gograng a few days ago, and now he is at it again. I wish he wouldn't."

Next day, the post having arrived, I remained in camp. Paljour went up the Chang-lúng again, intending to cross to Chang-lúng-yokma to hunt after fresh yak tracks, as this was the time of the year for them to put in an appearance, and this was their usual road. The day before, we had seen some old tracks at the mouth of the valley, and the prints of the colonel's boots following them into Gograng: so one herd had evidently crossed over a few days previously, and Paljour inferred that others would now be travelling along the same track.

On the 4th of August I started for the upper valley, for Paljour had been unsuccessful in his search the day before. I took two yaks and the small tent; the other tent remained at Madmar. We went up the right side of Gograng, whose slopes command a good view of the opposite valley, where all the game is supposed to be. I came across several antelopes, but would not fire for fear of disturbing other game. We made camp in a small nala with steep sides well concealed from view. After the tent was pitched, I took a walk down the ravine and spotted a wolf, who had just topped the ridge to my right. I ran back for the rifle, but he was two hundred yards off before I could fire, and I missed him. He looked small, and was yellowish-white in colour, somewhat similar to the antelope; I could distinctly see his white paws (*Canis pallipes*). In the afternoon we went along the base of the range towards the head of the valley, and after a rough three hours' walk I sat down, and Paljour went on to explore. He had not gone two hundred yards when he beckoned to me, having seen five nyan quite close; they were, he said, the very five of the day before, over which I had so blundered in the Changlung valley. They had bolted in this direction, and Paljour had promised me another shot in a couple of days; he was as good as his word. We stalked for about five hundred yards, and came on the animals at exactly the proper point; they were about one hundred yards below us. I had a capital rest on a rock, and the biggest ram was again the nearest, grazing with his right shoulder towards me. I did not aim under his tail this time, but straight for the shoulder, and made a most satisfactory shot. The ovis ran down the hillside for about twenty yards and rolled over. The others fled across the stream and valley to the opposite range, and I had no chance of another shot. Paljour said we should meet them again in a couple of days. The nyan was a large animal, the biggest of the lot —an ugly beast, with long lanky legs, a big stomach, and the hair coming off his skin in patches; but his head was a noble trophy. The horns measured forty and thirty-nine inches round the curve and seventeen inches round the base. This was the best head I secured. When Paljour came in, he showed me little splashes of lead sticking to the ram's hair. These, he averred, were from the bullets I fired at the ram two days before when he was crossing the stream, my shots having splashed off boulders. We moved camp across the main valley to the mouth of the Longser on the other range, explored the valley, and found it empty.

The Joint Commissioner at Leh laid me under an eternal obligation by sending me two servants in place of the rascal Saráp; they arrived with the post. No one was more grateful for this kindly thought than little Yákúb, who, it will be remembered, was the only one of my Indian servants who did not collapse at the foot of the Baralácha Pass. He was the only servant I had had from that time to the arrival of the men from Leh, for Saráp counted for nothing. Yákúb had all the work of the camp to perform, and he did it manfully and well, with the help of the coolies and yakmen. He had to pitch the tents and take them down almost every day, make things inside comfortable, do all the cooking for me and for himself, look after Chamúrti, whom he groomed every day and fed with cakes when there was no grazing;—all these duties, be it noted, in addition to a long march almost daily. He had no caste prejudices; he drank my tea from my teapot and ate the same food that I had. His only luxury was a pipe, and he would have dearly loved a glass of whisky after a day's labours; but during the whole of my long journey he never once abstracted a drop, though the temptation must have been sore indeed. These traits are not common in a Hindústani Musalmán. My experience with this man showed how useful a servant of his stamp can be when untrammelled with the prejudices of the caste-beridden peoples of India. In addition, Yákúb was cleanly in his habits: he brushed his teeth every morning with a civilised Western tooth-brush, and, more remarkable, he used soap every day! He was also the handiest man I ever came across: he mended my boots and clothes, patched the tent, kept the saddlery clean, was a capital horseman, a first-rate taxidermist, a born shikári, and by no means a bad cook. All these accomplishments were acquired in the household of the late General Gott, where he was brought up from boyhood. Of course he had his faults: though a little man, he had a big ugly temper, and made himself feared and hated wherever he went; he also had a weakness for liquor, when legitimately procurable, and he was an unpleasant customer in his cups.

On the 7th of August I made a long and final journey to the head of the Gograng valley. After passing Pangta we came to a large glacier, along which the four nyan had bolted, after their patriarch had been slain. Moraines lay on every side, and round the foot of the glacier was the usual indescribable chaos. The walking was most difficult, but we crossed below the glacier at its very snout where water and snow were frozen, and the walking was comparatively easy. About the centre of the glacier, where the main stream issues from beneath, the muddy water gushed up with great violence in the form of a natural fountain about two feet in height, falling in an ever-moving dome. The breadth of the glacier at its extremity was about three hundred yards, and its perpendicular height about fifty yards. Peaks, pinnacles, steeples, and needles of frozen snow were visible above. Besides the dirty stream rushing out from below, little rills were pouring from all sides, as if the icy mass were sweating in the sun; one jet spouted from a small hole in the solid ice. I saw no sign of transparent ice. The whole mass had the appearance of a solid mountain of consolidated snow, quite different from other glaciers I had seen. It was a grand scene, and the weird surroundings took strong hold of my imagination; they had a similar effect on my companions, who said it was a "bad" place, which should be passed by as quickly as possible, and Paljour's steps were hasty as he led the way across. We went up the valley till it divided into two narrow ravines. The smaller seemed to be a short side nálá, down which flowed a stream. The other, no doubt the commencement of the main Gograng valley, could be viewed for some distance; it was choked with a serpentine glacier. We could see nothing beyond but a steep, stony mountain ridge streaked with snow, evidently the summit of the valley, and the dividing line. After Pangta the small higher valleys have no separate names; the whole of the upper portion is called Phú-Gograng, or "Head of Gograng." After passing the glacier with the muddy fountain, the hillsides become very stony and abrupt. We reached our farthest point, but found no sight whatever of game; there was no animal in the valley larger than a marmot. No doubt my predecessor's two months of wild shooting had frightened every animal away, for the rest of the season at anyrate.

The official map of Chang-chen-mo, it may be observed, and probably that of the whole of this part of Ladakh, perpetuates many serious mistakes.

We began our return from the head of the valley at noon, and found the tracks of the four nyan which had fled across in this direction when the big ram was shot; we followed them up the hillside in the Pangta valley, and found the beds where they had slept, but could not discover the animals themselves. They had had a good scare, and must have been lurking somewhere near the sky-line—a very unusual thing for these large animals. I was not very keen about them; none of the four had a good head; I had secured the best.

The next day I returned to Madmar camp, gave up the

hunt in Gograng as hopeless, and returned to Kiám, passing Gogra camping-place on the way, where I halted for breakfast. This camp is on the right bank of the Gograng stream, just below its junction with Chang-lúng stream. "Go" means door or gate, and there is really some resemblance, for Gogra looks as if it were the gateway into Gograng. That night at Kiám there was a severe storm; the Gograng hills were covered with snow nearly down to their bases, and something stronger than the normal gale began to blow up the Chang-chen-mo valley. Kiám camp was very uncomfortable, as the position is much exposed. This probably was the turning-point between the short summer and the shorter autumn which ushers in the very long winter. I may note that the change occurred on the 9th August.

CHAPTER XIV

DONG (WILD YAK) SHOOTING

Start on the hunt—Shoot an antelope—The first dong track—Paljour takes up the scent—A black spot in the distance—Resolved into a bull-yak—Seventy yards range—I miss the target, four feet by six—The second shot tells—The bull slows down—Circumvent him at last—A butcherly business—The usual reaction—Piercing cold—The Tibetan gale—A snowstorm—Exhaustion—Tea and blankets—No remedy—The frozen dong—A splendid trophy—Bullets and their wounds—Hunting twenty thousand feet above sea level—The temperature falls—No water procurable—Yákúb's excitement over the dong's head and hide—A keen sportsman—Invents a bow—And hunts the tailless Tibetan rat successfully—Weight of the dong's head—Length of the horns—The hunt continued—Tibetan grouse—More wild yaks—A successful stalk—·500 bore bullets and their effect on the dong—Shepherds and sheep—How the Maharájah trades—The Champa robbers—Their depredations—Varying temperatures—Three wild yak bagged in a week—A record performance—Give up the hunt—Weights and measurements of heads and horns—Details of cost of expedition.

ON the 10th of August we started for Keipsang, with four yaks and fifteen days' provisions, for a long search after wild yak; crossed the valley and went up gradually to what is called the Konka-la in the map, a name which is not known locally. The path runs just under the conical red hill which is visible from Kiám camp, the "pass" is just under it, and the Keipsang valley opens out to view as soon as the crest is reached. The ascent is hardly perceptible. Just as we topped it, Paljour spied nine antelope on the stony plain below, and we went after them at once. They were below the bank of the stream, and we got very close, but just then the biggest buck topped the bank about a hundred yards away, then there was hurry and confusion, and I missed the big one. A second shot, however, broke his fore leg, and a third shot bowled over a smaller one at over two hundred yards. I was using the Winchester again. We followed up the wounded antelope for a long time, but could not find him.

The sun was hot, I was blown and tired—and the usual thing happened. How often does not the "usual thing" happen! The wounded buck had hidden himself somewhere so effectually that I gave up the hunt and handed the rifle to Paljour to carry. He went along the ridge, I lazily following; suddenly the antelope appeared on the sky-line, on a level, but at some distance from Paljour, and about a hundred yards from me. The buck stood for some time motionless, and had a good look at us—tableau! We all three stood like statues. As the buck went over the ridge, I rushed up for the rifle, and had six shots, missing every time; nothing under six shots would have relieved my feelings. The wounded animal made for another slope higher up, and I had two good hours' further toil in the hot sun before he was mine; the moral is, of course, always obvious, but *cui bono*? Like other fellows, I shall do the same thing till the end of the chapter.

Next day was my red-letter dong day. We left camp at six to explore the upper Keipsang valley for traces of wild yak; but with little hope. We had not gone very far along a kiang track when Paljour noticed the broad hoof-marks of a large yak leading up the valley. He decided that it was four days old, but was worth following, especially as the animal was travelling in the direction we were going. After a short distance the track bent towards the stream flowing at the bottom of the valley, and the marks showed distinctly in the damp earth. Paljour began to think the footprints more recent, and quickened his pace; presently he came to some droppings, and exclaimed, "It is only two days old!" Farther on we passed more dung, and Paljour with great animation declared that the animal had passed along here only the day before. The tracking was carried on with great diligence now, for we were evidently on the track of a very large bull, and he could not be far off. As we got farther into the folds of the valley our caution increased, and old Paljour, who led the way, became the embodiment of circumspection. We made a careful survey of the ground ahead from every bend in the valley, and scanned every slope and hollow with the greatest minuteness; our advance was consequently very slow. It was necessary to exercise such care, because the wind was blowing up the valley to our quarry. It thus became a regular game: if the dong scented us first, he would win; if we saw him first, we should score. At one of these turns, while Paljour, myself, and the coolie boy carrying my tiffin were lying prone on the slope of a rise, Pamber, the boy, drew Paljour's attention, albeit dubiously, to a black spot on the slope of a distant stony hill. Paljour said it was a rock; we had made many such mistakes before. Even after a careful look through the binoculars, none of us could say positively what it was, but, when the long telescope was brought to bear, we found that the supposed rock was our quarry—an enormous bull taking his rest. He was certainly not less than two miles away, and was high up on the slope, so he could not possibly scent us; we had won the first move in the game. We dropped under cover at once, and lay there nearly two hours, till nine o'clock, waiting till his bovine lordship had finished his "Europe morning"; but he did not move excepting once, to change sides. We could not go farther along the bottom of the valley for fear of the wind, so Paljour decided to go back to the first side valley on our left, and then strike up the hillside for the crest of the range. It was a toilsome grind to the sky-line, and, after proceeding along the crest, we peeped over. The old bull had at last got up, and was feeding in a side valley next the one in which he had been lying. We trudged over the intervening ridges and depressions till we came to the one where he was grazing. He was busily engaged, hardly taking his mouth from the grass for minutes at a time, and not moving ten feet in any direction; he was breakfasting, and had evidently a good appetite. We crept down till we were on a level with him, but there were still two hundred yards between us, and we could get no closer. I determined to wait till he came nearer, or went down the next depression. He did neither, but remained grazing on one spot not ten yards square. I got tired of watching, so had a biscuit and stretched myself, leaving Paljour to watch. I should say I had half a dozen naps within fifteen minutes, and a fresh dream during every nap—about two minutes to a dream. After this quick succession of nightmares (or day-mares), I sat up, and then suddenly came a puff of wind from behind us and towards our game, which made Paljour and myself start up together. We hurried back at once to the next depression, dreading every moment lest the dong should get our scent and be off. Paljour now changed his tactics and went down nearly to the bottom of the main valley, and then proceeded up along that, till we came to the dip in the hillside in which the animal was feeding. Then we ascended till we got on a level with him again within less than a hundred yards. By sitting up, I could just see the top of his back moving above the swell in the ground which separated us, and I cocked the rifle, ready to fire whenever he showed his shoulder; but he gave a turn and lay down facing us. By raising my head, I could see his horns and the top of his head; six inches higher, and our eyes would have met. Here was a fix: the tension was getting unbearable, when Paljour pointed to a rock in front of us forty yards away, and whispered that if we got there I could have a shot at his shoulder. So we backed, and got behind the little rock, and there found ourselves within seventy yards of the still unconscious game, but his horns and head were still facing us, and we were on the slope below him—he had us completely under his command. The only alternative was to rise slowly and give him the shot in the chest as he rose. This was a ticklish business with a single rifle, and only a ·450 at that. If the huge beast charged, he could easily grind us into the hillside. However, it had to be done, or my only chance would be lost. I rose slowly up, not in a very comfortable state of mind, but with my nerves braced and steady; the bull rose too and stared. I fired with deliberate aim, and missed. The bullet passed his left shoulder, and clapped loudly on the hillside in the distance. It was the hand of Providence. I was quite collected and steady, and the target, seventy yards off, was four feet broad by six feet high. Had the bullet struck, the maddened bull would have been down on us, and one, if not both of us, would have been killed.

Things turned out differently. The dong rushed round the hillside to my right, and I had time to put in another cartridge, and gave him another shot at a hundred yards as he rushed along. This shot was a hundred times more difficult than the first, but I placed the bullet fairly in the centre of his body. I heard it tell loudly on his ribs; but the yak only went the faster. A third bullet went after him as he topped the swell, but there was no visible result. We, too, ran round the swell, but lower down, and found the bull standing on the slope of the next valley looking rather sick. I fired again, but with no result. The bull now attempted to go up hill, but could not manage it; he turned and ran down to the level of the main valley, and started to go along the bottom, but soon subsided into a short, quick walk. His gait was very characteristic; it was evident his temper was up, as, witness the angry flourishes of his bushy tail. The effect was heightened by the swaying to and fro of his long black shaggy hair, which hung all round below his knees like a thick curtain; seen from behind, it resembled the swaying of a kilt when the wearer is stepping out his best. The whole action of the old Bos seemed to say, "I don't want to fight, but by jingo if I *do*!" His pace, however, decreased by degrees as I watched him through the glasses, and soon became very slow, for the poor beast had a mortal wound. It was past noon now, and, as I had no intention of letting the poor brute escape thus wounded, I sent Pämber back to bring up the camp, resolved to follow the bull, and finish him off as quickly as I could.

I had a snack, and we started again. At this unlucky moment the wind changed again, and blew right to the dong; the consequence was, that after passing a turn we saw him rise slowly from the ground and resume his slow walk. We had to stop and keep him in view. The valley was narrow, with steep stony hillsides, and there was no way of heading him, except by climbing right up to the sky-line and getting round to the head of the valley. It was a terrible task labouring up those steep hillsides in that rarefied atmosphere; the highest point we reached could not have been much under twenty thousand feet. The bull came slowly on up a narrow gully. The track, no doubt, was well known to him, as it led into the Chang-lúng valley, and so on to Gograng, and he was evidently travelling to that grazing ground when we discovered him. We had no choice but to get on the steep slope above him and cut him off from the pass. We got up the side of the hill on our right and then mounted slowly to get out of his view, but the hill was so steep that it was a long time before we could effect our purpose, and the climb was a most trying ordeal. We did at last get him under cover, and then worked round and placed ourselves between him and the only possible line of escape. Then the miserable wind changed again; the weather had become cloudy, and now, just as we were well placed, the icy blast came straight down from the Keipsang-la, and through us (literally) on to the wounded animal, bringing with it a cutting sleet-storm. We became desperate, rushed down to the bottom of the gully, and went for the bull helter-skelter. He, of course, scented us, and was standing up facing in our direction, when we sighted him a hundred yards off. He did not seem inclined to move either up or down the nálá, which at this point was not ten yards broad, with almost perpendicular sides, and gazed at us steadily, as immovable as a rock. We thought discretion the better part of valour, and hastily clawed ourselves up the hillside on the left; it was like a rocky wall, with very insecure footing, but we negotiated it in quick time, and came on the old bull again at forty yards and above him. I opened fire on the poor brute, but he took several solid bullets without attempting to escape, and at last succumbed to his many wounds.

The shades of evening were closing round us when he sank and died: the icy gale shrieked and tore through the rugged gully, and a snowstorm was fast shrouding everything in a white mantle. I had bagged my first wild yak, and had won " the blue ribbon of Himálayan shooting," but felt no exultation. I was sorry for the poor beast, and besides, my very soul was shivering within me from the intense cold, and the void within craved for a full pot of hot, very hot, tea. Fortunately, the yaks had come up with the camp; we had not gone half a mile when we met them. I had the tent pitched, and was under shelter and taking the nourishment I so much needed in a very short time. The storm continued, and the cold was intense —everything was frozen, so I got under the blankets and made myself as snug as I could. The arrival of the tent was just in the nick of time; in half an hour darkness would have overtaken us out on that bleak hillside. I had been out on the hill thirteen hours at a very high elevation, most of the time undergoing severe physical toil and no small mental excitement. The reaction which should have set in with the cessation of work did not come, and I could not sleep. The fearful weather, which only two folds of cloth kept from me, added much to my discomfort.

Next morning, when the storm lulled, we visited the bull. The snow had shrouded the hills and valleys in white, and so dazzling was the brilliancy that I had to put on my goggles, though there was no sun-glare. The morning was bitterly cold, and it was still cloudy. We found the dong frozen; he had died in a folded-up sitting position, and felt as hard as a rock, being coated with hardened snow. Nothing could be done with the huge bulk till the sun came out and thawed it. The operation of cutting off his head alone took more than two hours; the skinning and cutting up took the whole day. The trophy was a magnificent one: I had never imagined such massiveness and beauty. The second bullet I fired hit in the right ribs, went through the liver, and was found on the ribs on the left side, splayed like a mushroom about twelve-bore size. It was a solid bullet of 320 grs., and had 125 grs. of powder behind it, fired at a range of a hundred yards; this speaks well for the Winchester Express. I fired this shot when the bull was running round the hill after I had missed him with the first; it was no doubt this shot that killed him, though it took nearly ten hours to complete the work. I could discover no other fatal injury. Another solid bullet went into his stomach, one broke his fore leg, another a hind leg, both at the knees. When at close quarters I fired into his left shoulder; but in the excitement of the moment I must have used the cartridges with hollow bullets; I made a careful examination of his shoulder, and found that these light bullets had not penetrated beyond the mass of hair and hide even—the base of one was sticking in the skin!

One thing is certain, ·450 hollow bullets driven by 125 grs. of powder produce no more effect on the shoulder of a wild yak at forty yards than on a solid rock. I gave old Paljour a tip of four rupees for this successful hunt, and Pámber, the boy, one rupee for having first sighted the bull. The old shikári thawed under the influence of the silver, and he gave me the following information regarding the wild yak:—They are divided by Tibetans into three classes: (1) the largest is named *Taingan*, a hoary monster with grizzled face, shoulders, and flanks; (2) *Traisir*, a huge beast with grizzled face only: (3) *Tainak*, a young bull, jet-black all over. The one I had shot was evidently a "Traisir," to judge by his grand grizzled head and face. If a tame bull with white about him goes to a wild cow, the progeny has a white tail: if a wild bull gets to a tame cow, the produce is fierce and stubborn, and the horns of the young bull have to be cut off at the tips to prevent mischief. It would therefore seem that tame and wild animals are apt to get mixed; but this can happen only in Tibet proper, where wild yaks are so common. Paljour said that only in Tibet are wild ones found with white tails.

In the evening I returned to the camp at Trak-karpo, losing a good chance of a fine antelope through the freaks of a kiang. These worthless animals have an entirely mistaken idea of their own importance. When they sight the sportsman, they promptly assume that they themselves are the animals stalked; but, instead of going clean away like sensible beasts, they rush about in the most idiotic manner and within easy range of the disgusted hunter; their temperament must be very excitable and nervous, and their intelligence of a very low order.

The cold in the Keipsang plain was getting worse daily; at night everything liquid was frozen, and there was great difficulty in getting water till the sun came out, when a regular transformation scene set in at once. I paid a visit to Kiam camp to see about the preserving of the dong's head and hide. Four tame yaks had full loads carrying the hide, head, and meat, so we made an imposing entry. Yákúb was struck dumb with the magnitude of the head and hide. Old Paljour had a bad half-hour in explaining to him, with his imperfect command of the language common to both, the exciting details of the chase. Yákúb was a keen sportsman. As his camp duties did not allow him to accompany me, he manufactured a pellet-bow out of a broken bamboo alpenstock, and went out on regular hunts after the tailless rats, that abound in great numbers in all grassy spots. There was no lack of excitement in this novel sport, as it was really difficult to stalk within killing distance of these small creatures with such a weapon. He collected a small heap of their pretty fawn-coloured velvet pelts. About five hundred of them put neatly together would make a dainty rug.

The dong's head gave Yákúb several days' congenial work, and he set about it without delay. The first thing we did was to weigh the head: it was exactly 100 lbs. The horns were 34 inches in length. The nyan head I shot in Gograng weighed 23 lbs. I found two large flocks of sheep at Kiám; one had just brought salt from the Mangtza lake in Tibet, and the other was bound for the same place. Their road lay through Kiamgo-Traggar valley, where my future dong-shooting would be, so I arranged with the shepherds that they were to keep a day's march behind me as far as Lanak-la, and returned to Trak-karpo in the evening.

Next morning we left the Keipsang by another Konka-la (a slight rise only), and entered Kiamgo-Traggar at once. A small white rock is in the centre of the opening, named also "Trak-karpo"; the waters of several valleys meet at this white stone, and run united to the main stream. The march from Keipsang into Kiamgo-Traggar was a most trying one—a long series of stony slopes and valleys, one after the other; not a blade of grass, not a drop of water, was visible anywhere. In one of these stony depressions Paljour spied two birds with a young one; we went after them, and Paljour picked up the youngster, lying like a stone on the ground. It was about the size of a common grey partridge, and was exactly like that bird in colour, but the legs were short and feathered like those of a grouse. I carried it some distance in my hand after the old birds, which kept moving off a few yards before me—the hen pretending to be disabled, and fluttering along just as I have seen pheasants in the Himálayas, when trying to distract attention from their helpless broods. The old birds were marked like the pintail grouse of the plains, similarly shaped, but much longer in the body: they were evidently specimens of *Syrrhaptes Tibetanus*, the Tibetan grouse. They are described by Bower in his book *Across Tibet* (page 294). He found these birds in this same valley.

At 12.30 we reached the opening of the Lúngún side valley, our intended camping-place, and were making eagerly for the opposite side, where there was a stream, when, looking up the valley, Paljour made out a dark object about a mile off: the glasses showed it to be a dong. Here was a fix! I was dead tired with seven hours' tramping, had had no breakfast yet, and now a tremendous stalk (the wind was wrong, as usual) had to be undertaken at once. We went back on our tracks a bit, and, after a hurried snack, began the ascent of the hill. We had to go to the very sky-line before we could cross over to the proper side for a safe and close approach. The ascent took us fully two hours, and when we got into position, about a hundred yards from the bull, he did exactly what the first had done—lay down, facing us straight! I did the same, glad of a little rest to pull myself together, while Paljour kept watch. Half an hour passed, when the shikári said, "He is up." I raised myself and saw the bull going fast up the side valley, in which he had been sleeping—no doubt he had got a puff of our wind, and was alarmed. I ran as fast as I could, and had a snap-shot at 150 yards with the Winchester as the bull climbed the hill in front. The shot turned him, and from his sudden change of course I made certain he was hit: he turned quite suddenly, and came in a curve to our right, and above us. I imagined that he could no longer ascend on account of his wound, like the Keipsang bull. As he made this curve, I had time to put in four more shots with the double Express, but at very long ranges.

One took effect, and broke his right hind leg below the knee; this crippled him, but he made a regular bolt round the steep and stony hillside above us, with the intention, evidently, of getting into the upper part of the valley. We ran, too, in the same direction, but lower down the slope, to cut him off. His progress, however, was slow, as I could see from the dust—he was out of sight owing to a curve in the hill. I slackened my pace, but Paljour, not noticing this, went on and got above me; he was thus between the bull and myself. As the bull turned the swell in the hillside, he suddenly came in sight of Paljour, and, instantly changing his course, charged furiously at the old man, straight down hill. Paljour retreated towards me, best pace, shouting to me to fire; but at first I could not see the bull, and when he did come in sight the shikári was directly in line with him. I shouted to him to get out of the way, but he was too flustered to understand. Fortunately, above me, and about ten yards off, a small rock jutted out of the hillside, and Paljour screwed himself under it, into the smallest space. The infuriated bull stood above the rock, only a few feet from the man, evidently at a loss. He could hear his enemy distinctly, for Paljour was shouting continuously, at the top of his voice, for me to come and hide under the rock beside him. It was clear that both man and animal were unconscious of each other's proximity: one was mad with rage, and the other was off his head with funk. There was no time, however, to admire the tableau, for the monster above me was bent on mischief. I put a ·500 Express bullet into his chest, and down he came straight for me. I backed a few yards to get out of his course, and fell into a stony hole, cutting my legs very severely—the hand of Providence again! In the hole I was out of sight of the furious animal, which thundered past, about three yards off. I had just time to twist myself into a sitting position, and deliver my second barrel into his shoulder as he rushed by. That finished him. He fell twenty yards below me, sprawling on his belly, with his legs spread out, thus checking the otherwise inevitable roll down hill. His head was raised, and he was bleeding copiously from the mouth.

The scene, though it lasted only a few moments, has left an indelible impression on my memory. Our respective positions in this transaction were, I should say, unique. The blazing sun behind the bull, as he stood over Paljour, setting off his grand proportions, Paljour jammed under the rock, bawling at the pitch of his voice, and myself quivering with excitement on the stony hillside! It seems a laughing matter now, but at the time we were all three desperately in earnest. At anyrate, Paljour thought the situation critical, for when the bull rolled over he came down to me, put his head on my feet, crying, "You have saved me, you have saved me!" He patted the rifle affectionately, exclaiming, "*Bahút achha bandúk, bahút achha bandúk!*" (a very good gun, a very good gun), and was altogether hysterical for a time.

After we had recovered somewhat, we went down to the dong, which was still alive, and I was debating in my mind whether I would spend another cartridge on him to put him out of pain, when Paljour shouted something at him, abusive, I suppose, in Tibetan. The sound of the human voice roused the savage brute's fury again; he moved angrily, but it was his last effort. The poor beast rolled over and went down the stony hillside, over and over, for a hundred yards, bringing up on a level bit at the bottom, on the flat of his back, dead. The camp came up presently, and we pitched near the carcase.

Next morning he was cut up. He was much smaller than No. 1, but was a compact, sturdy beast, of immense

"THE INFURIATED BULL STOOD ABOVE THE ROCK."

power. His horns were four inches shorter than those of the Keipsang bull, the points worn away and chipped, but much thicker at the base. When Paljour noticed the condition of his horns, he said, "This is a *khuni*," meaning that the animal was a murderer, and that he must have killed a man. He related the story of a Tibetan, who was attacked by a wild bull the year before, beyond the Lanak-la. The man's stomach was torn open, and he was killed on the spot. Dongs whose horns are worn and battered are always vicious and dangerous; they are constantly fighting, and attack everything they encounter. This bull had all the appearance of a morose old rogue; he probably was the identical brute of Paljour's story, as I shot him within two days' march of the place where the Tibetan was killed. The wild yak's face was greatly grizzled, his teeth were worn down, and one was missing. Paljour said his age could not be less than twenty years, while the Keipsang bull could not have been more than fifteen. As he lay, he gave me the impression of a well-trained prize-fighter, while the figure of the first monster I shot put me in mind of a large and portly gentleman, in the prime of life, who took no care of his muscles. The chest and shoulder shots were well placed, and made short work of the huge beast; as both were fired within ten yards' range, the result was only natural. The bullets were solid ·500s, and had 135 grains of powder behind them. The penetration was very great, and the effect inside tremendous. Both lungs were torn through from right to left, and the chest shot had gone through the body so far that we could not trace the bullet. Mystery attached to the first shot I fired from the Winchester. It had seemed to disable him—or was it pure cussedness that had caused him to change his course when he heard the shot and come round the hill towards us? The flesh between the thighs was blue, and looked as if a bullet had made a passage that way, but examination was such a nauseating business that I did not carry my explorations very far. One fact, however, was certain: there was no bullet-hole in the hide of that portion of the body. Paljour had his own theory about the entrance of the bullet from behind, but I could not accept it, as there was no sign on the part indicated.

The sheep, fifteen hundred, in charge of fourteen men, came up during the day and camped close by. They were anxious to go on, as they travel by night only, and intended to cross the Lanak-la by sunrise next day. Five hundred of these sheep belonged to the Maharájah of Kashmir, or, let us say, to his officials. In this way he had large flocks of sheep all over the country. The profits in the salt trade on this number of sheep go to him: the only advantage the owners get is the produce of the sheep, but the number belonging to the Maharájah must never diminish. If they die, or are lost across the border, it is the people's loss, on the "heads I win, tails you lose" principle. These men had wonderful stories of the Champa robbers across the border, and seemed to be in great fear of them. The Champa (nomadic) robbers (called also *Chakpa* by Bower) are probably the *Golok* plundering tribes mentioned by other travellers. They are mounted on trained horses, that gallop up and down mountains at full speed. A rest is fixed between the ears of the horse, from which the horseman takes aim with his long gun. They have their tents fifteen days' march in the interior, and mounted parties infest the roads. Sometimes, when their supplies run short, they undergo great privations. There is no redress from their plundering, because there is no appeal nearer than Lahsa, three months' journey distant; besides, these sheepmen say, the Champas pay a tax to Lahsa for the privilege of plundering. This party with their sheep were going to Mangtza-tso (lake) for salt, ten days' march beyond the border; it is the lake that Carey passed on his journey to Polú. The year before a party of Rúpshú men, themselves nomads, were plundered as they were returning from the lake by these robbers. The men who were now going up came from Pobrang. They said they had no arms, and offered no resistance to the Champas, who were terrible fellows. The shepherds took all the meat of the dead dong and buried it high up the hillside under large rocks. They said they would return in about a month, when they would take the flesh home!

I noted the temperature inside the tent during my stay in the Lalúng valley. At 9 P.M. the thermometer showed 46°; at 6 A.M. 24°—a difference of 22° between evening and morning. At 4 P.M. it was 66°, or an extreme variation of 42° in the twenty-four hours. These figures speak to the climate of these parts in the middle of August.

Next morning we went up Kiamgo-Traggar in the direction of Lanak-la, the travelling-path of *Poëphagus grunniens* when he is seeking pastures new. We reached the opening of the Kalúng valley at nine o'clock, and at the same time Paljour discovered the tracks of a large dong going in the same direction that we were. We followed them for two hours, first down into the plain, where there was water, then through grassy plots and over stony plains. There were two, a large bull and a smaller one. I gave up the search when the things came up; but Paljour followed the beasts up a small valley, and then returned, saying the dong had gone up very high. We proceeded farther to find a good place for camp, and when turning a spur, Pámber, the boy, pointed out two black spots near the sky-line, which the glasses soon resolved into the bulls. The large flock of sheep that passed this way last night must have disturbed them, and they had climbed high; but for this circumstance, I am sure we should have found them on the level in one of the grassy plots. We backed round the corner at once and made camp under the hill, well concealed from the dongs above, and at two o'clock began the stalk, passing up the Kalúng valley until we got past the point where our game was. We had to go this distance to get the right side of the wind, which was blowing up the valley. It took us an hour's steady climbing to get near the top of the ridge, and, as we approached the point we were making for, I thought to myself that if the bulls appeared on the crest above we should be fairly caught, and that the rifles ought to be uncovered and loaded; but such is the perversity of human nature that I only thought, and put off action until the very thing that was running in my mind happened. When we were eighty yards from the ridge, an immense black form rose slowly above the sharply-defined sky-line and came slowly along the crest, looming twice its actual size against the deep blue above! We flattened ourselves among the stones in an instant, I tearing madly at the cover of the ·500 Express, while Paljour presented two cartridges with a trembling hand. The bull, however, did not see us, and the wind for once was right. The beast seemed half asleep and very lazy; he moved along very slowly, and gave me a splendid chance. The first bullet told loudly, and was answered by a flourish of the bushy tail, but the second shot missed him. I just had time to reload when the other bull came along, but only the top of his back showed above the crest, and the bullet passed over him harmlessly. We rushed over the ridge, and followed the tracks till we had the two animals again in sight in a small valley below, and about a mile away. The big bull, standing with his head down, seemed hard hit, and the smaller stood close to him in an attitude of inquiring sympathy. We stalked down and found they had gone on, but very slowly, so followed the tracks round a couple of side valleys, and at last came on them standing quietly in a narrow depression; it seemed as if they were trying to hide in the best way they could in this fold of the barren hillside, for the smaller one turned his head and looked in our direction in the sly fashion of a wild animal trying to escape notice. The big bull was twenty yards ahead of the youngster, who was the most alert, and was evidently looking after the safety of his older companion. I fired at the wounded animal with the Winchester and missed; and missed twice again as they bolted! The distance was over 150 yards, and I had not a clear view. I now put up the second sight, and my fourth shot, at certainly not less than 300 yards, rolled over the big bull like a rabbit; the fifth shot did exactly the same to the other. Here was luck! Old Paljour was surprised out of his stolidity; he raised a shout, waved his greasy headgear, and salaamed me several times. I was certainly elated myself at the sight of the two bulls kicking up the dust on the hillside below me. We had not gone fifty yards towards them when the smaller one got up and limped along the level track with his leg hanging useless from his shoulder; he fell twice, and I thought he could not go far, so did not fire again, but he mended his pace by degrees, and ran right round the valley and over the dividing ridge, before I realised that he was getting out of my hands. That was the last I saw of him. The back of the old bull was broken, and he never moved from the place where he fell. I ended his pain with another bullet. My first shot, when he came over the ridge, hit him in the fleshy part of the right hind leg. I aimed, or thought I aimed, at his shoulder when he loomed against the sky-line as big as a haystack, but the fluster I was in at the moment may be imagined—this huge target was only eighty yards off, and I was within six inches of missing it altogether.

I fired my last shot at wild yak on the 16th August. I had bagged three—and lost one through my own foolishness. I began the hunt on the 10th. I think this is a record that has not been touched yet—three wild bulls in six days. I might have continued for another fortnight and collected a good supply of these enormous heads; but for what end? The hunting and stalking are the most exciting in the world; the climate, the ground, and its surroundings the most trying. The chase of the wild dong, therefore, must be classed amongst the severest tests of a sportsman's quality; but a bag of three good bulls quite satisfied me. I have a horror of big bags—an unconquerable disgust at my own butcherliness comes over me when I stand over a noble animal that has been slain by my own hand: this feeling increases with every trophy added to my collection, till it forces me to drop the pursuit of that particular game and follow something else. In the present instance remorse got the better of me after the third bull, and I left the travelling trail of the wild yaks to pick up a couple of antelope heads in another part of the valley. The escape of the wounded bull haunted me and made me unhappy for several days, though I spent some precious time trying to retrieve him; he crossed the range of mountains to the north, and must have made his way to the Great Plain beyond, and died in lingering misery. May I be forgiven!

The head of the second bull (the murderer) weighed only 84 lbs., and the horns were 29 inches in length. The third bull's head weighed 94 lbs., and the horns were 30 inches long.

Before proceeding to other scenes, a few details of the cost of my expedition will be useful. The yaks, ponies, and coolies had been with me for one month and six days, reckoning from the time they were hired to my return to Pobrang, where they were discharged. For that period the expenses were as follows :—

	Rs.		
Hire of eight yaks	76	12	0
Hire of two ponies	19	3	0
Hire of goats	3	6	0
Wages to Paljour, 8 annas a day (I kept him on as far as Tänksé)	20	0	0
Wages of Pämber and another man	8	0	0
Cost of four sheep	4	0	0
Bakshísh	5	0	0
Total, Rs.	136	5	0

Or three rupees twelve annas per diem. These figures prove that this kind of sport is not really expensive when managed with ordinary prudence. Of course the carelessly rich or inexperienced sportsman will probably have to pay double. He should, however, bear in mind that the extra money he dispenses will not find its way to the people who have actually done his hard work, but into the bottomless pockets of the rascally Kashmiri shikári, or of the confidential English-speaking servant who runs the whole show, including his master. The simple remedy is to pay each individual with your own hand.

CHAPTER XV

STAG AND BEAR SHOOTING IN KASHMIR

To Leh, capital of Ladakh—Route from Leh to Kashmir—Leave it at Shargól—March to Súrú—Story of General Zoráwar Singh and his death—From Súrú to Súknis—A human skeleton—Details of fatal accident to Dr. Genge and his party—The Súknis bear and his harem—Master of the village crops—Cannot find him—Stag-shooting in the Upper Wardwan—Hauking (driving) is unsuccessful—A stag calls—Go for him—Just in time—Difficulty in "haláling"—A hysterical coolie—A fine trophy—March for the valley—My first bear—Bad weather again—A forty-eight hours' snowstorm—Bear-shooting is ruined—A sociable snipe—Cross over into the valley—Five days' hard work—Result, a stag and a bear—Shooting tour comes to an end—Joined by Yákúb and Chamúrti—The latter's adventures—Yákúb lionises at home—Is fêted by nawabs—Takes to drink—And dies.

My next objective was Leh. I left Pobrang on the 28th of August, and reached the capital of Ladakh on the 2nd of September, crossing Chang-la, 18,000 feet, an ascent of three and a half hours, on the way. The distance is 74 miles as I made it, 77 miles according to the official list of routes.

Tánksé is the largest village on the road, and all supplies for the trip to Chang-chen-mo are always collected here and from the neighbouring villages. The valley for several miles, above and below, is most fertile, and can supply sufficient quantities of necessaries for a small party going on a three months' excursion. If the sportsman makes his start from Leh, he should send his camp on ahead, and make the foot of the pass himself in one day. The second day will take him easily into Tánksé, and the third to Pobrang.

The road from Leh to Kashmir is a well-known line of travel, and I take up my story at Shargól, where I again left the beaten track; this place is the sixth march from Leh. Yákúb went on with the ponies and things by the straight road to Srinagar, while I, with eight coolie-loads, struck off to the left for Sórú at the head of the Wardwan valley, where I intended to have some stag and bear shooting before concluding my travels. My first march was to the foot of a pass with no particular name—a distance of about fifteen miles—which took us ten hours to get over; the coolies carrying my loads were very slow, and gave much trouble at each village we passed. Beyond Shargól the traveller is in Baltistán, and the population is chiefly Musalmán. I saw only a few Bhóts (Tibetans), Lámas, and gónpas (monasteries) during the march. The next day's march was a very stiff one indeed. I changed the coolies for four baggage animals, and got along better. We passed over the crest of the range between two peaks marked on the map 18,026 feet and 18,653 feet; the pass itself cannot be less than 17,000 feet—a very high one for these parts. From this point I had a grand view of snowy peaks to the north and north-east, beyond Nabra and its big glaciers, but no snow was visible on the rocky, broken mountains between me and the distant peaks. This was the first really extensive view I had had of Ladakh. The next descent was very long and trying indeed—zig-zagging and doing the serpentine along a very steep hillside all the way to the bottom of the valley—the Phúlúng. We came to the first village, Labbaks, at half-past two; but my camping-place was Sánkú, so we trudged on in the heat. I was thirteen hours on the road, and did only twenty miles; a most trying day's march.

Khalík, the servant I had brought from Leh, an Arghún or half-caste, beguiled the tedium of the journey by relating the story of Zoráwar Singh, the famous general of Mahárájah Guláb Singh of Kashmir. He was the conqueror of Ladakh, and subsequently lost his life in Tibet during a great battle, while he was on his march to Lahsa itself. The half-caste's story was shortly this: The name of the place where the general was killed was Parang; he was on horseback during the battle, and was hit by a bullet in the thigh; he dismounted and sat on the ground, where he was shot again in the chest, and died as he sat. The Bhóts (Tibetans) were so afraid even of the dead hero that they would not approach his body for two days. Then they cut off his head and sent it to Lahsa, and ate the rest of the body, that they might assimilate the courage of the gallant old Sikh! The head is still preserved in the biggest monastery of the city, and is worshipped with great ceremony as the head of a famous conqueror. The Bhóts won the battle by *jádu* (magic); it snowed very hard all the time, and the bullets would not come out of the Sikhs' guns.

To Sórú was the next march, seventeen miles up the left bank of that river; the valley is very fertile, and the road, for the greater part, good. I remained here for a day, collected ten days' supplies, and started for my next point, the village of Súknis at the head of the Wardwan valley; it was a rough journey, and took four days' hard marching. The first stage was about twelve miles up the Chillúng stream. Several ancient moraines and landslips had to be crossed, and the stream was considerable even at this season. Marmots were numerous; they are bigger than the Tibetan variety, are of dark chestnut colour, and have black muzzles. We negotiated the pass next day, after a very difficult ascent over glaciers, moraines, etc., which took us more than four hours, at a rate of about a mile an hour. The descent on the other side was very steep and long. I had breakfast on top of a huge rock, under which, close to the path, lay the bleached skeleton of a man. It was that of a Kashmiri who died of exhaustion and cold many years ago while trying to cross; his body was placed in a hollow under the rock, and covered with large slabs. The skeleton was, however, plainly visible from the path; it was quite perfect, and had never been disturbed.

After two more descents, reached Kún-nág at 4 p.m.; the distance of the whole march was about twelve miles. The pass, named "Lanwi" in the map, is at the head of the Kaintal valley, in which Dr. Genge and his camp were buried under an avalanche of fresh snow a few years ago. I missed seeing the place where the accident occurred, as the pass by that route was closed, but heard the details of it from an old Kashmiri shikári at Sórú.

Dr. Genge was shooting ibex in the Kaintal valley, and had bagged one and wounded another. His camp was under a precipice in a perfectly safe place, according to the experience of the men with him; but during the night a dreadful snowstorm came on, and several feet of snow accumulated on the mountain slopes above. An enormous mass was loosened, by its own weight, no doubt, and rushed over the precipice in an avalanche. The servants' tents were quite close under the rocks, the doctor's a little farther out. His body was found subsequently some distance off, with his bed, etc., but the tent remained where it was, crushed and broken. The body was found only half covered with snow. It is singular that the body and furniture were found at a distance from the tent. The occupants of the servants' tent were found dead in the position in which they were sleeping. Two coolies who had been sent for supplies to Sórú tried to return with them, but the storm drove them down again. They crossed five days after, and, finding no trace of the camp, inferred that the sahib had gone to Súknis, but, finding he was not there, came back with twenty men and discovered the camp buried under the snow. Many years before this another Englishman and his party were buried under an avalanche in the Múngil nálá, Wardwan valley, as they were returning in the evening from hunting ibex. Considering the number of men who, year after year, travel about in the Himálayas, it is wonderful that so few fatal accidents have been recorded.

I was now on the watershed of the Chináb, and everything was changed. The hillsides were carpeted with grass, and the first clump of birch-trees graced the farther bank just in front of my tent-door. The next camp was Pajahoi, opposite the opening of the Wishni-waj valley. I made my first attempt after bears here, but was unsuccessful. Shepherds and sheep were about, and I heard of a sahib and mem-sahib in a nálá lower down; so not only had the stag season opened, but the sportsman (and his wife) were up and after them. At this camp the tent was soaking wet with dew in the morning: I never saw dew in Ladakh. I reached Súknis on the 22nd of September, and from this point began my hunt after stag and bear.

Oh for the good times of twenty years ago, when stags and bears in the Kashmir valleys were less rare than they are now, and the sportsman had not to work so hard for a couple of good heads and half a dozen brown bear skins! He then simply "raced" for his valley, and, if his head shikári was a good intriguer, got in first. He pitched his camp low down, where it remained fixed, while he, with a very small following, roughed it higher up on the grassy slopes, and shot his game at his leisure. When he wanted a rest, he came down to his main camp for a couple of days. Now the best shooting ground is strictly preserved, and where access is allowed, "shootists" (not sportsmen) simply jostle one another, running out long distances on receipt of information, and then running back after the quarry has been shot or missed.

I had to do some hard tramping and climbing before I bagged two stags with very ordinary heads, and two brown bears, which in these days may be considered a good reward for three weeks of very severe and continuous work.

As soon as I reached Súknis, I heard of three bears, and crossed the stream to the left bank for them, but I never had the luck to come across the animals, though traces were frequent on the paths and hillsides. There was one particular old male whom the villagers had known for years, and they were most anxious that he should be wiped out, for his ravages among their crops were very serious; and since he had imported a couple of females to keep him company, their presence had become intolerable. The old Bruin was completely master of the situation after sunset. Shouting, tom-tomming, torches and fires had no terrors for him; he simply went where he liked, wandered about all night, and in the grey dawn retired up the valley with his harem, to repose quietly during the heat of the day. I was shown the path used by these animals night after night; the soft earth was worn into oblong holes by the bears' feet, and the bushes alongside had torn hair from their fat sides. The men with me worked hard, but they could not hit off the hiding-place of the big bear. These animals probably travelled several miles morning and evening, and perhaps lived in another valley. I was unable to waste many days over them, as the stag-forest was yet some distance down, and I was anxious to begin business there.

I took my camp down to the village of Basmin, seven miles below Súknis, and thence took twenty-five coolies for a beat on the slopes overlooking the right bank of the Wardwan river. We first went down a couple of miles, and then worked up a wooded spur for three hours, and an awful grind it was. Just as I got placed, and the men were moving to their several points, a stag called in the forest opposite, about four hundred yards away—the first call I had heard that season (date, 25th September). I had taken a few mouthfuls of breakfast, but stopped in a hurry as the welcome sound reached my ear, and went up hill to get above the stag. He called about four times. We had not been gone long when there was a tremendous shout from the coolies, a short distance below the animal: they had come upon some hinds! We returned crestfallen to our former position—but I did not resume my breakfast. Nothing came of this beat, nor of the next one, so I gave up in disgust, and was coming down hill when a coolie started a stag that was lying at the foot of a pine-tree. This is nearly always the result of driving in Kashmir when a single sportsman tries to circumvent these deer. Against my better judgment, I was induced to try this one by the Kashmiri shikári I had hired from the village; he knew where the stags were, and went straight to the place with this body of men to turn them out before the muzzle of my rifle. He wished to save me trouble, he said! He had, however, increased my troubles by, at anyrate, two days' extra toil up and down the steep hillsides to find he disturbed the game by still-hunting. I gave up the beating business on the spot, and vowed never to have

"BOUNDING THROUGH THE GLADE."

anything more to do with that kind of sport again. There were evidently several stags in the forest—signs and forms were numerous. There was trouble in the camp next day about supplies, and I had to remain there making arrangements till three in the afternoon. I was eventually obliged to write to the police officer at Maryo, two days' march down the valley, to send me help. The *rasad* (supplies) difficulty is a frequently recurring one in this country; villagers are not willing to sell goods when their long winter, a season of semi-starvation, is close at hand. I started in the evening with two coolies and a local man, with food and bedding, for a good hunt after stags. On the way we met a man who said four shots had been fired on the hillside I was making for; the local man with me said it must be the Siddík of Gurdraman, a village above Nowbúg, who had a gun (an old rifle); he had been shooting in Múngil. I met him afterwards near Súknis, coming my way; but I could hardly believe the story of the four shots, so went on and camped at dusk high up in a dry watercourse, where we were belated, as we had spent a long time getting over a very difficult place just below. Water was very scarce, but we eventually discovered a little in a rocky hole. We started at six A.M. next day, and, after a short pull up hill, saw a stag crossing an open glade high above us; he soon got our wind and bounded off prettily into the nearest birch clump. The rising sun caught his flank, and the inside of his left thigh flashed the rays back to us almost with the brilliancy of a mirror. We saw nothing more that morning, and made camp at the foot of a fine old pine-tree in the heart of the stag ground. This was really a comfortable, not to say luxurious, abode compared with the narrow watercourse where we had passed the night. Firewood was abundant, the shade was very welcome, and the invigorating pine-scented air filled my lungs. In the evening we went out and watched the open hillside for a stag. For two hours we saw and heard nothing; the sun went down behind the range, the evening breath of the forest grew colder and colder, and my thoughts turned longingly towards the cheerful log-fire and the meal awaiting me. My appetite grew keener, and at last persuaded me to leave just at the very time a stag was likely to appear. I lay down, at length, before the fire, and was getting comfortably warm, when a stag roared in the very direction whence we had just come.

We were not two hundred yards from the open glade, and we covered that distance in record time, though the shadows were dark and the ground was by no means level. The local man led the way and spied the stag, from the edge of the forest, crossing the open towards a spring farther down. I tried hard to get a view, but could not see the beast. Darkness was fast coming on, and the surrounding forest made darker the clearing which the stag was crossing. He must have winded or seen us, for he went back at once the way he came, but slowly, and called again. We raced round the hillside, and at last I caught sight of him going at a leisurely pace towards the opposite wooded slope. I took steady aim with the Winchester, and heard the shot tell. He disappeared in the bottom of the depression, and we waited to see if he would appear on the opposite slope; there was no sign of him, and I made sure he was down. So we went on cautiously, and discovered him lying on the level, facing us. It was now almost dark. If he rose and went only a few yards into the forest, we were certain to lose him; so I fired again and missed. The stag sprang up and made for the forest, but I had just time to give him another shot, which dropped him as he entered the birch bushes—a most lucky shot. The two men with me rushed down for the halál, but to their horror they could not find the animal in the darkness, and their hopes of lawful meat for supper began to fade. But they did find him at last, guided by his dying struggles. Then they shouted that two men could not perform the ceremony, by reason of the animal's struggles and because it was so dark. One of the coolies from the camp, who had brought up the double Express on hearing my first shot, was still with me, and when the shikáris shouted that they could not cut the beast's throat between them, the absurdity of it quite upset that coolie; he roared with laughter, jumped about on one leg and then on the other, bit his hand and arm to keep himself from laughing, and behaved so comically altogether that he set me off too. The idea that two strong men should be unable to halál a dying stag was so funny to this simple villager that it nearly sent him into hysterics. When he was sufficiently recovered, he went to help, and I returned to the fire, much elated with a stroke of luck which I certainly did not deserve, after deserting the hillside at the very time that brings the chance of a shot. I had a rough camp dinner, drank to my luck in a tin pot of hot Swiss milk, in default of anything stronger, and turned in. Next morning I took the measurements of my trophy. Length of horns, 37 and $35\frac{1}{2}$ inches; girth above brow antler, 7 inches; divergency at tips, $38\frac{1}{4}$ inches; tines, 10.

This is very near the size that Ward says (page 65) "should be considered a prize worth working for." The divergency seems small, compared with that of the largest Ward had seen—fifty and fifty-six inches. The body of the stag was short, sturdy, and compact, quite different from the shape of the huge animals that are shot in the valleys on the Kashmir side. The more rigorous climate of the Wardwan valley, and the harder life, I suspect, tend to give this compactness of body, which is more suitable to their surroundings. The first shot that hit was a solid Winchester bullet of soft lead weighing 330 grs: it struck him behind the right kidney, which it severed, went through the stomach, and was found under the skin on the left side, having passed through the small ribs; this was good penetration. The second shot, fired at him on the ground facing me, carried away one of the brow antlers—a great misfortune; the third, when he was among the birch bushes, broke his back.

I remained in this valley four days longer, and worked hard for another trophy, but was not successful. Stags were by no means numerous, though I heard a call now and then, and came on tracks frequently; also their wallows where they had rolled in the mud and torn up the ground round about. Their travels in search of hinds had begun; they moved about so much that meeting them became a mere chance. I gave up the chase after those four days and went back to Súknis.

I left that village next day to cross over into Kashmir. I had ten coolies and a local shikári, who promised me bear on the road, and perhaps a stag on the other side. The path led up straight from the village, and the ascent to the top of the pass was long, and sometimes steep; the pass itself is a depression leading into the Kassal valley, an extensive one with a considerable stream running down to the village of Basmin. We camped in a grassy plain, below a large rock, across the stream. I got my first bear on this march. Signs were abundant and fresh after the ascent began, the animals having dug up the pathway in several places in search of roots. All these upper valleys must be good for brown bear, but for a long time Bruin in person did not appear. At eleven o'clock I was breakfasting on the hillside, when Kamál Shikári got the first view of him digging on the hillside to the right, about a mile off. Before we could get near him, he had gone down over to the other slope and was out of sight, and the wind changed. But the bear luckily was at the bottom of the valley, and so the wind for once was in our favour. We found that the bear was having a bath in the stream, and he seemed to enjoy it extremely; the sun was very hot, and I envied him. After several rolls in the water, he came out and wiped himself vigorously on the grass, especially under the neck, which showed the white collar distinctly. Then he shook himself and frisked about, and again betook himself to the more serious business of searching for grubs, gradually ascending the opposite slope. We worked cautiously down and then up, eventually catching him up; but he was constantly moving, and, though I had him covered several times, I could not get a good chance. At last he stopped for a moment, broadside on, a little above me and about fifty yards off, when I gave him a solid bullet from the Winchester, on receipt of which he bolted down the hill and round towards my right. I lost sight of him at once, on account of the slope and the huge rocks about; so ran to get a view. Unfortunately, a huge rock prevented my seeing the bear, and the bear from seeing us. He came full tilt in our direction till he passed the rock on my right, certainly not five yards off; then he stopped suddenly, gave a loud grunt, and stood up on his hind legs. We were very much taken aback at this sudden apparition; and Kamál, the shikári, standing next to me, improved the situation by uttering a loud cry, throwing up his hands, and falling on his back, just like a woman. The "whoof!" of the bear had knocked him over, but the animal had no idea of attacking. Before I could fire, he had turned round and was off like the wind up the slope. I had to run out and get clear of the rock before I could fire, by which time the bear was nearly fifty yards away, but another bullet cut short his career, and he subsided on the spot. Kamál regained his legs and his senses as the rifle cracked the second time. When he saw the result of the shot, he ran up to the dead animal and fired volleys of abuse at him: the Kashmiri shikári all over. I daresay he was not afraid, but the suddenness of the rencontre quite upset him. He *said* his foot slipped! Shortly after, he pretended to become seriously ill while crossing the pass—the Kashmiri again. The Kashmiri is the oddest mixture of childishness, cunning, bluster, and swagger; they are also perfect at skulking and shamming. The best plan is to ignore their groans and pantomime of suffering; if they complain, offer them their wages and tell them to go home.

I was unfortunate in the weather again at this place; we were literally snowed up for two days and could not move. After forty-eight hours' continuous snow it was twelve inches deep about the tent. The coolies had finished their stock of food, and, fearful of being snowed up, clamoured for a start. So I was obliged to move down towards Kashmir. It was a great disappointment, for signs of bear were numerous, and I made certain of making a good bag after the weather cleared. During all this snowy time a single snipe had been lying up by the stream close to my tent; I heard his plaintive "scape, scape," often, day and night, as if he too were protesting against the ghastly weather. I put him as I started, and he flew off in the direction we were taking, evidently having made up his mind to clear out, as I had done. Bear tracks were fresh in the snow, all in the direction we were going,—even they had a poor opinion of the weather! We gradually ascended to the foot of another

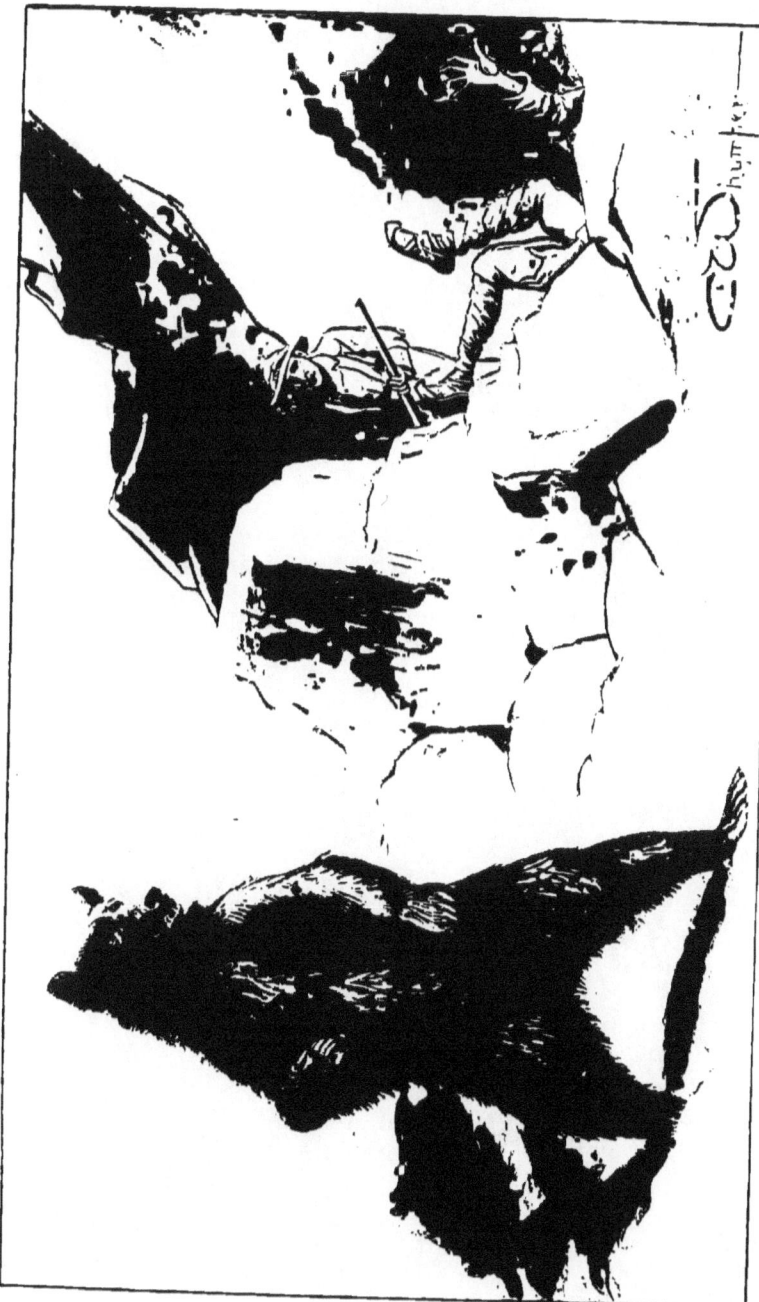

"HE STOOD UP ON HIS HIND LEGS."

pass: the way was rocky, but not steep. On the other side was a steep descent of a mile or so to the Lang-nai —a long and narrow valley. There was very little snow on this side. We camped at the huts of some Gújars. The weather was bad again that night, and in the morning the snow fell very heavily: it was thick on the pines and birches in the hanging forest across the gorge— a beautiful winter scene, seen dimly through the falling flakes. All day it snowed, and all day I snuggled under the blankets: the coolies, too, in the huts were fairly comfortable. Next morning it had cleared up, so we made a start; but the little tent had to be left behind, as it was frozen and too stiff to pack. By two o'clock I reached Lidú, where I found Yakúb and the large tent, from Srinagar. I found that the sporting colonel, who was before me in Chang-chen-mo, had forestalled me here also; he left the village five days before my arrival. He got a stag here, but, I was told, his shikáris shot the animal!

I stayed at home for two days, had a good rest, and then went up again into a valley next the Lang-nai, by which I had come down, to make a final try for bear and stag. After five days' hard work I got one of each, and was quite satisfied.

I arrived at Srinagar on the 20th of October, and remained there a week, collecting and packing up my trophies, then made a start for the plains by tonga dâk—Yakúb following with Chamúrti and the traps. The pony had fared well during this long and rough journey, though he was on short commons so often, and had had many adventures in his own line: the most serious was his fall from an unsafe bridge on the way from Ladakh. The man who was leading him knew the frail nature of the bridge, but he also knew that the water was very cold, so he chanced the bridge, and Chamúrti fell over, but the man got across dryshod—his bones somehow must have ached for some days after! The pony was not in the least hurt, though the drop could not have been less than twenty feet, and he turned completely over, legs up, and fell on his back. He was up in an instant, came out of the water, shook himself like a dog, and promptly turned to on the grass! The saddle was seriously damaged, but was still serviceable. I think it was the saddle that saved Chamúrti a broken back. Yákúb wound up the tour in style. When he reached his native town, his friends, including several nondescript nawabs (nobles), gave a banquet in his honour. Of course he was well plied with liquor, and the narrative of his adventures in the far-off land from which he had just returned must have inflamed his naturally quarrelsome disposition. At anyrate there was a row before the feast was finished, and little Yákúb distinguished himself by clearing the banquet-hall of hosts and friends alike. He always carried a light Gurkha *kukri* (knife) in his belt—he used to say he was so small that he wanted something to protect himself with. On this festive occasion that kukri came to the fore, and the guests disappeared like the smoke from their own hukkas. Then Yákúb, mad with fury or drink, got into the street, was disarmed by the police and bestowed in the lock-up—whence I had to bail him out at midnight. I had subsequently to part with him, on account of weakness for liquor. He then tried his fortune in the Central Provinces, came back, got among his nawab set again, and in six months drank himself to death. I am afraid the distinguished company he kept was his ruin. At anyrate they deprived me of a servant whose like I shall never see again.

PART III

BEHIND THE HIMALAYAS—A PEEP INTO TIBET

CHAPTER XVI

THE BASPA VALLEY

A three months' tour—Description of the valley—The river—Villages—People—Climate—Theóg—Mattiana—Saráhan—Meet my friend—Rájah of Basáhir—He has tiffin—Is a keen sportsman—Well educated in English—Kilba—Headquarters of Forest officer—Large staff of woodcutters—How they are fed—Lay in my supplies—How I managed my transport—Enter the Baspa valley—Villages on the road—The course of the river—A transformation scene—Sángla village—The level valley—An ancient lake—The passes—Sheep—Sheep-stages—Difference between Tibetan and Himálayan sheep—The upper valley and river—Bad road—Miserable huts—Wild women—More information regarding passes, roads, etc.—Chitkúl.

ONE summer I obtained three months' leave, and determined to devote it to a shooting trip in the upper valley of the Baspa river. In Ward's *Sportsman's Guide to Kashmir* a sketch is given of this trip, and the sport likely to be had in that part of the Himálayas; and this induced me to go in that direction. As I eventually crossed from the valley into a corner of Tibet never before visited by Europeans, some account of my journey may be of interest, though I cannot say that my expedition was successful as regards sport.

The Baspa and its long valley are not generally known, being quite off the beaten track, and rarely visited except by a stray sportsman or a forest officer on duty. The Baspa stream runs into the Sutlej about fifteen miles above the Wángtú bridge on the latter and a few miles below the large village of Chíni. A glance at the map of Basáhir will show that an enormous snowy spur, or rather range, springs from the main buttress of the Tibetan highlands, and runs down almost straight to the Sutlej below the above-named bridge. The main range, or Tibetan buttress, extends in a northerly direction as far as the frontier village of Shipki, where it is pierced by the Sutlej. The great angle formed by these snowy mountains is subtended by that river from Shipki to the Wángtú bridge—the Baspa valley forming the south-westerly portion of this enormous triangle. Its length from the source of the stream to its junction with the Sutlej is not less than fifty miles, and its breadth—that is to say, the level portion of the valley through which the river runs—nowhere exceeds two miles, while in many places it is less than one. Villages are few; the population is scanty. Twenty miles above Sángla the principal village is Chitkúl, the highest inhabited point in the valley.

Owing to its position between two lofty ranges of perpetual snow, the climate of the valley is severe for at least nine months of the year. The inhabitants are a mean and mongrel lot, for whom existence must have very few joys, and whose life, to an outsider at least, appears not worth living. On their southern border their neighbours are the high-spirited and high-handed Garhwális, and on the northeastern they have the exclusive Tibetans. The Baspa people carry on the trade between these two peoples, and are bullied by each in return. The Garhwális supply the rice and other commodities which the Baspa men take to

Tibet and exchange for the wool and salt of that country. They have also, it seems, to propitiate the Rájah of Garhwál by annual offerings, in addition to the dues paid to their legitimate ruler, the Rájah of Basáhir. Moreover, it often happens, in the upper portions of the valley, that the one annual crop yielded by the soil is destroyed by an early winter; when the miserable people are frequently left dependent on the doubtful profits of their trading and the produce of their flocks of sheep. The struggle for existence is extremely hard, as the wretched appearance of the people fully attests.

I had sent my travelling kit on ahead some days before. So, finding everything ready for a start, I walked out of Simla before sunrise on the 2nd of May. I made two marches, and slept at Theóg. Next day I reached Mattiana, having met on the way two Bhótias (Tibetans) returning to their village near Chíni. One of them had been to Gartokh, in Tibet, three months ago. He told me it was a seven days' journey from Shipki, and that he had shot two wild yak on the way, and had seen many *Ovis ammon*. According to his statement, a couple of Europeans could travel anywhere beyond Shipki, without hindrance; he was quite positive on this point, and volunteered to take me. A large party, he said, would not be allowed. This was curious, as the experience of every European who has attempted to cross into Tibet has been just the reverse. I got this information out of the Bhótia only after much questioning, as his intelligence was limited. At Saráhan my friend M. of the Forest Department came in—a most pleasant surprise, for, though I was making for his headquarters on the Sutlej, I had no hope of meeting him for some days. His Highness Shamsher Singh, Rájah of Basáhir, whose summer residence is here, paid my friend a visit during the day, and was very friendly and pleasant. He spoke English well, and seemed fairly educated and intelligent, but was rather deaf. He was a small old man, and rumour said he drank deeply. On the present occasion, however, he declined whisky, saying this was not the time of the year for it; soda-water, pure, was the proper drink now. But there was a twinkle in his eye as he defined the seasons for drink. He stayed to lunch, and put away the chicken cutlets with evident relish, though he ate with his hands, sending after for the *chilamchi* (brass wash-hand bowl) when he had finished, and having a thorough wash-up at the table. The whole performance was indeed quite a revelation in this land of caste prejudices. The Rájah is a keen sportsman, and takes great interest in guns and weapons of all kinds. I obtained his signature to the two *purwánas* (permits) I had procured at Rámpúr, and he signed his name in English.

I halted at Kilba for a couple of days to rest and to make ' final arrangements. This village is the headquarters of the Deputy Conservators of Forests. Woodcutting is carried on to a considerable extent; and as most of the labour has to be imported from the plains, a large number of men are always scattered among the forests, for whom provisions have to be supplied by the Forest Department, from Rámpúr, or even farther. The carriage of these supplies takes some days, and when, through any unforeseen circumstance, delay occurs and the stock of food runs low, the scattered men are in some danger of being starved. Villages are so few, and the population so scanty, that the people have little to spare for strangers, and consequently Government has to undertake the feeding of its employés.

The difficulty of obtaining supplies is a never-ending annoyance to the tourist or sportsman in the Himálayas. Long experience had impressed this on me, so I set about collecting my supplies, and received most kind and valuable help from my friend. In fact, but for his assistance, not only now, but during the whole time I remained in the Baspa valley, my journey would have been impossible. I was not long in collecting the food and other necessaries I required; he also made over to me four Balti coolies to carry my luggage, and promised four more as soon as a party arrived from Simla. I thus had eight men during the whole period of my trip, and was freed to a very great extent from the difficulties of local carriage. The traveller's principal aim is to be as independent as possible of both local carriage and supplies in that part of the country where he intends to pass most of his time. If he is fully equipped in these respects, his presence will not inconvenience the people, and he may depend on their good-will and assistance.

I was advised to collect supplies from each village I passed. In this way, by the time I reached my shooting grounds beyond the last village, I had enough to last me to the end of my trip. Myself, three servants, and eight coolies, made twelve mouths to feed, and the consumption would be about nine seers (2 lbs.) of flour and three seers of other eatables, or twelve seers per diem—nine maunds (80 lbs.) for a month. Half of this quantity I obtained from my friend's stores, and it was not difficult to make up the other moiety from the villages as I passed along.

I began my long tramp on the 13th of May. M. accompanied me to below the village of Sápni, and then returned, leaving me to my own resources. The Baspa is a large clear stream where it falls into the Sutlej, a pleasant contrast to the muddy current of the latter. The valley is very confined here, and the hillsides are very abrupt. I saw a brace of Kólsa pheasants and a number of very pretty small birds, one species with very long and slender white tail-feathers. I have seen them at times in the plains in wooded country during the cold months, so that these little mites must be great travellers; they are very quick in their movements, flashing through the green foliage like white lightning: I have never seen one in a state of rest. I passed Chánsu—or rather the fields below it, that are on a large piece of flat ground, which ends in a precipice facing the river. The edge of the precipice is lined by splendid deodars, the roots of which are so interlaced with the soil that they prevent the land from crumbling away into the river. It is wonderful how these large trees retain their hold in such a place; if one fell, it would go straight down into the river several hundred feet below. The road traveller to-day passes through cool and pleasant forests all the way; but the valley is so confined, and the hillsides so abrupt, that there is no extensive view in any direction, until a sudden transformation scene takes place at the bridge over the Baspa, a couple of miles before reaching the village of Sángla. Some distance before coming to the bridge, the river dashes down its steep and rocky bed in frightful turmoil, resembling a river of milk churned into foam. Nothing could be better calculated to enhance the surprise that is awaiting you as you come round a mountain spur to the bridge. The furious torrent with its deafening roar shows the turbulence of a Himálayan river in its roughest mood, from the bridge. On your left, whence you have come, the raging waters disappear; on your right, a broad and limpid stream gently murmurs over its pebbly bed. Looking up stream, the valley is seen broad and open, the hillsides covered with forest, and higher up topped by a snowy range; on the left, bare and forbidding mountains edged with rugged and pointed peaks. In front flows the now placid stream, and, farther on, level fields, thickly dotted with spreading

SANGLA VILLAGE

walnut-trees. Walking through the fields along the footpath, the village of Kamru comes in sight, high up on the hillside, also the Rájah's "Kot," or fort—a conspicuous object, black and grimy from age, smoke, and dirt. The houses of Sángla are just visible through the walnut-trees, a long way off on a spur—the camping-place. Tradition has it that this portion of the country was in former ages a lake; and the country round shows every indication of the truth of the legend. The head-man of Sángla refers to the river in ordinary conversation as *Samúndar* (sea), and there is a temple dedicated to Nág-deota (the serpent deity) in the village. The sudden change in the course of the river at the bridge indicates very clearly the point where the lake burst through and made its way to the Sutlej. A couple of hundred pounds of dynamite, used now on the hillside near the bridge, would certainly close the passage again and re-form the lake above.

I experienced here a decided difference in the climate—I felt really cold in bed during the night! Walking through the village in the morning, I visited the Nág-deota and Láma temples, and noticed an array of stags' antlers and barhal horns in the public buildings between the two. The head-man of the village, by name Dhián Dás, and the pújári (priest) of the Nág temple, are intelligent men, and gave information about the passes without any hesitation. They told me that the Garhwál passes were open, but no traders had come across yet. The "China" (Chinese, meaning Tibetan) passes would not be fit for travel for another month. These men said it was twenty days' journey from this to the place in Tibet where they go with their rice to trade. They mean "sheep journeys," which are short stages—the most the laden sheep can do in a day, grazing as they march. These short stages are called by the people of the country "*ádhi-róti*," or half-a-cake journey—a very expressive term. The Sángla people buy rice from the Garhwál traders, and, loading it up on their sheep in small bags, take it to Tibet, where they barter it for wool and salt: the former article, they said, was now very dear. A very curious reason was given in explanation of the fact that Tibetans do not come to trade in this direction: their sheep, it was said, cannot cross passes, filing along narrow mountain tracks, one after the other. This is because they are plains sheep, accustomed to wander in "open order" on the flat table-lands of their mountain home! If they were driven along a narrow track, they would huddle over each other and would come to grief.

I did a good trade here, and was now not at all anxious about running short of supplies during my stay in the upper valley.

There are two, if not three, level stretches of land at the bottom of the valley, like steps descending from the country above. The river runs broad and smooth along the level, and then cuts its way by a narrow channel through the steep slope down to the next plain. To me it appeared that these steps were at one time a succession of lakes, connected by a streamlet, and that their waters were gathered eventually in the largest and lowest, above the present site of the bridge. When the opening to the Sutlej was formed, all these mountain lakelets were sucked dry by the big river, and in the course of ages the Baspa cut through the soil and formed its present deep channel. The hill slopes are well wooded, and small forests of pines and other trees are frequent in the valley, but I saw none of large girth. Approaching Rakcham, the path changes to every variety common to mountain tracks—over slippery granite rocks, then along several log bridges, across chasms between huge boulders; and at two places, notched logs, by way of ladders, to ascend masses of rock on one side and to descend from them on the other. These specimens of a Himálayan road occur within a space of two hundred yards. Those of us who wore boots or shoes had to take them off and climb barefooted. Just below this break-neck path is Rakcham itself, a black and grimy village of half a dozen wooden houses, planted in several feet of foul mud. Most of the miserable huts are built against the rock: these are filthy in the extreme, and the inhabitants are filthier still. The women are extraordinarily timid. Whenever I met them on the road, or even passed them at a distance working in a field, they invariably took to flight, and hid behind rocks and trees till I was out of sight—for all the world like wild animals, from which, I am sure, they were not many degrees removed. It was very cold and cloudy in the evening. The elevation of Rakcham is 10,445 feet.

There was slight rain in the night and snow on the mountain-tops. The morning was pleasant, but foggy, much warmer than the previous evening. After 2 P.M. the cold rapidly increases, as from that hour the wind generally begins to blow down from the snows, and lowers the temperature considerably. A trader from Rám-Serai, in Garhwál, who came over with rice twelve days ago by the Rúpin Pass, said the passage was not difficult. Rám-Serai is eight marches from Rakcham. My informant professed ignorance of the names of the stages in Tibetan territory! Even in this remote corner, the exclusiveness of China is felt and respected. This man, no doubt, had been warned by the Tibetans to give no help or information regarding the country beyond the pass; all I could get out of him was that the country is bare and stony, and that sheep are not grazed there.

I left Rakcham at 9 P.M. and reached Chitkúl at 1 P.M.,

seven miles. The road runs along the right side of the valley, ascending and descending the hill slopes. The forests were thinner and the trees smaller; I noticed stunted birches growing on the level of the valley for the first time. It was rainy and foggy in the evening, after a sunless day. Barhal are said to be found farther on. I prepared for a start with a light camp, leaving most of my things in charge of a servant at Chitkúl, in a house I got from the head-man.

CHAPTER XVII

THE UPPER BASPA

Bad weather—A plurality of fathers—"Garókchs"—The village god—How he was propitiated—Proceed to the upper valley—My first barhal-stalk—A "bootless" tramp—A good shot—Anparh, the shikári, is not wasteful—The side valleys of the Upper Baspa—Dangerous pathway—A stone-shoot—Narrow escape of my servant—Balti coolies behave well—A chance at a ram—A good shot—The wily ram shelves himself—Yákúb's ascent after lawful mutton—The ram is perverse—Halálcd at last—"Never again," says Yákúb—A grand panorama—Anparh's tactics—Temperature of the valley—Heavy snowstorm—Elevation of the camp—Of the Gúgérang Pass—Tibetans and their sheep—An ugly specimen of humanity—I fall ill—Uncertain weather continues—Flowers peep out with doubting hearts—Indisposition, blue devils, collapse—A quick recovery.

It snowed during the night, and next morning all the valley was white and the tents covered. At six o'clock the thermometer marked 36°. The bad weather was unfortunate, as it delayed my progress, but it had this advantage, that it would drive the game lower down, and stalking would be a much easier business. It began to snow again at half-past seven, but I arranged with the *garókchs* (priest) to go with me after barhal; he was the son of the man that M. recommended me to take. The father went out with my friend when he came up here last year, and I was informed that he was dead, but the priest now told me that *that was another father!* This puzzled me a good deal, and inspired my Musalmán servants with horror and disgust. The fact is, polyandry is rampant in this valley; and it is impossible for a son, be he ever so wise, to know his own father within, say, half a dozen, or whatever the number of the brothers in the family may be! In this instance a father had died, but not the one known to my friend.

The word "garókehs" is an awful one to pronounce; it means the priest, or the man in charge of the village god. The nearest approach to it in English is as I have spelt it, but the proper pronunciation of the word is impossible to an unaccustomed tongue without danger to the muscles of that organ. The man who volunteered to come with me was strong, intelligent, and keen on shikár; but he said the *deota* (god) of the village must be propitiated before we could hope for sport. M., he informed me, went out and got nothing; then he made an offering of two rupees to the god, and immediately had excellent sport. This logic was irresistible; I gave in at once.

All arrangements being reported complete, I went down to the village, had the deota taken out of his abode, and asked him to be kind. He was brought out in a sedan chair fixed on two long and flexible poles, like the familiar jhampán of the hill stations. It was made of red cloth with a silver roof embossed with faces; above this was an umbrella-shaped construction, with long locks of hair taken from yaks' tails. The chair was carried by two men, backwards and forwards, a few paces in front of the priest, my future shikári's father. When the god came opposite him, the chair was shaken violently up and down and then inclined towards the priest; this was done twice. On the second occasion my servant offered two rupees to the son, who was standing close by. He mumbled something, meaning, I suppose, that it was not enough—so one rupee more was placed in his hand. He then took the money to his father; the god was shaken more violently than ever, and brought to a standstill. The priest bent down and seemed to have a conversation with the god. After this the son approached and told me that the deota was *rázi* (propitiated), that I was at liberty to go anywhere, and I should get good sport. Of course their music accompanied these holy functions—two big drums and a brass pot. The god had a firm seat on his chair; the shakings he got made me anxious lest he should tumble out, and such an accident would perhaps have been fatal to my prospects.

The next march brought me up close to the barhal ground, and I sighted a flock for the first time, but they were high up in a grassy valley, and it was too late in the day to attempt a stalk. We met a large flock of sheep from Garhwál, that had crossed the Barású Pass the day before. They were bringing rice to Chitkúl. The village god, whose name, by the way, is Mathi, was taken to-day to Rakcham, to bring rain, which was wanted for the crops. The day was sunny and hot at times; then windy, rainy, and cold. The rain came from the upper valley and passed down towards Rakcham; so Mathi scored.

We started at five o'clock on a very cold morning, and went straight up from camp after the barhal sighted last evening. The ascent took us first up a stony nálá and then along a hillside that became steeper at every yard, but at last we got up to the snow. I had on an old pair of boots with soles as slippery as glass; my progress was not at all satisfactory, and soon, in fact, became dangerous. I had at last to take my boots off and trust to my stockinged feet. I felt much safer, but on the sharp points of the frozen soil I feared my soles would be cut to pieces. We were, however, near the ground where the wild sheep had been sighted, and excitement kept me up. No traces of

the animals could be found, so we went up farther, crossing
the steep sides of two more ravines. At last the barhal
were sighted on a slope above us, grazing along towards
the snow. We crept along until we came to a rocky
ridge, beyond which we could not go without instant
discovery. A ravine full of snow lay between us and the
game—distance about two hundred yards. At first only
ewes were sighted; they were evidently alarmed, for they
were moving off in their usual leisurely way. Suddenly
Anparh, the shikári, called out, "*Ménda, sáhib, ménda*"
(a ram, sir, a ram), and I spotted him following the five
ewes. He was going up very slowly, and whenever he
stopped he had his tail towards me—he did not seem to
understand the alarm of the females. Something must have
frightened them, but evidently they had not seen us yet.
At last the ram stood for a moment showing his left side.
I fired and missed. He then turned, went up some distance, and stood again, giving me a slanting shot at his
right shoulder. This time I hit him in the small ribs, the
bullet passing up towards his neck. He walked up a few
yards and then rolled down dead. The distance could not
have been less than 250 yards. The sun was facing me,
and I could hardly see the foresight through the glare, so
had little hope of making a good shot; but I had a rest to
fire from, and the Henry Express shot up to the mark.
Yákúb, who had accompanied me, was disappointed about
the halál; he shook his head as he scanned the ground
between himself and the dead game, and let the meat go
with a sigh of regret. The coolie went across and rolled
the ram down to the snow, and then dragged it along to us.
It was skinned and cut up on the snow. Anparh and his
companion did not waste a morsel; he first cut the tes-
ticles off and put them carefully by in his waistband; he
even made an attempt to collect the blood in the emptied

paunch, to the horror of Yakúb, who called him a vulture. The horns measured only 16½ inches—not worth keeping—and all the hair was coming off the skin. The beast's age, according to the rings on the horns, would be eight years, and they were small for a ram of that age.

My feet were not cut, not even the soles of the stockings, much to my surprise, after the agony I had suffered; I had made certain of being laid up for several days. It would be a great thing to be able to walk barefoot when occasion required, but the practice necessary to acquire this accomplishment would be an experience that few, I imagine, would undertake.

I was out again at 5 A.M. on the hillsides between Dwárea and Chitkúl; we went up steadily for four hours, and at last sighted three barhal, but in such a situation that we could not get at them until they crossed a ridge. When we got up to the same point, no living thing was in sight. Somehow we had made a mess of the stalk, though it appeared an easy enough one. I concluded that one of the ewes of the flock had been acting sentry on the ridge, and gave the alarm as soon as we showed ourselves. The view we had of the snowy valley opposite was the grandest I had seen here yet; it is like an amphitheatre topped by white peaks all round, and the level bottom also covered with snow.

Up the valley the stream comes round a tremendous precipice, and the path follows it on the right bank. Farther on, the track passes along the steep and crumbling slope of mountain—an awkward path, as we discovered. Stones, large and small, were continually falling from above, and we were obliged to run back the first time we tried to cross this dangerous bit. The bad footing compelled slow progress, but the frequency of stone showers recommended speed. It was a ticklish undertaking, but we managed to dodge across, untouched by sundry projectiles which came whizzing down. The Balti coolies, though carrying heavy loads, crossed nimbly, timing their passage by keeping a steady watch above. The stones seemed to be detached by the wind, which raged in fierce gusts along the crest above us. The fall of a fairly large stone could be followed by the puffs of dust as it ricocheted down the hillside. Only one coolie and the khidmatgár remained to cross. Just as they came to the dangerous bit, we saw a fall of stones coming, and shouted to them to go back. The coolie returned promptly, but the fool of a khidmatgár, after retreating one step, lost his head and stood stock-still. We, not forty yards from him, watched the stones hurling past on both sides of him, but by marvellous luck not one touched him! The man just turned his back on the hillside and stood screwed up while the shower lasted; but the fright dazed him, and when the danger was over he would not move until, shouting having failed, a coolie went and led him across. It would not have required a large stone to knock him over into the river fifty yards below, where he must have been drowned. The four Baltis were capital fellows: they carried enormous loads, were extremely willing, and put their hands to everything in camp. As we were reaching the camping-place, Súancho by name, some likely barhal ground came in view, and I started on ahead with Anparh. Shortly after, we sighted nine wild sheep coming along the hillside towards us; we went on to meet them, but they soon got suspicious, and went back. Anparh said they were coming down for a drink.

At six o'clock next morning we made a start up a narrow gully, then up very steep, crumbling, stony slopes and steeper grassy hillsides. I stayed at some rocks, and Anparh went about looking for the barhal, but he came back unsuccessful. The coolie at last descried three animals grazing on a distant hillside; they seemed to be ewes, but after breakfast, and when the sheep had gone over the slope, we followed, in hopes of a ram being in the flock. We went down some very bad places and up those tiresome crumbling slopes for an hour, peeped over the ridge, and made a careful survey. No barhal in sight; it was very disappointing, for the climb had been severe. At last Anparh discovered five barhal lying down on a distant ridge, and sharply defined against the sky-line, and oh, ever so much higher than the point we had attained after such fearful toil! I examined the beasts carefully with the telescope, a very powerful one by Steward, and made out five splendid rams—two of them with grand heads; one had apparently only one horn. They were, however, masters of the situation; we could not move an inch beyond the rocks, where we were hiding, without instant detection. Here we remained four hours. This is the kind of thing which tests the patience of the most enduring sportsman. I was scorched by the mid-day sun on one side and cut through by the icy blasts from the snows on the other, till the rams left their secure perch and disappeared. We were just preparing to cross over, when two ewes came over the ridge, some distance below the point where the rams had taken their siesta, and ran down in our direction: we were baulked again. After a time the females disappeared, and at the same moment the old rams came in sight again, and seemed inclined to follow them. So we prepared to descend the ridge on our side and catch them lower down.

But this was not to be. We were just on the move when Yákúb peeped over for a last look and exclaimed, "The rams are running up again!" We were endeavouring to discover the cause of their retreat, when a flock of one ram and five ewes appeared just below us, running up the hillside we overlooked; the latter did not seem to be alarmed, but the wary old rams took the hint at once and returned the way they had come. I then fixed my attention on the flock below, and took a shot at the ram as he stood for a moment about 200 yards off. I had put up the second sight, and the bullet, of course, went over him; but the next shot hit him in the root of the tail as he was going up hill, and stopped him at once. The distance was not less than 250 yards. He went up to some rocks and lay down, evidently very sick. I had four more shots at him in that position about 300 yards off, but failed to touch him. At last Anparh went down, got above him, and drove him towards my right front. He was too badly hurt to go fast, and at last jumped or rolled down to the bottom of the ravine and there remained, for stones failed to move him, and at last we had to go down. As we approached, he slowly mounted some rocks about thirty yards above us, a most difficult climb, and lay down again. I would not fire, as the poor beast was mortally wounded. Though his perch was only a few feet above our heads, it seemed impossible for a biped to reach him. He was dying before our eyes; he lay stretched on the ledge, just broad enough to hold him, while Yákúb, knife in hand, was eyeing him with an expression which eloquently reflected his distress that good mutton should escape his fleshpots, though almost within reach of the arm shaking with eagerness to halál! The temptation was too great; he volunteered to go up if we would give him a hand. It took us about ten minutes to get the man up, and, just as he was getting the knife out of his belt, the ram kicked in his dying throes, and pushed himself over the ledge, falling with a crash to the bottom of the nálá, nearly on our heads. The angry and dis-

"CROUCHED ON THE ROCK ABOVE, KNIFE IN HAND."

appointed Yakúb, crouched on the rock above, knife in hand, glaring down at the carcase, was a picture. But now there was still less time to lose if the mutton was to be made lawful, so we got the little man down as quickly as we could, and the ceremony was performed; it was a mere detail, of course, that the animal was stone dead before the knife touched his throat. As Yakúb wiped his knife on the ram's body, he said, "The Baltis may say what they like, but I am not going to risk my life again to get lawful meat for them!"

It seems that these men, who are all Musalmáns, were greatly scandalised when they discovered that the first ram I had shot had not been halaled, and they spoke feelingly on the subject of good mutton falling into the hands of the heathen. My servant, in a weak moment, promised that the next animal should certainly be fit for orthodox mouths, hence his gallant efforts; but it was his last attempt in the good cause. Ever after, a Balti coolie formed one of my shikár party for the express purpose of halaling bagged game, but my luck was so bad that the man had not many opportunities of using his knife.

We left the carcase on the snow, taking only the head with us down to camp. On my way I came across a frozen waterfall, a beautiful sight. The ram was brought down next morning and cut up. I sent a quarter of wild mutton to my friend's wife at Kilba, whose kindness in looking after my commissariat could not be sufficiently acknowledged. The horns of the ram were $17\frac{1}{2}$ inches in length, and girth at base $11\frac{1}{2}$ inches; they were not worth keeping. The bullet broke the hind leg near the backbone, entirely smashing it; the spine too must have been injured, as the hind-quarters of the animal seemed paralysed when he endeavoured to get away. The bullet was the usual Eley's ·450 Express, driven by five drams of powder.

A No. 3 shot was found in the neck of the ram; Anparh said that people travelling through the valley sometimes bagged wild sheep with shot! Anparh tried his best to allure me back to the village with wonderful tales of enormous rams to be found in the valleys near it. I was too old to be taken in, but allowed him to go home for a couple of days to keep him in good-humour. He was now the most important personage in my party, as he knew the pass and road into Tibet, and could speak the language of that country. I began to see now that there was not two months shikár in this valley—nor even ten days; and I was maturing a plan to steal over the Gúgérang Pass into Tibet, and perhaps, if I was lucky, to get a few shots at *Ovis ammon*. Anparh was my stand-by, but he fought shy of the idea, and displayed great apprehension whenever the subject was broached, even in the most general way. But by cautious handling, and bakshísh, I was sanguine that I and Yákúb would be able to bring him into a proper frame of mind by the day when our dash across the pass was to be made. We therefore humoured him a good deal.

The thermometer at 4 P.M. was 48°, at 8 P.M. 30°, and during the night it fell below freezing point, as a glass of water on the table had a cake of ice on its surface. This was not bad for the end of May at the bottom of the valley, for these temperatures were taken inside the tent. Next morning we went towards Dúnti, on the path up the valley, to look for barhal, but saw nothing. The road was bad in places, but fit for laden coolies. Clouds were hanging about, and the cold increased, and towards evening it came on to snow and rain, the fall on the hill-tops being very heavy. The snow continued through the night, and the tents were covered. The thermometer at 9 P.M. was 28°, at 6 A.M. next morning 26°, and at noon 60°. It cleared up at last, and the cloudless sky was that intense azure seen only from these elevated regions. The snowy mountains looked very brilliant in the bright sunshine, and contrasted beautifully with the intense blue above. A delicious breeze blew up the valley, and my enjoyment was complete as in the evening I went on the back path a couple of miles down the valley, less for game than to meet the post, for which I was getting impatient.

Snow again during the night. Gerard, in his book on Kanáwar and this portion of the Himálayas, says that the fall of the Baspa river is 250 feet per mile, and that Chitkúl village is 11,400 feet high. Súancho, where I was camped ten miles above the village, would therefore be 13,900 feet above sea level, and the Gúgérang Pass, which I intended to cross, not less than 18,000 feet. About 5 P.M. I heard a shepherd's whistle, and, rushing out of the tent to have a look at the new arrivals, found the Jádhs (as the people of the Baspa valley call the Tibetans), with a flock of sheep, had arrived from their country. Anparh had told me they could not possibly be here for twelve days at least. There were eleven men and four hundred sheep. I sent up two of the coolies to bring one of the Tibetans down to the camp, but none would come. When all the sheep had passed, the two last men ventured down, but it was difficult to carry on a conversation. The Balti coolies managed a few words in their own language, but the result was not satisfactory. One of them was a hideous old man with his two front teeth projecting over his lips; the other was a decent and very intelligent-looking young man, much more reserved and dignified than his companion. The latter asked for a smoke, and we gave him some tobacco in a chilam (Indian pipe), which he said was good. They were nine days from their village, the name of which I could

not make out. The young man looked more like a
Chinese Tartar than the old one, and was evidently of a
superior breed. Their heads were bare except a short
plaited tail behind. They had two miserable dogs with
them—very poor creatures. The sheep were large and
strong, and carried very heavy fleeces, which they would
leave behind in the Baspa valley. They all carried salt
in small woollen bags. There was no snow this evening
in the valley, but higher up there was a storm, and the
breeze was blowing down instead of up. There was a
heavy fall of snow at night, the heaviest we had had yet;
it must have come from the higher valley; usually the
storms came across the range from the Garhwál side
At 6 A.M. the thermometer was at freezing point, but
the sun came out strong, and the snow rapidly disappeared.
A very cold wind was blowing from the upper valley, and I
stayed in the tent, having contracted a bad cold during
the night. A particularly fine evening; the young moon
in the very blue sky was a glorious sight. Next day the
breeze was cold and dry, and the sun very hot. The
rhubarb stalks were springing along the level of the stream,
and I saw one plant whose central stem was ten inches
high. Very few flowers were visible—in fact, the little
yellow scolloped one was the only flower that had as yet the
courage to peep above the ground; and this at the end of
May! Anparh and the coolies of his village came in
the evening.

My cold left me, but indigestion and nausea took
possession, and I had only two cups of beef-tea during
twenty-four hours. These complications were caused by
my four days' inaction at this camp. I left Súancho
camp and reached Dúnti after a very wearying march of
four hours. All strength seemed to have left me, and I
was hardly able to get up the shortest ascents; I never

felt so helpless in my life. The depression of spirits, too, was great. After every tug up the road I was on the point of giving orders to return, for I felt so utterly played out that I imagined I could never reach the next stage, about three miles on. But I got in at last, and, after a rest and some food, things began to look brighter. My illness was slight, and could not be accountable for such an utter collapse of energy and strength; the high elevation had something to do with it. At these great altitudes it would seem that the slightest illness prostrates one entirely, and I can easily understand how people of weak constitution, in bad health, or with diseased organs— hearts or lungs—succumb so quickly from exposure on lofty mountains. My walk did me good, for the indigestion disappeared. Just as we started from camp, we saw nine barhal grazing on a grassy slope above, but they seemed to be all ewes, and I was not fit to go after them.

Dúnti is a large plain, and the river runs along its left edge, at the foot of the range. Anparh informed me that the hill-tops here are under the special protection of the god Kardú. This information, as I foresaw, was preliminary to the usual ceremony of propitiation, in which Her Majesty's head, in silver, plays such an important part. My guide was far too diplomatic to make the suggestion at once. He bided his time for the appropriate moment—probably when a ram with splendid horns would be sighted, looking down on us from a distant peak. That would be a propitious sign for me, and for Anparh also. I would in imagination have a foretaste of the successful stalk, while Anparh would say to himself, " There is the messenger of the good deota demanding his rights."

CHAPTER XVIII

THE UPPER BASPA—(*continued*)

Another stalk—Ends in failure—But bag a ram next day—Excellent though unsanctified chops—The god Kardú is squared at last—Features of the upper valley—A tramp among the hill-tops—17,000 feet above sea level—Freezing cold and melting heat again—The Tibetan gale drives us back—Driven to bed in desperation—An airy bedroom—Nature freezes most audibly—Give up my intended tramp—Take a walk round the base of the peak—Return to camp—A snowstorm—Beautiful effect in moonlight—A dash for Tibet—Anparh—An enlivening episode—Garhwális "lift" a complete Tibetan encampment—They try to trade on their own account—Tibetans object.

THE next day was given up to correspondence, as the post had at last come in. I went for a walk in the evening by the hillside down the valley, and sighted a flock of wild sheep. Anparh conducted the stalk, and did it well; but at the critical moment a loose slate slipped from under his foot, and as he put his head over the crest of the ridge, he was seen at once—a whistle, and the whole flock of ten scattered in all directions. The ram was lying down not fifty yards from our position, and as Anparh peeped over, their eyes met, and the barhal vanished before I ever saw him. No doubt the noise of the falling slate had directed his gaze, and we had come too close—as great a mistake when you have a trusty Express as it is to go to the other extreme. In the present instance, however, we had lost sight of the game, as the ground was very much broken. While the animals were clambering up the rocks above us, I had three snapshots, but missed; the sun was low down, and blazing full in my eyes, so I had not a fair chance. Returning late, long after sundown, Anparh spied some ewes across the river a long way off, and, as meat was wanted in camp, I had another shot, but the bullet fell short; the distance must have been over 300 yards. I had four hours' good rough walking and scrambling, and did it well, though the cold in my head had by no means left me.

The next morning I was more successful: I got a wild sheep after a long and tiresome stalk. Yákúb declined to go down and cut the animal's throat, so Anparh and his friends (including myself) had the meat all to ourselves: there were glum faces among the Balti coolies! A great deal of fat came out of this barhal, and the chops I had for dinner were capital. Now that I had drawn blood in the dominions of His Majesty Kardú, Anparh thought the time had come for the usual offering, but he was considerate. Instead of demanding silver, he asked for two seers (four pounds) of flour and a quarter of a seer of ghí (butter). I was informed that when Wilson Sahib came here five years ago he was taken seriously ill, and had to offer a goat to Kardú before he got well. It struck me at once that Anparh was making capital out of my recent illness; but I did not demur, and the articles were weighed out to him. If I could get this primitive man to lead me across Gúgérang into Tibet, even for a few days, I should regard it as ample recompense.

On the 1st of June I started for a four days' tramp among the hill-tops, the only way, apparently, of circumventing the old rams. After a tremendous grind of three and a half hours we made camp on an open grassy space under the great peak, 21,221 feet high, which overlooks

Dúnti. This was a very trying trudge indeed, and, though it was ten o'clock when we stopped, water had not yet begun to flow, everything being still frozen hard. We must have been at least 17,000 feet up. The last part of the ascent was distressing for the lungs: I coughed much, but had no other disagreeable symptoms. My appetite, however, did not suffer, and I made a good breakfast. Only four of us remained up—myself, Yákúb, Anparh, and a coolie; I sent the other men back to the main camp. The sun after a couple of hours was blazing hot; no shelter of any kind could be had, but when a breeze sprang up it was cool enough. We went out at three o'clock, in the direction of and above Súancho. After noon the wind had begun to rise, and by the time we started it was blowing a gale up the valley, frightfully cold and penetrating. I had on an overcoat, a cap well over my ears, and thick, warm gloves, yet I felt miserable. Anparh and the coolie were much worse off, but they held out manfully. We carefully searched all likely places, but saw nothing. We were just above the spot where the five rams had been sleeping a few days ago, but all the hillsides below us now were empty—and for a good reason, I afterwards reflected: I had fired eleven shots down there only a few days before. Súancho did not seem very far off, and, in fact, looking from above, the extent of country seemed very small. Looking up from below, I was under the impression that there was no end of shooting ground, but reversing the view gave an idea just the reverse. The piercing wind at last drove us back to camp, though we could not have been away more than an hour, nor have gone more than half a mile. I took refuge at the fire, where Yákúb was cooking the cakes for dinner, and stayed there. The pungent smoke was at last too much for me; but I shrank from going to bed because of the cold.

AN AIRY BEDROOM

So I went to Anparh's fire and spent some time turning him inside out on the manners and customs of his family and people. I was soon tired of this, for the juniper smoke almost blinded me and also made my head ache.

My bedroom was certainly open and airy enough: the vault of heaven was the roof, and a level spot on the hillside the floor. I tucked myself in comfortably, spread the waterproof sheet over all, and made Yákúb secure it all round with heavy stones. The wind had died away, the clouds had disappeared, and the stars were brilliantly shining. But a look at the thermometer at 6 P.M. had told me that the temperature then was 30°. Everything round me was freezing fast and hard; the tinkle of the rill of water from the snow-bank above, flowing a few feet from my bed, was fast growing fainter, till at last it ceased. I could not sleep; in my anxiety to ward off cold, I had made myself too warm, and I had difficulty in breathing. I imagined I could hear things freezing round me. The waterproof over me was coated with the hoar-frost which, in the lovely moonlight, I watched spreading over the grass by me. The grim peak, 21,000 feet high, just overhead caught my eye every time I peeped out. So much for sleeping out in the open at 17,000 feet above sea level.

I was up at 5 A.M., as I heard Yákúb at the fire; he was busy thawing his shoes, which he had left out, and which were frozen as hard as boards. He seemed impressed, but said that he had passed a good night, though at first he felt too warm and was suffocating. Everything was frozen, and ice had to be melted to make the tea. I soon made up my mind that I had had enough of it. My own suffering and inconvenience were severe enough, but it was ten times worse for those with me; and as there was no sport to compensate, we should be much better down below. I explained this to the men, had the things packed and everything ready for a start in five minutes. The coolie took a load and made for camp, whence he would send up others for the rest.

We went higher up, to the base of the mighty peak above, on a last attempt to find the big rams. We spent hours skirting giant crags, passing over grassy slopes and snow-beds alternately, but at last gave it up in despair. There were no signs of game, neither fresh nor old. I came to the reluctant conclusion that shooting in the Baspa valley was a delusion and a snare, at least at this time of the year, and was sorry for having wasted my leave in it. I broke my good old alpenstock in getting down a snow-bank: a faithful friend in many a ticklish place was that thin and elastic bamboo. On the way down we picked up the skull of a barhal ram, with horns 24 inches round the curve: they were bleached and worn by the weather, and must have been lying on that grassy slope for years. I came down to camp so disgusted and disappointed that I had no appetite for breakfast. I felt dyspeptic and down-in-the-mouth, and had also a sore throat—the only results of my trip up above.

There was a heavy snowfall during the night. All the valley and hills got a new mantle, and the night scene under a brilliant moon, after the storm, was beautiful. The opposite hillsides were stencilled out in fantastic patterns, the open spaces intensely white, the hollows in shadow intensely black. The silence over all gave the finishing touch.

The time having arrived, we made serious advances to Anparh on the subject of the journey into Tibet. I was resolved to waste no more time in this valley, and, as a good deal of my leave remained, I determined to attempt the pass at the head of the Baspa, and have a peep at least into Tibet. My present position at the head of the valley was an opportunity of which I determined to make use. The only difficulty was a trustworthy guide and interpreter; Anparh was the man, but, as I have already said, he had hitherto fought very shy of the idea. I had tried all my powers of persuasion on him, and my servant frequently had him in his tent, plying the chicken-hearted aborigine with all the temptations that his imagination could suggest. We were thus delayed, working at Anparh, when one evening, as I was strolling up the valley, I suddenly spied a man across the river, and shortly afterwards a large flock of laden sheep. This seemed strange, as there was no road on that side and no grass to feed the sheep. I hurried back to camp, brought up Anparh and showed him the men and sheep. He at once said, " It is those rascally Garhwális who went into Bhót (Tibet) by the Kúnchúrung Pass to trade on the sly, and are now returning with some Jádhs (Tibetans) to show them the way, and making for the Barású Pass." We went down to the river-bank to have a talk, and as soon as the Tibetans saw us they rushed down to the stream on the opposite bank, salaaming and gesticulating very excitedly, shouting (for the Baspa was noisy) a torrent of words quite incomprehensible, of course, to me. The Garhwális kept aloof on the hillside, seeming intent on driving the sheep; but two of them came down and tried to prevent the Tibetans from telling their story. This was most singular, and I was in a state of extreme curiosity before Anparh got at the facts.

These Garhwális, it seems, were the very same men who came down the Barású Pass when my camp was at Dwária, and whom I met in the evening going down to Chitkúl. They would not trade at the latter village, but went across the Charang Pass into Kúnchúrung, saying they would trade there; but that was only a blind. They

drove their sheep through that valley and went over the
Shólarang Pass into Tibet, intending to trade direct with
the Bhóts, and thus save the "middleman's profits." It
seems that the trade mediation of the Baspas between
their neighbours is more than a mere practice; it is a
recognised custom among these various peoples not to
trade direct, but to barter with the Baspa men, who pass
on the goods, making, of course, their own profit out of the
transaction. This unwritten law is strictly observed—by
none more so than by the inhabitants of this valley, to
whom a general infringement of it would be ruin. The
Tibetans, who are bound down very strictly by the laws
of their country in the matter of crossing frontiers, or of
allowing foreigners to do so, had never travelled into
Garhwál; but the hardy and enterprising inhabitant of the
latter country is not sufficiently self-controlled to respect
the mutual law, and he breaks through it now and then,
as in this case. As soon as the Kúnchúrung people
discovered that the Garhwális had stolen a march on them,
they sent information to one Rám Bahádur, the Basáhir
official, who looks after this portion of His Highness's
territories. This gentleman communicated with the
Tibetan authorities, and, when the enterprising Garhwális
arrived in that country, they were at once seized, their
sheep and property confiscated, and they themselves sent
about their business without even a day's food—so they
said. They came back by the Gúgérang Pass, and met a
party of Jádhs. They fell on these people at once, took
possession of their sheep and food, and made prisoners of
the owners. This occurred four days before I saw them.
The Garhwális took them across the Baspa, high up the
mountain side, then came down by the Nílang road, and
were travelling along the opposite side of the valley on
their way to Garhwál when I saw them. This was

evidently a reprisal for the treatment they had received at Zárang at the hands of the Tibetans. I invited both parties to come across, saying I would hear both sides; but the Garhwális became defiant, gesticulated wildly, flourished their sticks, and refused to have anything to do with me; they would take the sheep on, happen what might, and started off, forcing the Jádhs to accompany them; but the latter broke away, and the principal among them rushed to the river-bank, fell on his knees, and, joining his hands in an attitude of supplication, bellowed piteously for protection from his enemies. The Garhwális followed him, handled him very roughly, throwing him down and trying to drag him away. But he lay prone on the bank, and shouted and roared louder than ever. I and my men, with a deep and rapid river rushing between, were helpless spectators of this scrimmage. The Tibetan, however, resisted so vigorously that his assailants left him after administering sundry thumps and kicks. The other Jádhs had fled up the river to find a crossing-place, and the Garhwális went on with the sheep. Though Anparh was much incensed against the Garhwális and abused them roundly, he soon cooled down, and threw them a pellet of tobacco across the stream, as they said they were dying for a smoke.

The Jádhs came into my camp two hours later; they had had to go far up the valley to find a safe ford. I gave them a good feed of bread and meat and tea, and a nip of whisky all round at the end. They were grateful, and so cheerful that one would not have thought they had been so recently plundered of all they possessed. The tea was put into a dégchi (cooking vessel) full of water and boiled on the fire, then some salt was thrown in, and, when the decoction was ready, every Tibetan produced his cup from inside his coat, and the tea was ladled out. Some sugar was put in each cup, and then each man dipped a bit of his cake into the liquid (it was very thin indeed), and ate decently and slowly, though they must have been hungry enough. They then smeared the cakes with ghí, and when the meat was boiled, finished off with that. The head-man, who turned out to be the Panbóh or head-man of Zárang, remarked that there were three kinds of tea, and that this which he was drinking was the best. As it was Pálampore orange pekoe, his taste was undeniable. Dánam, the head-man of Zárang, was a small man, well dressed and clean-looking, well bred, and evidently of a class superior to his companions; something like a well-to-do head-man of a village down in the plains of India. This was the gentleman who went down on his knees and roared for help on the banks of the river, and who was hammered by the Garhwális. His conversation and gestures were very sprightly, and he talked incessantly, describing his misfortunes and abusing his enemies. But everything was done in a gentlemanly and well-bred manner (quite different from his companions, who treated him with respect, though in eating and drinking there was perfect equality), his bearing free and unembarrassed in the extreme. He was always addressed as "Panbóh," a word I had not heard before; it evidently bears some relationship to the Burmese "Boh," with which we have now become so familiar. Another man, by name Temdians, of village Tángi, a zamíndár, was a very ugly specimen of humanity; he had a very pronounced hare-lip, and his front teeth projected hideously from the aperture; his dress was dirty in the extreme. These Tibetans had been deprived of 227 sheep, 220 bags of salt, 2½ bags of porridge flour, half a bag of wheat, 1 bag of tea, 5 sheep-loads of ghí, and other matters. All the sheep had heavy fleeces—the most valuable part of the plundered property. When the Panbóh and his party left us, Anparh went with them, and a coolie was sent off in the morning to Chitkúl, that the authorities there might stop the Garhwális before they could cross the Barású Pass.

A snowstorm came on shortly after my visitors left; but apparently it takes a good deal of bad weather to stop a Jádh. His head is bare in all weathers, and he wears only one woollen coat nearly down to his heels, a waistband round his middle; this is his full costume at this season. The coat is very loose; when the weather is warm, he slips his arms out of the sleeves, and the upper part of his garment hangs down below the waist; when the cold is bitter, he pulls his coat a little tighter round him. The waistband converts the upper part of his coat into a capacious receptacle next his skin, in which he carries all his necessaries—cup, pipe, tobacco-bag, flour-bag, and other sundries—not forgetting a small book of prayers, which is taken out and diligently read when there is nothing else to do. This latter circumstance impressed me. Every Tibetan is educated, at least in such degree that he can read and write.

My servant reported that Anparh had at last agreed to pilot us across the Gúgérang, on the distinct understanding that the period was not to extend beyond fourteen days, and that he was to be paid one rupee a day while he remained across the pass. He said he would take me to the villages of Tángi and Zárang, which are on the other side, and see what game could be had beyond those places. He protested, at the same time, that no wild yak or *Ovis ammon* were anywhere within reach. My intention was, if possible, not to return this way, but to get back by Púling, Súmdo, and Nilang, and down the Bhágirati (one of the sources of the Ganges), to India. Anparh, however, did not know that country. There was snow again at night; in the morning everything was hidden in a white sheet.

Dánam Panbóh had said there was nothing to be had in the Zárang direction, and that last year two sahibs, whose names sounded in his mouth like "Charley" and "Davis," had crossed the frontier some distance away to the east, and in consequence the Tibetan officials in charge of that portion of the frontier had all been beheaded, their bodies sewn up in leather bags and thrown into the river. He could not name the place where this had occurred; but as soon as I mentioned Darjiling and Jálap-la, he at once repeated those names several times, and said those were the places. Since then, he said, fresh orders had come, enforcing greater strictness in guarding the passes and preventing Europeans from crossing. This was the only result of the much-trumpeted Macaulay Mission!

The night of the 4th June brought a very hard frost. Even stones and rocks were glazed into shining smoothness till the sun touched them. I went out at 7 A.M. to look for barhal, in the hope that the inclement weather had driven them down from cloudland, and after a short walk I saw some on the slope below the peak where I spent that memorable night 17,000 feet above sea level. I watched the barhal till there was a chance of getting closer; but as this did not occur till ten o'clock, I sent for breakfast. With the telescope I could make them out quite plainly: there were twelve lying about with their legs stretched out and their heads on the ground, just like so many dogs. The only ram in the flock lay at full length, the picture of repose; I could fancy I heard him snoring. They were all manifestly enjoying a mid-day nap in the warm sun after the bad weather of the last few days. After half an hour's rest and breakfast I began the ascent, a most trying one, as the slope was frightfully steep, and the wind became colder and stronger at every step. It took us fully two hours to reach the point from which I was to have my shot; and then, on looking over, not an animal was to be seen! This was a horrible disappointment. In going up we had made a couple of mistakes, and had shown ourselves each time; the wild sheep had not been so sound asleep as we thought them to be, and had seen us. Perhaps if Anparh had been with us we would have been more successful, as he had perfect knowledge of the ground. We had taken the shortest way—there was another and a longer one, which it doubtless would have been more prudent to follow. Yákúb collapsed at the end, and came down suffering from pains in his chest and head. We got down to the tent at four o'clock, very fagged, but hot tea soon set us both up again.

While at breakfast, I saw three men going along the path up the valley; they turned out to be Jádhs on their way to Zárang, sent by Dánam Panbóh about his sheep. This was not a good sign for my trip; doubtless, word had also been sent about my intention. I tried to keep my arrangements as secret as possible, but Anparh was such a coward, it was hardly likely he had held his tongue. On the other hand, I flattered myself that I had made a good impression on the Tibetans, and that my lucky interference in their favour, when the Garhwális were carrying them off, would ensure some grateful return on their part. Shortly after the three Tibetans went up, eleven more came down the valley. The three men who had escaped from the Garhwális got back to their village in three days, and this party of eleven had at once started in pursuit. They were a wild and very dirty lot; two of them were only boys, and three of them Lámas. These latter had their hair cut very short, and all three were clothed in very dirty red chógas (long coats).

The Garhwális with their plunder were stopped opposite Súancho. The coolie I sent down to Chitkúl met my men coming up with the things I had left in the village near Dwareah, and the porters left my traps on the road, crossed the snow-bridge, and met the plunderers. They remained there all night, and next morning came on to the Barású valley. Here the Garhwális refused to go down farther or to cross the Baspa. They were, however, detained with the sheep, while all the valley assembled to decide the dispute. The Garhwális stoutly held their own, though they were starving, and appeared a masterful set of fellows, showing much more spirit than either Kanawaris or Tibetans in this affair, though they were manifestly in the wrong. The former were in mortal dread of them, and would not oppose them openly, though anxious to help their friends the Jádhs. The Kanawaris are in a miserable position owing to their situation between two disputants, their trade—in fact, their existence—as I have said before, depending on both.

CHAPTER XIX

FIRST STEPS IN TIBET

Dánam Panbóh recovers his sheep—A young Tibetan—His intelligence more apparent than his moustache—Tibetan officials—Anparh is unwilling to make a start—Makes up his mind at last—Arsamang camp—The way up—A scene of desolation—Rampant moraines mounting on each other—First view of Gúgérang Pass—Reach the crest—And enter Tibet—A Balti coolie falls ill—Too much "púltas" the cause—A new dish—Fraternal devotion—Péchang—The Baltis meet an old friend—Are greatly comforted—Ascend a side valley—No game seen—Unique scenery on the road—A disrupted mountain—Stunted trees appear—Ráná—Nánútatto—Green fields appear—Yellow furze.

THE party of Tibetans who went down with their sheep some days ago, and who passed my camp when I was at Súancho, came in on their return journey, and informed me that the Panbóh had got his sheep back from the Garhwális, and that he was going on to Sángla to trade. The affair was settled by compromise, both parties getting their sheep. I entertained these Jádhs at four-o'clock tea. The youth mentioned before was by far the most intelligent of the lot, and his free-and-easy bearing on the present occasion was pleasant to see. After tea I presented him with a pair of scissors; he at once got hold of a newspaper and cut out a pretty ornamental pattern, which he placed against the breast of his coat and admired very much. I then gave him a small looking-glass, and he at once put it before his face, and, with his finger on his upper lip, began an anxious scrutiny of an incipient moustache. These men refused to take me to Zárang, as it was forbidden, but said the Panbóh was the responsible man, and could do what he liked. The official over him was the Chaprang-Zong (Chaprang, governor), and over the latter a very great man called the Garh-póng, about whom they had very hazy ideas indeed, like ignorant villagers all the world over. I visited them in their camp in the evening. Their sheep seemed semi-wild animals, and difficult to manage. There was snow again at night, a very heavy fall that lasted for two hours, but the morning was bright and warm. Two men arrived in the evening from Dánam Panbóh, with a message to say I was not to go on without Anparh, and that he himself would come if he could arrange his business soon. He had also given strict orders to all the Jádhs going up that my advent was on no account to be made known to the Chaprang-Zong. The two Jádhs were to remain with me until Anparh arrived. The Jádhs with the sheep went on this morning, leaving a sick one behind, which the Chitkúl coolies ate.

Anparh turned up at last, but he was very loth to go, having no doubt been talked over or frightened by Dánam Panbóh, for whom he wished to wait. I also discovered that the message brought by the two Jádhs was misdelivered or misunderstood. Their instructions were that I was on no account to go on until the Panbóh arrived, and if I persisted, the messengers were to precede me and send word to the Chaprang-Zong! Anparh, no doubt, had betrayed my plans; under any circumstances, concealment was hardly possible after meeting so many Tibetans. My determination was, however, fixed, and I kept Anparh to his promise. As soon as the messengers saw me preparing to move, they started on ahead to give notice. Chaprang is forty-five miles at least from Zárang,

so the official at the former place would not be able to
organise any opposition for some days at least; and I
should put in a week's shooting across the pass in the
interval. They seemed most anxious that I should not
enter any village. Both Anparh and the Panbóh said
they should come to frightful grief if I forced my way in.
I had no intention of doing that, but intended to go as
far as I fairly could, and started with ten loads and fifteen
days' provisions. Anparh was very much alarmed,
imagining that I was going to force my way to Zárang;
and though I repeatedly told him I would remain on the
other side of the pass and shoot until the Panbóh arrived,
when I should abide by the latter's decision, I had great
difficulty in getting him to advance beyond Nithál.
As far as Nithál, the valley is open, wide, and level as
below. At that point two valleys from above meet; the
left is the one up to the Gúgérang Pass, my road.
Immediately after leaving Nithál this valley contracts,
becoming very rough, broken, and winding, blocked with
fallen rocks and masses of snow; the path is on the left
bank of the stream, some distance up the hillside. So
shut in is the valley, that steep hill-slopes are all that can
be seen. Arsamang, the camping-place, is a small flat
with two stone enclosures, where the shepherds stop on
their way up and down. Anparh found on the path a
dead sheep, which he brought in to eat. Arsamang is a
miserable place for a camp; there is not room even for a
small tent; water is obtainable some distance down, but
no fuel. On the way up I had to bully a Chitkúl coolie
with a stick, as he threatened to throw down his load and
return. The Balti men, as usual, behaved well.

The night was pleasanter than at Dúnti; though this
camp is much higher, it is more confined, and there was
no wind—though it blew strong and cold till dusk, when

everything was hushed, and the silent darkness felt oppressive. The path next day led us over tremendous moraines, that seemed to have jammed together on their meeting from all points of the compass. In the Nagdim valley, farther on, we toiled up another enormous moraine, and descended into a level valley down its almost perpendicular side, covered with treacherous snow. Several of the coolies slid down, load and all; one lost his balance, and had a bad fall: then we came to a level valley, sloppy and boggy from recently melted snow. There was not a dry inch of ground—and this was the halting-place for breakfast. More hard walking brought us to a great amphitheatre of snow, encircled with jagged peaks, and in the centre of the very broken sky-line the Gügérang Pass was pointed out—a slight depression flanked by two castle-like crags. An immense field of snow stretched away to the south, surrounded by lofty snowy mountains; the scene was desolate, but very grand. We went up along the snow till we came to the foot of the pass, and thence had a very stiff but short ascent to the crags above—a hundred yards more, and we passed between jagged rocks into Tibet, with a roaring wind at our backs. It was terribly sharp and cutting, and it made me literally run before it till I got under the turn of a hillside. We saw three dead sheep on this descent. When we reached Péchang camp, which we did at 5.30, one coolie was thoroughly done up, and gave in; they had been very severely tried. Péchang is a cold place: no wood, bare rocks, water, and snow, and an awful wind for ever blowing. The coolie who gave out coming up the pass was a Balti, who had been complaining of pains in his interior. I discovered in the evening that, owing to the scarcity of fuel at Arsamang, the Balti coolies could not cook their food; so they mixed the flour with water, making a mass of dough. Then the party sat round, and each taking a handful of the dough, dipped it in ghí before swallowing it. It took several doses of chlorodyne to give the sick man relief. The exhilarating dish described is called "pultas," otherwise *poultice*. The Baltis have slightly changed the word, and therewith its meaning. The word must have been picked up in the hill stations, where these men go to earn a living as navvies. The man who was taken ill had a brother in our party, and he showed right brotherly affection. After carrying his own load up a bit, he would go back and carry up his brother's. He did this for about two miles of the worst part of the journey just below the pass.

We left Péchang at half-past six, and went steadily down the valley till ten, when we came to a side valley leading down to the villages of Kúnnú and Chárang. We saw six wild sheep up this valley and halted for a stalk, but they turned out to be all ewes. Anparh was very anxious that I should return this way, without going farther down towards Zárang. I humoured him, and halted for a day. There was much less snow on this side. The hills are rounded towards their bases, the tops are jagged and naked peaks, and no vegetation whatever is visible. There was, however, a little grass lower down, and large patches of the prickly Tibetan furze with yellow flowers. There was another yellow flower on a small plant that comes up in a bunch, not very high, with separate stalks and green leaves, rather common in some places. When the Balti coolies saw these, they were greatly excited, evidently recognising a flower of their native land. Each plucked a quantity, presented some to me, and stuck the rest in their caps. They were wonderfully brightened up by meeting this old acquaintance. The last year's dead bushes furnished the only fuel; fortunately, though a strong wind was blowing down the valley, it was not cold.

Yákúb was laid up from the effects of the previous day's hard work.

I made an excursion to the side valley on the left—the way by which Anparh wished me to return. The mouth of the valley is very narrow and steep, a sheep-path ascends the hillside along rocks and crumbling ground—a hard pull up. Then the path enters suddenly on a level plain, and the features of the valley entirely change. A sloping plain, covered with yellow furze, comes down to the stream, which runs in a deep bed. Barren rocky hills, ending in fantastic ridges, bound the plain. In the left front a long level valley, with a stream running down the centre, curves down from the Gúgérang direction. From the right front another smaller valley comes down, with bare and gently-sloping sides. Above these is the snow-capped ridge which divides India and Tibet. Though the ground, as far as the eye could reach, in every direction was splendid for wild sheep, I did not see a single animal. Their tracks were visible all over the hillsides, and the game had certainly been here within the last three days, so perhaps a leopard had cleared them out.

We left next day, as there was no temptation to prolong our stay, and came down the valley by the path which runs along the hillside, above the stream, for about a mile, then comes down and crosses over to the right bank. The current was strong, and up to the coolies' thighs in the centre. The path follows the right bank, and then brings one suddenly upon the most extraordinary sight I saw on this trip. The hillside on the right bank has slipped down bodily, and gone right across to the left bank in an enormous mass of rock. The slide is at a considerable angle, but the stream has worked its way out by the left bank at the foot of the slip, and makes a fine cascade, shooting out towards the right bank, and falling into a pool below. An enormous archway has been formed under the fallen mass, by the rock crumbling away and falling into the stream. This opening partly spans the right bank and partly the stream, but diagonally, so that the waterfall, when you look through the archway, seemed to be rushing at you as it turned the foot of the landslip at an acute angle. The effect was very strange. Fifty yards farther on, another mass of rock had slipped to the edge of the stream, and stopped there at a very sharp angle. The shape of this mass was exactly like the flintlock of an old musket; the cairn at the top had been placed there, no doubt, by the Tibetans, who have a great habit of piling up stones on any conspicuous spot. It is considered a praiseworthy act to raise these landmarks, and, in fact, they are necessary in such a country to indicate the way. For the same purpose little heaps of rocks were piled up all over the landslip. These collections of stones will be found on every remarkable spot that catches the eye. A little farther down large boulders and masses of rocks have fallen into the stream. For more than a mile the mountain seems to have made a wholesale movement downwards, and the valley, for that distance, is entirely blocked with the ruins. Probably this was the result of an earthquake, but no such disruptions are seen on the opposite side of the valley, where one vast precipice falls sheer to the water's edge. After this disrupted bit of country is passed, the valley opens out, and the stream again flows in a level bed. The range on either side is barren and forbidding, black and rugged on the left, receding and crumbling on the right. The path goes along the débris for two or three miles, the valley gradually opening out at the same time. At 10.30 we reached Rámá camp, where a considerable stream joins the main river. It is almost equal in volume to the latter, and this side valley, therefore, must be of considerable length. The main valley, at this point, is level, and about two hundred yards broad, but stony. There were a few bushes and stunted cypresses on the left range; these were the first trees I had seen since I left the birches at Súancho. It was much warmer down here, too; the temperature at 3 P.M. was 54°. No signs of human habitation, fixed or temporary, were anywhere visible, and no one appeared from either direction. Drizzling rain fell nearly all the evening. A coolie, with the post, turned up after dark—a most welcome arrival.

While it rained below, heavy snow fell on the ranges above, especially towards the passes. I sent three coolies back to Dúnti to bring flour and rice, not wishing to run short of supplies here. The bad weather continued all day, so I occupied myself in diligently reading stale newspapers.

Anparh confessed, one fine morning, that it was no use breaking my heart in climbing these hills after imaginary rams. There were none, but some could be had lower down, at a place called Nánútatto. I took him at his word, and broke camp at once, reaching the place at noon. After the first hour's march we came to a considerable stream, which flows into the main valley from the left. We had to cross the main stream above Nánútatto, and followed a path below enormous precipices, whose feet are washed by the water, leaving little room for traffic. After this we ascended till we came suddenly to some fields of barley—the first cultivation. The valley is more open here, and the hills undulating, and receding from the now narrow stream. There were several patches of cultivation on both sides of the valley, but they were not in a very flourishing condition, and had no one, apparently, to look after them. The hills looked promising, the slopes being covered with grass, and yellow furze abounded; above these, and not far distant, are crags and precipices. As I came lower down to Nánútatto, wild rose bushes were numerous, and some very pretty wild flowers that were new to me, but no trees. The furze grew stronger and lustier the lower I went down. Where the sun strikes down with unusual warmth, and the spot is sheltered, the bushes of it are very large and dense, and the blossoms more plentiful and vigorous, giving a warm glow to the otherwise bare hillside.

It was strange that no one had yet come from below to look after us, especially as the Panbóh had sent intimation of our coming: perhaps the Chaprang-Zong's had not yet had time to reach Tángo.

CHAPTER XX

AMONG THE TIBETANS

Camp discovered by two old women—First Tibetans arrive—Marriage customs—The real Panbóh of Zárang—He stands on his dignity—Tibetan manners—A Tibetan game described—Tibetan ponies—Her Majesty's silver countenance changes the aspect of affairs—Anparh's dilemma—The agreement ratified—The return visit—I hold an exhibition—The Panbóh and the penknife—Tea and biscuits—Tibetan mode of expressing satisfaction—Napier Johnstone—Tandúp—His classical oblation—Primitive way of cleaning a dish—The Panbóh polishes his fangs—Tibetan humour—Preparing for a feast—Buy some curiosities—A welcome present from Mrs. Chering—Tibetan gratitude—The feast—The Panbóh and his followers depart—True version of the Garhwáli episode—Chinese exclusiveness—Lámas of Tángi interview me—A present of three articles—A regular passport system—How trade is carried on.

NEXT morning, on my return from a walk, I found several Tibetans in camp: they had come from the village, and it transpired that early in the morning two old women came from Tángo, which lies just on the other side of the next slope, and, horrified to find their fields occupied by my camp, rushed back and gave the alarm. Among the men who had now come was the elder brother of the young man to whom I had given the scissors and looking-glass. He had gone on a visit to his wife, and had most likely taken her these valuable presents. In this country the custom, so Anparh informed me, is for the wife to always live in her father's house, where the husband visits her periodically, but never brings her home. He takes all the sons, the mother keeps all the daughters. All the work and labour performed by the wife is for the benefit of her father, not that of her husband. No wedding ceremony takes place: young people meet at the fairs which are frequently held, and arrange their own marriages. After this preliminary, the young man begins his visits to the young woman as above. I don't think Anparh had the imagination necessary to invent such a singular custom for my special amusement, so perhaps what he said was true. Late in the evening arrived the real Panbóh from Zárang. The man I rescued from the Garhwális, it now appeared, was only his younger brother. The genuine Panbóh, who was an old man, sent word that he was too tired to see me that evening, and put off his visit till next day. The truth was, he had been indulging too much in chhang (Tibetan beer) on his way from the village, and did not feel equal to high diplomacy in consequence. Several other men arrived after him, all mounted on stout little ponies, mostly greys. I was told that all the swells of the six villages under the Panbóh were to assemble here and hold a parliament over the stranger who had entered their borders: the president would be the Panbóh. I arranged through Anparh to bribe him, as well as other influential members; and promised a feast and chhang at Tángo after everything had been settled in my favour. All I wanted was to get back by the Sangyókh-la to Nílang, the frontier village, and, if possible, to get a view of a real Tibetan village. Everybody appeared to be in high good-humour, and the Jádhs were singing at the top of their voices.

The Panbóh continued to make excuses, and these culminated at last in his refusal to visit me at all. He said, in the first place, that he could not allow me to go an inch farther towards Tángo, and that I must return the way I came. If I had anything to say to him, I must come and see him. The old gentleman was standing on his dignity. Anparh was our go-between, and seemed very despondent. My curiosity was far too strong for my dignity to be a stumbling-block, so I expressed my anxiety to visit the Panbóh and his companions behind the huge boulder, on the sheltered side of which he had taken up his quarters; but there was no use going till all the men who were expected had arrived, and they came dropping in till late in the evening, and then more were expected. The Panbóh could give no definite reply till all the influential men had held this important meeting, and I had been fully discussed; so I had to put off my visit till Anparh could tell me that all was ready. In the meantime I had my breakfast and the Tibetans their tea, which they were constantly brewing in copper dégchis (cooking vessels) of Indian manufacture, as fresh arrivals appeared. At eleven o'clock Anparh announced that the time for my visit had arrived, and I walked over to the Panbóh's airy residence, not a hundred yards from my tent.

I found him seated with his back to the rock, and the usual three stones, with a fire in front of him for brewing tea. He looked very dignified and solemn, and invited me to be seated. Tabra Panbóh was a man of fifty or more years of age, decidedly Chinese in feature, of fair complexion, with hazel eyes, as far as I could make out, for they were very bleary, and the lids and surrounding skin very much puckered. He wore a Chinese felt hat and the Tibetan costume, and was smoking a hukka with a brass chilam (bowl). His companions sat round about him. There was very little of the Chinese about them: a wilder-looking, uglier, and dirtier lot of men I never saw. Every type of ugliness was represented among them, and not one in any respect resembled another. This is a most noticeable feature among these people; there seems to be no racial type. The difference also between the common herd and the head-man and his connections was very marked; the latter seem to belong to a foreign and distinct stock, Chinese-like. There was only one thing in common between them—their terribly bad teeth: they had not among them a set of teeth that could be looked at without disgust, and the Panbóh, I think, had the worst. His two eye-teeth stuck out beyond his lips like canine fangs. His younger brother and the son of the Tángi head-man were decidedly Chinese in feature, and they were the only decent-looking men in the assembly. After a long palaver and much wrangling, no decision could be arrived at; but all said they did not know of any road leading to Nílang, and that I could not go that way; that I must return the way I had come. I could not be allowed to visit any village. The orders against foreigners entering the country were very strict, and if I persisted in going farther, their heads would be cut off; and so on. The final reply, after much chattering, was that all had not assembled yet, and no definite answer could therefore be given. A fresh party arrived while I was there, and the head of it dismounted some distance off and came up to the assembly, leading his pony. When he caught the Panbóh's eye, he doffed his Chinese felt hat in quite a graceful fashion, just in the European style, and the greetings also very much resembled our own. By the bye, these Tibetans have one very English habit indeed—that of whistling. Riding or walking along the road, they whistle; when engaged in any work by himself, the Jádh whistles; and the little boy, sitting on a rock watching the ponies grazing, is sure to be whistling.

As the business was for the time over, four of the

party got up for a game, the name of which I heard, but which was unpronounceable by English lips. The younger brother of the Panbóh got it up. One hundred and eight pebbles (the sacred Tibetan number) were collected, and each of the four players provided himself with nine small pieces of stick, each one of a different recognisable pattern; the stakes were four annas from each player. Two brass dice, dotted in the usual way, excepting that one side was crossed from angle to angle by two lines, and the iron tea-ladle, were produced. A cloth was spread on the ground, the players sat round, and the pebbles were placed in a circle between them. The sticks of each player were passed through the pebbles according to the pips turned up on the dice. The great object seemed to be to pass one's sticks through the stones as soon as possible, throwing out those of other players that were passed over. The man who puts all his sticks through all the pebbles first, wins the stakes. The game took a long time, and gave rise to much excitement and noise; each player rubbed the dice with energy on the spread cloth, on the side of his boots, on the back of a Láma, or with a pinch of dust "for luck," accompanying the action, which was energetic and prolonged, with various gestures and the words, "riri, riri, luri, luri." The dice got well polished, and I should say would soon be worn out if many games were played. After seeing the first game through, I left and had a look at the ponies. They were small, well-formed, compact animals, with fine heads and broad chests; they could not have been over twelve hands high, but there could be no doubt of their strength and steadiness, for they carried their riders, who were big men, with ease.

I returned to the tent much discouraged by the result of my interview, making up my mind that I must return the way I had come. Anparh came and said the final decision was that I could not be allowed to go any farther. I was in despair, and sent Yákúb and Anparh back for a last effort, the former with some rupees in his pocket. This last move had the desired effect. After a time they returned and said the Panbóh and his friends were willing to let me go to Nílang by the Sangyókh-la, provided I made a short détour so as to avoid villages, and also provided that a consideration was forthcoming. I went off to the assembly at once with Anparh and Yákúb, and it was at length arranged that Anparh should go bail for me, and give a written agreement that I should not enter the villages. The noise and talk and squabbling over this business was indescribable. Anparh cut a most wretched figure; his very small modicum of courage gave way entirely. He had little confidence in me, and no doubt thought that as soon as he was bound down by the agreement, and in the hands of the Tibetans, I would sacrifice him to my own wishes. I never met before such a chicken-hearted individual for a highlander. At length we got him to the sticking-point, and Yákúb dribbled out the rupees: first he put five into the hands of the Panbóh, who looked disappointed; then five more, and so on, the Panbóh's face expanding in smiles as each dose was administered, till the magnificent sum of twenty rupees was reached. At this point it became evident that the man's face could expand no more, and the dole ceased. The next business was Anparh's oath and written agreement. But it now appeared that Anparh could not write. The difficulty was got over in this way—no doubt another Tibetan custom: Anparh took up a small stone, round which he wrapped some white woollen string. This implied that if the agreement made was infringed, Anparh would have to pay that weight in gold. This solemnity was ratified by the attachment of my seal to the woollen string, the Panbóh producing a cake of sealing-wax from the depths of his waistbelt for the purpose.

The negotiations having been satisfactorily concluded, I made over to the Panbóh ten rupees to cover the expense of the promised feast. He transferred the money at once to Anparh's two Chitkúl coolies and two of his own men, who instantly started for Tángo to bring the sheep and the chhang, and I returned to my tent happy. The Panbóh and his companions soon after followed to pay the return visit. A blanket was spread in his honour, and I sat on a stone, the rest round three stones, the *sine qua non* in Tibetan social functions. We were closely packed. One old man pressed my left elbow close to my side, and another ancient did the same on my right. The biggest cooking vessel in the camp was soon on the fire for the usual brew, which, this time, was the best Kángra valley orange pekoe procurable. A handful of tea was put into the cold water and allowed to boil, while pinches of dry tea were served round to each man—smelt, tasted, and approved, then carefully tied up in knots and stowed away. While the tea was cooking we held a show. I first brought out the binoculars, through which a flock of barhal high up on the opposite hillside was viewed with exclamations of astonishment and delight. The glasses passed round down to the smallest boy, whose head hardly came up to my waist. He was the ugliest but merriest and most free-and-easy urchin I ever met. His shrieks of delight and his grin, after he had got the focus, were most gratifying. But this excitement soon palled, and inquiries were made for "the long thing." Someone had seen the telescope used in the morning. The Steward's "Viceroy" was then brought out and placed in position on a boulder by the fire. After the peep-show with this, my watch went round, and everyone earnestly repeated "tik-tik-tik" for the next five minutes. The sight of the works behind, when the case was opened, struck them dumb. It was impossible to explain the use of the watch. An attempt was made for the Panbóh's benefit, but given up in despair. Anparh's linguistic qualifications as interpreter were not equal to the task, and I must confess neither were mine. I then produced my pocket-knife, the usual thumb-nail-splitting instrument with all the complications complete, and an electro-plated handle. It was not necessary to explain the uses of *this* to the Panbóh: his grave stare of admiration told its own tale. The uses of all the various instruments in the knife were explained to him, and, by way of practical illustration, I made Yákúb unscrew and screw in again one of the screws in the sole of my boot—an operation which threw the company into ecstasies, and roused in even the stolid Panbóh an agitation which he vainly strove to suppress. The knife had to be placed in his hand for an examination, which took several minutes. He returned it with longing eyes, and at length asked Anparh how much I would take for it! My answer was prompt—permission to visit the villages and country below! That was too big a price: the Panbóh shook his head and sighed.

Tea was now ready. A plateful of sugar and a spoon were placed before the Panbóh, and out came the wooden cups. Sugared tea went round several times, and was approved. A few Huntley and Palmer's biscuits were then handed to the Panbóh in a plate: he looked askance at them at first, but was persuaded to taste one; he put a bit in his tea, tasted, and approved. He called them "farfari." He then broke off tiny bits, and each man received a piece about half the size of my little finger-nail. It is quite remarkable the equality that obtains among these people: the Panbóh was treated as an equal by all, and he treated them in the same way. They seemed to have everything in common, shared everything equally, and must have very hazy ideas of *meum* and *tuum*, though honest and aboveboard as the day. Is this natural socialism? After tea and biscuit the Panbóh showed his satisfaction by holding up his thumb and saying I was a jolly good fellow. This is the Tibetan mode of returning thanks. Each one held up his thumb in the same way, with the fist closed, and repeated the same words. Now the whisky came round. It had to be explained first to the Panbóh that it was the same as his chhang, made from barley. He took a few drops in the palm of his hand and tasted it. Approval stole over his face; and a few drops went round in the usual way in the palm of each man's hand. Smacking of lips, wry faces, and grunts of satisfaction resulted. It was evidently too strong neat, and water was called for. Then a little whisky and water went round in the cups again, with universal approval. This, I will make bold to say, was the first time that "Napier Johnstone" was drunk by highlanders of this ilk; but the smacks, eye-twinklings, and coughs bore strong resemblance to the symptoms noticeable under similar circumstances in the far-off land of the grateful liquor's birth. As a special honour, I mixed a glassful in my own silver travelling-cup, and handed it to the Panbóh for his particular delectation; but the same thing happened—he took a sip and passed my silver cup round to each man present as before! It was drained when it came back to the Panbóh, who politely handed it over his shoulder, to my servant, and told him to have it cleaned. The spirits warmed their hearts, and I had again the emphatic verdict of their thumbs. Tandúp, my appointed guide, was not present when the whisky went round: he was called, and his share given him, shortly afterwards. He was a strapping young man, manly in bearing, with a heavy tread and swaggering gait in his long Chinese boots. He was the eldest son of the Tángi head-man, and brother of the young fellow I took such a liking to at Dúnti. He drank his glass very gracefully: sitting on his knees, he held the cup in his left hand, muttered a prayer, threw some drops over his right shoulder, then over his left, said a few words more, turned to his right, and poured a few drops on the ground, faced to his front, and drained the cup. This performance took him a minute or more. Some of the old fellows, after finishing their cups, licked them clean. The last ceremony was the presentation of a penknife, pair of scissors, and a small looking-glass (total value about a rupee) to the Panbóh. This completed this business. The first use he made of the mirror was to examine his teeth—what he had of them. Seeing that the two projecting fangs were not over-clean, he polished them up with the cuffs of his coat. It was explained to him that the glass and scissors were for Mrs. Panbóh. He grinned. On the handle of the penknife were the portraits of two royal personages; this was explained to the Panbóh, whereupon a coarse fellow on his right exclaimed, "Beware how you take another lady home; Mrs. P. will make you feel unhappy!" These people were very jocular and humorous, and had not a serious thought among them as far as I could see. Shortly after, the meeting broke up, and the Panbóh strolled back to his rock. Let me record his name here; it is Tsamdabi-ya. He was for fourteen years Chaprang-Zong, that is, Governor of Chaprang, a fort on the Sutlej about forty-five miles from his village. He was now in charge of these six villages and all the passes between Shipki frontier village, on the Sutlej, and Nílang. His salary was the revenue of the Tángi village.

The materials for the feast arrived in the morning—a sheep, rice, and chhang in the rough; there was none ready in the village. So a quantity of rice, cooked and fermented, was brought in a bag, and put into large copper vessels. After Tandúp had finished his breakfast, he sat down and began to strain the rice through a sieve by rubbing and squeezing it with his hands—a process which took some time, as there was a lot of rice. Anparh struck off the head of the old ram, and the blood was collected to the last drop in a vessel to be boiled. The Tibetans have a great horror of bloodshed—it is a part of their religion; and they prefer that some one else should kill their mutton. Their method is most cruel when they are obliged to slaughter an animal. They tie up the nose and mouth, and then let the poor beast rush about in the agonies of suffocation until death relieves it.

All the rubbish in the village was brought me for sale. I bought a Tibetan coat, bags, waistbands, etc., as curiosities. Two circumstances occurred during the day which pleased me much. Just before breakfast, the Buddhist priest of the village, a decent-looking old man, with a small boy behind him carrying a long wooden vessel full of milk, arrived with a message from Tandúp Chering's wife, to the effect that the milk was a present in return for my kindness in rescuing her husband from the Garhwális. The little boy, not much above my knee, was their son, and he had brought the milk on his back all the way up the hill, at his mother's bidding. It was deliciously fresh, and nothing could have been better timed for my breakfast. I sent the lady a small looking-glass and pair of scissors by the hands of her son, as a token of gratitude. After breakfast, a young man came with a large ball of fresh butter put up in a clean cloth bag, with another message to the same effect. He had been sent by his mother with this present, for the kindness shown to his father (another of the same party) in trouble. These little attentions were very gratifying, and showed the simple villagers in a very agreeable light indeed.

The Panbóh and his followers had their feast, and drinking and singing were carried on till the sun disappeared behind the hills. Most of the men then departed happy, but steady. Chhang, in fact, is very weak stuff, and an enormous quantity must be imbibed before anything like intoxication supervenes. Tibetans have an unfathomable capacity for it, and can generally achieve drunkenness when the supply is unlimited. The Panbóh gave me a final warning before he started,—that if I attempted to go by any other route but the one agreed upon, there would be trouble. The true story of the Garhwális' adventure was told me by the Panbóh. It was their intention to force their way into the interior of Tibet—not merely to the villages of Zárang, etc.—and deal direct with the traders of that part of the country. This was a very bold adventure indeed, and indicates a spirit like an Englishman's. But even these men, well known to the Tibetans as they were, could not manage to get much beyond the frontier, and were very roughly used indeed; they were detained just as strangers would have been, and, when they resisted, their property was seized and they were turned adrift. This action of the Tibetans seemed to prove that the regulation for the exclusion of foreigners is not especially directed against us, but is a part of the general policy of China. That it is not a Tibetan custom I am convinced. These people have often assured me that they would most willingly allow us entry if it rested with them. If the history of China's connection with Tibet is searched, it will be found that this exclusiveness is maintained by express orders from the Government of China, and that the Tibetans are simply obeying their masters. The odium, therefore, should rest on the Chinese, and not on the simple inhabitants of the country.

In the evening the Lámas of Tángi came with a present of one four-anna bit and a small piece of open-work cloth of China manufacture—said to be very precious and sacred; a lamb was also offered, but it had not yet arrived from the village. A present of this kind—that is, *three* things—is always made to great people. The Lámas were anxious to explain that they had brought these presents with no expectation of return, as they were only priests, and had no concern with worldly things, etc. But, at the same time, the present of five rupees that I put into the hand of the principal was most willingly accepted. The proper thing, I am told, to do with the flimsy rag (it looks like a bit of linen) is to tie it round one's neck. I did so, and put the coin in my pocket, for luck. There is no Tibetan currency—apparently all the cash in circulation comes from India. From what the Panbóh told me, it would seem that there is a regular passport system in vogue all over Tibet—no doubt introduced by the Chinese. He said the people of the country were forbidden to travel without a written permit from the authorities, even within their own borders: even traders had to get a pass. And there was yet further restriction: there were fixed trade routes and fixed markets, to which traders were limited. For instance, the villagers under the Panbóh were prohibited from travelling into the interior of Tibet; they could trade only with Kanawaris, and these latter could not proceed beyond Zárang. In the same way, certain traders from the interior were allowed to come to these villages with their goods and exchange them for Indian products, but are prohibited from going any farther. Trade is by barter, pure and simple, and any cash transactions, except on the very smallest scale, are impossible. The prohibition against strangers is so strict that even two Khamba beggar women (true Tibetans and no mistake), who were wandering about in camp, were not allowed to proceed farther in the direction of India. This system of restriction applies as much to Tibetans as to strangers from across the borders. The people understand it thoroughly well, and obey loyally. It is a *húkm* (order). The meaning of this Hindústani word, by the bye, was well understood here; and it was used with reference to myself pretty often.

CHAPTER XXI

A MARCH IN TIBET

Start from Tángi—A curious natural bridge—Tandúp, my guide—After rains again—A succession of blunders—A back view of the Himálayas—A Tibetan landscape—Force of the wind—The infant Ganges—The Sangyókh-la—Reach the regular trading route—Traces of barhal numerous—Run into a flock of rams—Make a large bag without any trouble—Púling Súmdo—Tandúp Zangbo—His manners and customs—His companion—Dismiss my Tibetans—Tandúp's wives—Presents for them—A good place for barhal-shooting—Rams about the camp—Meet the people from Nílang—I meet Paré—Information regarding game—First intimation of a wholesale murderer—Meet Bow Singh, the arch-impostor—Arrange a shooting trip with him—Bow Singh claims two nationalities—Meaning of the word "Jádh"—Bow Singh's temptation.

WE started next day along the Tángi road, which we followed for a mile, and then crossed over to the right bank of the stream at a point where the water has cut a way through solid slate rock, and where the channel is less than ten feet wide. A huge rock from above had fallen just over this canal-like passage, and formed a natural bridge. The descent and ascent from this boulder bridge are very steep, but mercifully short. We camped in a level field on the right bank, having taken two hours to cover not more than three miles. In the evening I walked along the hillside, down stream, and, through my telescope, examined the large and open valley in which the village of Tángi is situated, for I was in hope of obtaining a distant view, at least, of houses, but in this I was disappointed.

The valley is broad, open, and well cultivated. The village could not have been a mile away, but it was hidden by a spur of the hill. It was to avoid approaching this village that I was being taken this roundabout way. Tandúp went to pay his friends a final visit before starting on this journey; he came back full of chhang, and hardly able to walk, but in the highest spirits. He said he had to take a sleep on the road, as he could not manage to get along. His advent was heralded by shouts, songs, and whistling, some time before he appeared in person. He was exceedingly communicative, if one could only have understood him. He and Yákúb became great friends, but, in the absence of a common language, intercourse was limited.

The next march was up stream and up the hillside. This roundabout way might have been avoided by coming down from camp at Námútatto, crossing the stream and going straight up; but Tibetans hate getting wet, and this détour was made to take advantage of the aforesaid boulder bridge. The ascent took us five hours—it was gradual, but very trying. We halted on the ridge and had breakfast, with melted snow for tea. Tandúp was awfully done; he said he was hungry, but he breasted the hill like a thorough highlander. After breakfast we went down the ridge on the other side, and came to a stream which runs into that which descends from the Gúgérang Pass, opposite Námútatto. I had a stalk early in the morning after some wild sheep, but they had the advantage, and got away. Descending towards camp in the evening, I saw eight splendid old rams grazing on the opposite slope: their coats were of a slatey colour, and they had fine heads; but the country was so open that they soon saw us and were quickly out of sight.

I followed them up next morning, and sighted five of them high up in the valley on a stony hill, but they were a long distance off, and, mistaking them for females, I took no precautions, as they were not in the direction I was going. As soon as the barhal saw me, they made straight for the ridge, and only when they stood on the sky-line I discovered they were all rams! I *was* wild! After getting on to the open hillside, I saw two more animals, and, examining them carefully with the telescope, made them out to be rams. I went for them at once, and made a most cautious stalk, but when I was within two hundred yards, and looked over for a shot, I found I had been stalking two ewes. Two such mistakes at the very beginning of the day upset my equanimity, and it took me some time to recover. I then turned back, and again saw the five rams; so, turning to the ravine up which I had come, I had breakfast, and began my second stalk.

The rams were on a ledge of rocks, where approach from my side was impossible; but, shortly after, they left their perch and came down to the grass to feed. As soon as they were under cover, I slipped down and went up the opposite side as fast as I could. Here I made another mistake—my impatience spoiling everything. Instead of waiting under cover of some rocks until the rams came round the swell of the hill, I went on, very cautiously, to meet them. I had not gone far along the hillside when one of the barhal topped some rocks about two hundred yards, saw me instantly, and vanished. I ran forward to get a sight of him, and came face to face with another ram, not forty yards off, who was grazing quietly along in my direction. I saw his head only for a few seconds, and he too vanished; I never saw him again. Looking up hill I saw three rams making off, and had a snap-shot at a long range, and of course missed. This was a thoroughly unlucky day for me. There had been snow in the night, and when I began my tramp it was bitterly cold going up

"I DISCOVERED THEY WERE ALL RAMS."

the sunless ravine. My breath froze on my moustache, and my fingers ached even in warm gloves.

I resumed my march at 6.30 next morning, and went on up stream near its source. A gradual ascent brought me to a level piece of ground, whence I obtained a splendid view of the back of the snowy range—stretching from north-west to south-east. From this point the Himálayas do not look very imposing. There was a level plain below, encircled by rounded hill-tops, and vegetation was very scanty. The hillsides are covered with small broken rocks, which, at a little distance, give a round and smooth appearance to the landscape. It is the action of the weather, I think, which wears everything smooth. The wind, especially, has enormous force in these elevated regions, and tears along crags, precipices, and rough points with a noise like a mighty river over a rocky bed; indeed, the sound is so similar that I often mistook the rushing of the wind above for the echo of the stream below. In the course of ages the mountains have been rounded off, and undulations and curves have become the characteristics of the country; the ceaseless action of the elements has this effect upon the naked rocks. The force of the wind is terrible in these high regions; on an exposed ridge or hill-top a man cannot resist the pressure for more than a few minutes at a time. My theory may have no foundation in fact, but it is at least plausible. Vegetation is altogether wanting. The traveller in the midst of such desolation cannot but speculate on the causes which have produced it: there is nothing else to think of.

I came down to the stream at the level of the plain at noon. The sparkling rivulet that was murmuring past my tent door is one of those which are the true head waters of the sacred Ganges. They are the sources of the Bhágirati river, that rushes past the village of Nílang, and

is joined, lower down, by the small stream from Gangótri
—the sacred place of pilgrimage. The Bhágirati rises at
a higher elevation, has the longest course and the greatest
volume of the two, and has therefore more right to the
adoration of Hindús. The ridge I crossed in the morning was divided between the Sutlej and the Ganges
water systems. I had therefore doubled Sangyókh-la,
with no idea I had so easily crossed over into India
(politically speaking) again—especially after the experiences of the Gúgérang Pass! Geographically, however, I
was still in Tibet, and should not be in India proper till I
had passed Nílang. There must be a great gap in the grand
Himálayan rampart at this point, for there were no great
elevations in front of me. Nevertheless, camp Rangbocké
must be rather high; the Sangyókh is 16,800 feet, and I
was encamped only a few miles below it. In the evening
I went down stream for a long distance, but saw no animal
life of any kind. The valley was just redeemed from the
utter abomination of desolation by the sparkling stream
below, the heavenly blue above, and the glorious sunshine.
Returning to camp, I found many burrows of marmots
a short way from the stream; but they all seemed to
be deserted. There were signs of some beast of prey
near the burrows—it was probably a Tibetan wolf who
had settled down here until he had cleared the poor
marmots out.

We started next day at 6.30 A.M. and went up the
mountain side for about a mile, when we came to the
regular road from Nílang, that crosses the Sangyókh-la
and goes on to Zárang, etc., in the direction of Shipki
frontier village; this road is well defined, and much used
by beasts of burden. On the ridge by the roadside are
the usual heaps of stones with small flags of various
colours. A sharp descent led to the next valley; we

reached the camping-place at the bottom at 11 A.M., and, having had breakfast, started again. Travelling down stream, I found many barhal horns along the path and at all camping-places. One skull had a pair 25 inches long and 12 in girth at the base; the ram must have been a magnificent beast. He must have come to grief during the last breaking up of the snow, as the skull, which was very heavy, looked fresh. At one camp there were six pairs of horns collected in a heap. This valley is so close and confined that it must be unusually sheltered during the cold months and bad weather, and probably for this reason barhal frequent it in large numbers. It would be a good shooting ground in spring, before the animals had dispersed, or in autumn, after they had congregated here. At this season they are widely scattered, as grass can be had everywhere, and the old rams are away high up about the snow-line. Going farther down, I saw a dozen ewes, with lambs, running up a ridge, and shortly after saw two more run from the bed of the stream; they had, no doubt, been tempted down by the fresh green grass at the water's edge. I declined to shoot any of these females, though the men were importunate for meat, of which they had had none for several days; and, in fact, I myself had been living on tinned beef for a long time. Were it not for the lambs frisking up the steeps after their mothers, I am sure the sight of the fresh meat would have been too much for my scruples.

The coolies were on ahead, and I was some paces behind, when they turned an angle in the valley, and came plump on another flock grazing by the stream. There was shouting and excitement, of course. I got a rifle and ran at full speed to a large rock near the stream, which offered a good rest. The barhal were meantime rushing up the slope on the right with great clatter and dust. I did not shoot, as they seemed all ewes; but as soon as the flock reached the sky-line, to my surprise the animals seemed all rams! I promptly opened fire at about 200 yards, and the first shot brought down a splendid fellow hit through the shoulder—he collapsed on the ridge; the second shot hit a small ram in the hind ribs, and he went away to the right, very sick; the third and fourth shots were misses. All this firing did not seem to hurry the animals much—they went slowly along the ridge, still in sight. The fifth shot brought down another ram, the distance being not less than 300 yards; the sixth missed, and I ceased firing—three hits and three misses. I sent coolies to bring down the game, but, fatal mistake! a knife was put into the hands of one of them for the halál. Strict injunctions were given to cut the throats *low* down, but in their excitement the Baltis gashed the necks from ear to ear, thus ruining the heads for setting up. While the coolies were bringing down the sheep, I asked Tandúp how far we were from our camping-place—Púling Súmdo; he pointed to the ground we stood on, saying this was the place; so I had made this bag of three rams actually in camp. Literally in camp, for the tent was pitched over the tracks the flock made in their flight up the hillside. Such is the luck of shikár. I had been breaking my heart —and risking my neck—in the pursuit of rams for the last month without bagging a single animal; and here, at a turn in the road, I shot down three. The horns of the first ram were 23 inches round the curve, and $11\frac{1}{2}$ inches girth at base. Second ram 17 inches by 11 inches. The smallest ram was not recovered at the time. The third one was hit just above the root of the tail as he was climbing up, and never moved from the spot; his spine was smashed, and he must have died instantaneously.

I halted here, as Tandúp and his companion objected to

going farther; they had got us safely out of their country, and took no more interest in us. Tandúp was the source of considerable amusement to me during the time he was my companion. He was extremely good-humoured, and always in the most joyous spirits. With the help of one of the Balti coolies—the most intelligent of the party—I asked him one day what his surname was. After some difficulty, he at last understood what I meant, and said it was "Zangbo." It was not till some time afterwards I learned that the word simply meant "good"! He wished it evidently to be understood that he was "Tandúp the good." It fitted him very well; in the morning he was always the first astir, and, after putting on the tea to boil, he would prepare an extempore altar made of stones, topped with turf or grass, before which he would kneel and perform his devotions. His prayers were intoned in a low voice and with great rapidity, and he read out of his little prayer-book in the same manner. When this was done and his tea finished, he would turn his hand to any work, and, when the start was made, would lead the way singing, playing on his black wooden pipe, or whistling. He always carried in his hand his riding-whip, with which he tapped his boots. When he was tired, or had to climb a steep, he would sigh for his pony, flourish his whip, and yell out the noises used for making that animal step out; he lamented the absence of his mount a dozen times a day. On the march he amused himself driving the coolies along like a flock of sheep with shouts and jokes and horse-play, that kept them going. He belonged to the better class of country people; and, if he be taken as a sample of the rest, I am sure the independent country population are an amiable people, who deserve consideration from their neighbours. Tandúp Zangbo's intelligence, education, and manners were greatly in advance of those of the same class among the Indian population. His companion belonged to a lower grade; he was stupid, silent, morose, and bore a melancholy air, as if some secret grief weighed him down; but he read and said his prayers in the same fashion as his companion. I bought Tandúp's shepherd's musical pipe, and presented him with some tobacco and a pipe to smoke it. Tandúp was a much-married young man, and his wives were the subject of much conversation between the young man and Yákúb. They were constantly in Tandúp's mind, and my servant managed in course of the journey to collect some information about them. There were four, and their names were as follows:—(1) Sonam of Biár village; (2) Tashi of Zárang; (3) Dólma of Tángi; (4) Thaften of Chúsé. They all lived at their parents' homes, where Tandúp visited them periodically: the villages are only a few miles apart. Mrs. Thaften was the favourite, and consequently the best presents were reserved for her. These little things—scissors, needles, knives, etc.—completely won Tandúp's heart.

In the evening I took a walk up the valley joining the main one on the left. I had not gone a hundred yards from camp, round a bend, when I sighted a flock; but I was off my guard, and of course the animals saw me before I saw them. They ran up the slope and stood among some rocks within range; I had one shot, a steady one, but missed: this was aggravating, but I had only myself to blame. I returned to camp late in the evening, after a long trudge up the valley, having seen no rams after the first misadventure; but I saw ewes in several places. The valleys about here are certainly good finds for wild sheep; they were close to the road just now, probably because the people from below had not yet brought up their summer encampments so far. The spring and autumn are certainly the best seasons for a month's shooting in these hills; but the only game to be had is wild sheep. The journey from Mussoorie to Nílang would be an easy one. There are no passes to cross, and there is a good made road to within two marches of the latter place. The distance could be done easily in thirteen stages by laden coolies, and by double marches the shooting grounds could be easily reached in a week : a fortnight for sport, and another week for the return journey. So that within a month a keen sportsman could come out from Mussoorie, make a good bag of barhal in Tibet, and get back again. Or, if he were not in a hurry, good sport could be had on the return journey both with gun and rifle. This is worth noting by the jaded revellers of that hill station who are in need of a pick-me-up after the dissipations of the season.

In the morning I went down the valley and turned up the hillside on the right. I saw nothing but ewes; but by way of compensation had glorious views of snowy mountain peaks in the direction of Nílang, the first I had seen after some days. These peaks are probably Kamet and his neighbours. The wind on the ridge above was terrible— a good example of the Tibetan gale at its worst. Two rams came down from the hill I went up, and walked across quietly to the valley on the left, a few yards from the tent, while I was toiling on the heights above; and shortly after a young ram and a ewe came down from the same direction and grazed by the stream, not one hundred yards from the tent, for more than an hour; they then quietly went up the side valley. Yet another example of the vicissitudes of sport!

Going up the side valley after breakfast next day, I saw three rams, but they saw us first—and that was the end of that story. We went a long way up, but saw nothing else, and came back to camp at six. Some traders came up from Nílang that evening: one was the brother of the jemadár (petty officer), for many years in the service of a well-known European sportsman of the last generation, who spent most of his life in these parts. He was an old man, very friendly and communicative, and unusually intelligent; he had many stories about gentlemen who had come here for sport. He said one of them went up the valley which I explored to-day and brought back five splendid rams in one day; but he did not get back to his camp till midnight.

Next day, at a camp on the Nílang road, I found Paré, the old jemadár, himself. He also was going up with his rice and sheep to trade at Zárang and other villages. He said he had shot a barhal across the stream from his camp on this bank: four came down to drink. He had a very nice single ·500 Express, by J. Osborne, London—a present, he said, from his old master. I am afraid a goodly number of wild sheep have fallen to it since its crack was first heard in these wilds. I bought rice and other supplies from Paré. He gave me a man to show the ground, and said that the left side of the valley was the best for game. Paré gave me an awful account of a certain sahib who had deliberately shot with his rifle a number of men and a score of sheep! The men were innocent pilgrims on their way to Gangótri. He was secured after committing this crime, and was now in chains in Tírí. Paré also told me that a wild yak was found dead in the snow in Gandókh four years ago, and that he bought the head for ten rupees; it was the only one he had ever seen or heard of in these parts. If the reputation of the Baspa valley had not led me astray, I could have made a good thing of my three months' leave in this direction.

Next morning, soon after I started, I met two individuals whose swagger struck me at sight. They were both great swells: one wore a gorgeous gold-laced cap, and the other a Chinese velvet hat. These were Bow Singh, shikári, and his brother. I had heard of them, and they of me, and this meeting on the roadside was not accidental. After a short parley, Bow Singh accepted my invitation to show me the best shooting grounds in the neighbourhood. He had a double-barrelled Greener shot-gun (pin-fire), a good old weapon, and his brother shouldered one of my rifles. He was an oldish man, rather wheezy (from good living and over-much chhang), but probably would be A1 after the wild sheep of his familiar mountain slopes. At anyrate, he told plenty of stories of wonderful bags made by gentlemen who had been fortunate enough to secure his services. We halted at Goákh camp, and arranged here with Bow Singh (or Boosing, the right pronunciation of his name, and very appropriate too, from all appearances) for supplies, and yaks to carry them.

Bow Singh claimed to be Tibetan, but said he had left off wearing a pig-tail for several years; that is, from the time of the last Tíri Rájah's death, when every mother's son in the province had his head shaved "by order," the token of national mourning for the prince's demise. When he is down in Garhwál he is a Rájpút, but up here he is a Jádh, or Tibetan. I never got a satisfactory explanation of the meaning of the word "Jádh." Anparh said it was applied to all "bad" people who ate beef. When I replied that I must be a Jádh, he was rather nonplussed. Peoples living on the frontier dividing two distinct nationalities inevitably get mixed; and from personal experience I can say that it does not improve the breed: they are always bi-lingual—also a double-tongued, deceiving lot.

My servant let the cat out of the bag, and produced a considerable change in Bow Singh's tone of conversation when he was brought round to Gandókh and the *Ovis ammon* to be shot there. He said the leave of the Jádhs must be obtained first, bakshísh given, etc. It took some time to overcome Bow Singh's scruples; but he had set his heart on a red broadcloth choga embroidered with yellow wool. I tempted him with this magnificent robe, the materials of which I could obtain in Mussoorie, and told him he should have it provided he took me to the hunting grounds about which he had said so much.

CHAPTER XXII

THE LAST HUNT

A bad beginning—A very awkward ascent—Benighted—A good sleep and a square meal—An unsuccessful stalk—Massacre of the ewes—Twenty rams in view—The stalk—Forebodings of failure—Bad weather—A sporting official—New way of stalking wild sheep—The official and the pig-tail—Traces of Tibetan game—Bow Singh plays me false—Return to Púling Súmdo—Dismiss Bow Singh with a flea in his ear—A Tibetan official appears at last—An *Ovis ammon's* head—Splendid trophy—Return journey begun—Nilang—A good game country—An airy bridge—The great pilgrim route to Gangótri—Jángla bungalow—The story of a murderous "Sahib"—Bhattári—Journey ends.

AT six o'clock we started to ascend the hillside to Jaraphú, in our tracks of the day before; had breakfast there and went on again at two, having to negotiate a tremendous ascent that took us three hours. Luckily we were mounted; I had two small ponies and three yaks, and all the up-hill work was done on these poor animals, who had very hard work. The small pony that I had hired from Bow Singh was a sturdy little beast, who carried me well. My servant was astride a yak, the slowest animal in existence, but the surest-footed. The other animals carried the traps. The rotten snow on the steep slope gave very insecure footing, and all the animals lurched and slipped and slid, so that progress was painfully slow. More than once the baggage animals fell, and had to be set on their legs again by hauling at their horns and tails. This was a very painful operation, but the poor beasts bore it all very patiently. The ridge at last was reached, but it was almost knife-edged, and so smothered with snow as to be absolutely dangerous. So we had to dismount and descend as best we could. We dipped into a semicircular valley of moraines, round the bases of which slushy and half-frozen streamlets flow, having to walk through these, crossing a ridge here and there. Lower down, the moraines became more jumbled and confused, and walking over their broken surfaces was terrible indeed to me, who had on thin "Bisáhiri" shoes, which were no protection against sharp-pointed rocks. We got out of this awful ground just before darkness came on; but were obliged to proceed, as there was no camping-place and no fuel procurable.

We stumbled along down the hillside by the light of a clouded moon for two hours more, when we reached the banks of the Chhú-Hanmo stream. My shoes had gone to pieces, and I had been walking practically barefoot for a couple of miles, till I felt as if my feet were cut to shreds.

It must have been near midnight when we came to a halt. I threw myself under a huge tree a few yards from the water, too exhausted for any thought but one— rest. The yak with the bedding came in some time after, and I soon got between the blankets, but I was too tired to sleep. To complete the chapter of accidents, it came on to rain, and my bedding was soon soaked; but with the aid of a waterproof I managed to keep dry. I was too exhausted to think of food; and it was just as well, for most of the coolies lay up on the hillside above as soon as they were left to their own devices, and the man carrying the food, etc., never turned up at all. We had to send out to look for him, and he was brought down some hours after sunrise. This was quite the worst experience I had during this trip.

A good sleep in the morning, and a good square meal after it, made all the difference, and I felt so fit that by noon I was on the hillside with Bow Singh, on the hunt for rams. It was some time before we viewed any game, but towards evening five rams were sighted, and Bow Singh conducted the stalk. He went well, but made the common blunder of approaching the game *from below*. The consequence was, that when I got behind a rock within shot, and attempted to cover the game, I was discovered, and the animals stampeded. I had a hasty shot, and the barhal were round a swell and out of sight in a second. When they were next in view they were a long way off, and the shots I fired had no effect; this was most disappointing, as there were a couple of good heads in the flock, and there was no meat in camp, and everyone was clamorous. The mutton bagged at Púling Súmdo had vanished within two days, for the Baltis ate nothing else while the meat lasted. After this failure we worked up to the ridge, and saw on the opposite slope no fewer than twenty large rams grazing in various directions, but not far from each other. This was a grand sight. It was too late to attempt a stalk, however, so we returned to camp.

I enjoyed the luxury of a pony to ride up the ascent next morning. Shortly after dismounting we came across a flock of ewes, and, as the demand for meat was in my mind, I shot two. The sun had not touched the hill as yet, and a damp mist hung on the ground. My firing so bewildered the ewes that they forgot to bolt. After the first shot they ran a few yards, jumped on rocks and stared at me, not a hundred yards off; I could have slaughtered half a dozen. We crossed the ridge and went down into the next valley, where we had seen the rams last evening, and had a long climb up the other side, whence we sighted ten old rams. The stalk was long and tedious, as the animals were grazing and constantly shifting their ground, and we were below them. This time I insisted on getting above the game before approaching, and Bow Singh, who was leading, did capitally, as in the end he brought me face to face with the largest ram in the flock, not forty yards off. To reach my firing-point, however, I had to wriggle along in the prone position for some distance, and was considerably blown, when I ventured to lift my head. When I did, I beheld a venerable ram, gazing into my eyes; neither of us had time to speculate on the colours of our respective optics. I blazed into his chest; he gave me ample time, for I knelt and took deliberate aim; but, *horresco referens*, there was no result. I fired three more shots at the others scampering about, and again there was no result. Blank amazement and despair took possession of us; we looked at each other and sought some explanation. Bow Singh at last said that some of the rams must have been hit, so we went forward and saw two rams standing below the curve of the hill. One was looking very groggy, so I let him alone and fired at the other. I distinctly heard the stroke of the bullet, but both the animals galloped off at full speed. Two more shots, without result. I hit the first ram fairly in the chest, and I distinctly heard the bullet hit the second; but neither fell. The last ram was hit fair in the shoulder; the blood could be distinctly seen, and we followed him up hill for two miles, the blood flowing so copiously all the way that we made certain of finding him at every turn of the hill: but he went on into the next valley without stopping. I could think of but one explanation to account for these mishaps. I had finished my cartridges loaded with copper-tubed Express bullets, and was now for the first time using bullets plugged with wax. My theory is that these latter simply smashed up and spread out where they struck, not having, like copper-tubed bullets, sufficient stiffness to keep their shape till they had penetrated. I could not think of any other explanation. My supply of the other kind not being sufficient, I had procured an extra hundred, but never found out that they were not copper-tubed till I was far away in the Himálayas. I make a present of this experience to my brother sportsmen.

After a "Europe morning" (that is, staying in bed till late) I fell to tinkering those wretched bullets, picking the wax out of a few and driving in wooden plugs instead. This substitute I thought might stiffen them somewhat; but I was much disheartened, and very anxious to see the result of my next shot. After breakfast, we struck camp and marched up the valley in search of new shooting ground. The usual camping ground was boggy, so we went on till we found a dry place, at a point where two streams meet. The spot was evidently at a very high elevation, as it was very cold. A light drizzle had been going on all the evening. The back of the Himálayas is not favourable for a heavy downpour; the rain that does fall comes from the scraps of cloud that scrape over the snowy range and exhaust themselves on this side. It had drizzled like this every evening since I entered the Chhú-Hanmo.

It rained nearly all night down in the valley, and snowed heavily on the hill-tops. As it cleared a little at six, I ventured out to have a look at the ground, but after a time the rain came down again, and drove us back to camp. It was too early for the barhal to wander so high up at present; hardly any grass had sprouted, and not a flower was to be seen. Wet weather seemed to have fairly set in, and was interfering sadly with my sport. I was told a strange story of a traveller in these parts, who was probably an official of some kind on duty. He was proceeding this way towards the Tibetan frontier, and had his camp exactly where my tent was now pitched. A lady of the country (a low-caste woman) was travelling in his company, and he never came out of his tent till near mid-day, after a comfortable breakfast, when he would place himself in his lady's conveyance (a sort of hammock called a *dandi*) and proceed to sport; and he was successful too. From this very camp he stalked a flock of rams on the hillside above, being carried up in his hammock all the way: when he was within range, he alighted and shot three. This feat has not often been performed. He seemed to have made a mess of his official business, however: when he reached a place called Dókpa Sour, within the Tibetan frontier, he had a misunderstanding with the inhabitants, and cut off the pig-tail of one of the principal men. This led to unpleasantness, and our Government official was led back across the boundary, and warned never to show his face there again.

I saw this morning on the hillside very old droppings of the kiang. Down in the valley I picked up his skull, bleached by three or four years of exposure. The teeth were completely worn down, and the animal probably died of old age. Bow Singh said that they came here sometimes for the new grass, and went back in winter. If that is so, why should not *Ovis ammon* do the same? After two more blank days, wet and wretched, I began to feel sure Bow Singh was playing me false, and, sure enough, he showed his hand at last. He could not, he said, cross the border for fear of the consequences to him and his—the old story. I was greatly enraged, and on reaching Púling Súmdo dismissed Bow Singh, his men and his animals. Bow Singh's promises were a regular swindle. He had been with me ten days, during which I bagged only two ewes! Before paying him, I spoke my mind to him before all the people present; there were a good many, as several camps were pitched at the place.

Among the rest was a "Rájah" from Chaprang, in a nice little tent. He had been sent to keep an eye on me, though his purpose was declared to be the collection of Government revenues from Nílang. Further inquiry revealed that he was only the Múnshi, or clerk, of the Chaprang establishment: the people of Nílang called him "Rájah" out of respect. I had no doubt he had been sent down to watch me, probably on receipt of the report from Tángi, which the Panbúh sent to the Chaprang-Zong long after he had seen me fairly started. So perhaps, after all, I had not lost much by Bow Singh's manœuvring, as with this Tibetan official in my rear I could not possibly have got to Gandókh. The Múnshi paid me a visit while I was haranguing the people on the iniquities of Bow Singh; he wanted me to stop and have a feast. He was a well-mannered little man, but not a true Chinaman, I think, though wearing Chinese dress and long porcelain earrings in his ears. I was too much out of humour at the miscarriage of my plans to take much notice of him. To make me more savage, a man in the Tibetan official's camp brought me the skull of an *Ovis ammon* for sale. The horns were about 44 inches long and finely curved; the end of one was blunted. It was a splendidly massive head, and keen was my regret that fortune had not given me the chance of bagging a similar trophy. The animal could not have been long shot, as the blood about the skull was quite fresh. The man said it had been shot in the "Chang-thang"; but I did not believe this, as the Great Plain is beyond the Sutlej, and even beyond the snow-clad Gangri range. Probably the animal was bagged on this side of that river, perhaps on the very ground that I had been so anxious to reach! Never dreaming that he would accept it, I offered the man two rupees for the head; but he jumped at the offer. I did not buy the trophy, after all, for the weight of the head was quite a coolie-load in itself, and I had not a man to spare. The man judged the animal to have been eight years old, and said the horns were of ordinary size.

I made a long journey next day, starting at five in the morning, and reaching the village of Nílang at 5 P.M. The distance could not have been over thirteen miles, but the road was very rough, and the coolies travelled very slowly. The villages of Táding and Nílang pay one hundred rupees each annually as revenue to the Tibetan authorities at Chaprang, so they must really belong to Tibet. Nílang, or Chhángsa, its Tibetan name, is a miserable dreary place, almost deserted at this season, as most of the inhabitants are up the valleys looking after their flocks, or trading in Tibet. Excepting a few women working in the fields, there was no life or movement about the village at all.

Shortly after leaving Nílang next day, I began to *perspire* copiously. I had remarked, while in the higher altitudes, on the Tibetan side, that the most vigorous and prolonged exertion never had the effect of even making me feel moist, though I was most warmly clad. The change in this respect to-day was very marked; for a drizzling rain was falling, with a cool wind. Wild cypress, large and vigorous, were the first trees I met; then stunted and gnarled pines put in an appearance; lower down, deodar, stunted, mis-shapen, and small, their tops invariably cut off, most likely by the savage blasts of wind that blow along this valley.

The country and scenery were quite changed. The mountains on either side of the stream are masses of disrupted rocks, running up to precipitous ridges sharp and angular. In fact, I had entered on the Indian slope of the Himálayas, and, wonderful to relate, without crossing a pass! The only one on this route is the Sangyókh-la, or Kúng-lang as it is called by the Tibetans; but that range of mountains is a good distance within Tibet itself, and the pass appeared to me to be only a gentle slope. Of all roads into Tibet, I should say this one is the easiest, and gave the readiest access to that mysterious country. A traveller who did not delay on the way could easily make the Sutlej from Mussoorie in twenty days from the time of starting from the latter place; provided, of course, that Tibetan officials offered no obstructions. The high ground above the precipices on both sides of this valley is just the kind of country for téhr (wild goat), and no doubt many would be found near the sky-line; but I saw none from the path. In the winter months they would certainly be found in the sheltered parts low down, and then could be easily shot from the road.

At four o'clock on the following afternoon we came in sight of the Jángla bungalow, the first civilised habitation I had seen since leaving Kilba; I also got a sight of the iron suspension bridge over the Nílang or Bhágirati river, which leads up to the Gangótri valley and its holy places. Thousands of pilgrims pass along it every year, and to them it must be a boon indeed. The view was singularly effective: to the naked eye the bridge seemed to be only a plank, with a slight upward curve in the centre, just flung across the chasm at a narrow point. The name of the builder, Mr. O'Callaghan, still survived in the memory of the natives, though it is seventeen years since the structure was finished. Before this bridge and road were made, I believe, pilgrims had to cross the face of a precipice on the other bank of the river along a platform—a very good test of the faith of the mild Hindú; the passage was called the Bhairónghati. We put up for the night in the Jángla bungalow. An obliging clerk lived here, and also two fakírs, who gave me some very nice fresh milk. The clerk had been here ten years; his wife was ill from fever and dysentery, so I gave him some quinine, and recommended an early change of climate. The bungalow is built on the edge of the precipice overhanging the river, which is some distance below—a very wild spot.

I had heard various versions of the murderer sahib's doings since leaving Nílang, but probably none of them were true. The wife of the culprit was said to be in the village. If reports be true, this lady had no small part in bringing about the bloody tragedy with which her husband's name is connected. Farther on is the place said to have been the scene of the tragedy. The murderer is said to have slaughtered his victims on the level spot between the bridges over the two streams in front of the house. I found only the chaukidar's wife in the bungalow, but she was very reticent. An official from Tírí had been here for the last few days, and had just finished his inquiry; so everybody's mouth was shut, as is the custom in India when information is wanted. There seemed to be a feeling among the people here in favour of the sahib, scoundrel though he is, due, no doubt, to his family connections and to the wealth and influence which I learned were possessed by his mother.

At Bhattári I met the Tírí police official, who had been for the last three weeks inquiring into the murder case; he was returning to headquarters with his report. He gave me the history of the tragedy, which may be considered the official version, and therefore the most trustworthy. He said the murderer treated his wife very badly, and she had to leave him; she went to her people at Daráli, among whom were two men named Mián Singh and Nain Singh, the separation being effected by mutual consent. The mother, living with the couple at the time, approved of the arrangement. Six days after the separation the murderer went to Makpa village and forcibly carried off the sister of one Dharam Singh, a noted local beauty; his solitude was unbearable, and this was the way he selected to put an end to it. But his wife's desertion still preyed on his mind, and he was haunted with the idea that her relatives were conspiring to take his life. This morbid feeling led him to suspect everyone who came near his house; he drank heavily, too, and in the end probably quite lost his mental balance. A short distance below the house there lived a trader named Mala Ram, a Bisáhiri, who was a connection, by marriage, of Mián Singh's. The murderer went down to this man's hut and called for Mala Ram. He was wrapped up in his choga (cloak), and had a khúkri concealed under it. His manner at once betrayed his intention, and Mala Ram concealed himself, while his wife stood up and said he was not at home. The murderer suddenly drew his heavy knife, and, with two blows on the head and neck, killed her on the spot. The dogs began to bark at him, and a villager came running up to drive them off; he attacked the man and wounded him severely. He then went off to his house. He suspected everyone he saw of coming to kill him, and accordingly attacked anyone he encountered. He went down to the level between the two bridges, and saw two men; they said they were taking shoes to Mián Singh to sell. This enraged him. "You scoundrels!" he said; "you should have brought them to me!" and cut them down at once. Two men from the Makpa village then met him. The murderer cut off the top-knot of one and the ears of the other, because they belonged to that village. In this way he killed three persons, wounded seven, and destroyed twenty-one sheep. Probably many more people were murdered, as his friends were said to have thrown some bodies into the river. These were probably pilgrims, strangers about whom nobody asked questions. The day after these murders a doctor sahib arrived, and he persuaded the murderer to go down to Tírí and report in person what a fine thing he had done. He went, was taken prisoner and put in chains. The police officer called the murderer an "Isái," or Christian. By further questioning I discovered that this term was applied to him because he was neither a sahib nor a good Hindú. He was said to be the son of a *Dóm* (a low-caste man), and report had it that the mother had shared her money with the latter. From what the official told me, it was clear that the murderer had borne a bad character for many years, and, no doubt, had been going from bad to worse till this culminating point in his career. I may add that he was sentenced to five years' imprisonment and a fine of 20,000 rupees. He had the honour of being tenderly inquired after in Parliament.

I may close my narrative here. I reached Mussoorie on the 21st July, where I enjoyed a well-earned rest before going back to harness in the plains.

www.ingramcontent.com/pod-product-compliance
Lightning Source LLC
Chambersburg PA
CBHW030356230426
43664CB00007BB/618